PDF
HACKS™

Other resources from O'Reilly

Related titles

Information Architecture
for the World Wide
Web

XML Hacks

Amazon Hacks

Mac OS X Hacks

Mac OS X Panther Hacks

XSL-FO

Learning XSLT

XSLT Cookbook

JavaScript: The Definitive
Guide

Learning PHP 5

Learning Perl

Learning Java

Hacks Series Home

hacks.oreilly.com is a community site for developers and power users of all stripes. Readers learn from each other as they share their favorite tips and tools for Mac OS X, Linux, Google, Windows XP, and more.

oreilly.com

oreilly.com is more than a complete catalog of O'Reilly books. You'll also find links to news, events, articles, weblogs, sample chapters, and code examples.

oreillynet.com is the essential portal for developers interested in open and emerging technologies, including new platforms, programming languages, and operating systems.

Conferences

O'Reilly brings diverse innovators together to nurture the ideas that spark revolutionary industries. We specialize in documenting the latest tools and systems, translating the innovator's knowledge into useful skills for those in the trenches. Visit *conferences.oreilly.com* for our upcoming events.

Safari Bookshelf (*safari.oreilly.com*) is the premier online reference library for programmers and IT professionals. Conduct searches across more than 1,000 books. Subscribers can zero in on answers to time-critical questions in a matter of seconds. Read the books on your Bookshelf from cover to cover or simply flip to the page you need. Try it today with a free trial.

PDF HACKS™

Sid Steward

O'REILLY®

Beijing • Camb . . . . pastopol • Taipei • Tokyo

PDF Hacks™

by Sid Steward

Copyright © 2004 O'Reilly Media, Inc. All rights reserved.
Printed in the United States of America.

Published by O'Reilly Media, Inc., 1005 Gravenstein Highway North,
Sebastopol, CA 95472.

O'Reilly books may be purchased for educational, business, or sales promotional use. Online
editions are also available for most titles (*safari.oreilly.com*). For more information, contact our
corporate/institutional sales department: (800) 998-9938 or *corporate@oreilly.com*.

Editor:	Simon St.Laurent	**Production Editor:**	Brian Sawyer
Series Editor:	Rael Dornfest	**Cover Designer:**	Hanna Dyer
Executive Editor:	Dale Dougherty	**Interior Designer:**	David Futato

Printing History:

August 2004:	First Edition.

 This book uses RepKover™, a durable and flexible lay-flat binding.

ISBN: 0-596-00655-1
[C]

Contents

Credits

About the Author

Sid Steward works with publishers to make PDF do what they need. Sometimes, the solution is simply a script; other times, it is an entire document conversion workflow. He is a dreamer, a contrarian, and an idealist, all of which help him devise good solutions to interesting problems. His heroes include Bjarne Stroustrup and Vern Giles.

Contributors

The following people contributed material or expertise to this book:

- Simon St.Laurent (*http://simonstl.com/*) is an editor with O'Reilly Media, Inc. Prior to that, he'd been a web developer, network administrator, computer book author, and XML troublemaker. He lives in Dryden, New York. His books include *XML: A Primer*, *XML Elements of Style*, *Building XML Applications*, *Cookies*, and *Sharing Bandwidth*.

- Michael Fitzgerald is principal of Wy'east Communications (*http://www.wyeast.net*), a writing, training, and programming consultancy specializing in XML. He is the author of *Learning XSLT* (O'Reilly), *XSL Essentials* (John Wiley), and *Building B2B Applications with XML: A Resource Guide* (John Wiley). Mike is the creator of Ox (*http://www.wyeast.net/ox.html*), an open source Java tool for generating brief, syntax-related documentation at the command line. He was also a member of the original RELAX NG technical committee at OASIS (2001–2003). A native of Oregon, Mike now lives with his family in Mapleton, Utah. You can find his technical blog at *http://www.oreillynet.com/weblogs/author/1365*.

- C. K. Sample III maintains *3650 and a 12-inch* (*http://3650anda12inch. blogspot.com*), a weblog discussing the use of a 12" PowerBook G4 and a Nokia 3650. He is a doctoral candidate in English at Fordham University, focusing on 20th-century American and British literature, as well as 20th-century world literature, biblical studies, and critical theory. C. K. (Clinton Kennedy; no relation) works in Fordham's Department of Instructional Technology and Academic Computing as the Technical

Supervisor for the Fordham Graduate Center's North Hall Labs in Tarrytown, New York. His first "computer" was an Atari 400, and his first Mac was a PowerBook 5300CS. Originally from Jackson, Mississippi, C. K. currently lives in Bronxville, New York, with his fiancée, Kristin Landgrebe, and his pet Eclectus parrot, Misha, who just turned two years old.

- Darren Nickerson is a long-time member of the HylaFAX open source community and the founder of its online portal: *http://www.hylafax.org*. He is employed as a senior sales and support engineer at iFAX Solutions, delivering HylaFAX-based fax solutions to businesses worldwide.

- Ross Presser manages a small printing company's Windows network and develops humdrum in-house applications in several flavors of Visual Basic. During the few hours he is allowed to relax, he voraciously reads all kinds of text and kicks back to the music of Jimmy Buffett. He and his Parrothead wife live in southern New Jersey ("the part that has less pollution and more taxes").

Acknowledgments

I would like to thank my family and friends for their support, encouragement, and patience. I especially would like to thank my wife, Linda, for bravely adapting to my life of adventure. A special thanks goes to Chris DiBona for suggesting I write a book and then introducing me to Rael Dornfest.

Many thanks to Tim O'Reilly and the fine folks at O'Reilly Media who conceived *PDF Hacks* and then worked with me to create the excellent book you are holding. In particular, I am most grateful to Rael Dornfest for his keen oversight and to Simon St.Laurent for taking my manuscript in hand and turning it into a book.

A special thanks goes to Eric Tamm (*http://www.erictamm.com*) for allowing me to use his book, *Brian Eno: His Music and the Vertical Color of Sound* (Da Capo Press), in my examples. Visit *http://erictamm.com/tammeno.html* to download his book, or purchase the print edition from your favorite bookstore.

Thanks to Scott Tupaj for going through the code and double-checking the technical details. Thanks also go to Raph Levien, Edd Dumbill, Scott Tupaj, Marsha Steward, Stan Shoptaugh, Paula Morrison, and Mike Sherman (*http://www.svwh.net*) for their ideas, their careful review, and their thoughtful feedback.

Many thanks and deep gratitude go to the folks behind C++, STL, GCC, GCJ, and Debian.

Preface

Many people think of Adobe's Portable Document Format (PDF) as a proprietary format for delivering unchangeable content that readers can print out or view on-screen conveniently. That may be how most people work with it, but you can do many more things with PDF, with or without Adobe's tools.

PDF has come a long way since it first appeared in the early '90s. When Adobe began offering its Acrobat Reader for free, PDF spread across the Web as a paginated alternative to HTML. PDF has replaced or supplemented Adobe's PostScript language files as a format for exchanging print-ready layouts, and evolving forms capabilities have made PDF a more interactive format over time.

Although most people still think of Acrobat when they think of PDF, the format has become a standard for other applications as well. Adobe publishes the PDF specification, so developers can create their own tools for creating and consuming PDF. Ghostscript software, for example, is an open source toolkit for working with PostScript and PDF. OpenOffice.org enables users to create PDF files from its applications, and Apple has integrated PDF tightly with Mac OS X, including its own PDF reader and tools for printing to PDF from any application.

Many people treat PDF documents as finished products, simply reading them or printing them out, but you can create and modify PDFs in many ways to meet your needs. Adobe's Acrobat family of products, beyond the Acrobat Reader, includes a variety of tools for creating and changing PDFs, but there are lots of other helpful tools and products for working with PDF, many of which are covered in this book.

Why PDF Hacks?

The term *hacking* has a bad reputation in the press. They use it to refer to someone who breaks into systems or wreaks havoc with computers as their weapon. Among people who write code, though, the term *hack* refers to a "quick-and-dirty" solution to a problem, or a clever way to get something done. And the term *hacker* is taken very much as a compliment, referring to someone as being *creative*, having the technical chops to get things done. The Hacks series is an attempt to reclaim the word, document the good ways people are hacking, and pass the hacker ethic of creative participation on to the uninitiated. Seeing how others approach systems and problems is often the quickest way to learn about a new technology.

PDF has traditionally been seen as a pretty unhackable technology. Most people work with PDF using tools provided by a single vendor, Adobe, and PDFs are often distributed under the assumption that people can't (or at least won't) modify them. In practice, however, PDF tools offer an enormous amount of flexibility and support a wide range of ways to read, share, manage, and create PDF files. Even if you only read PDF files, there are lots of ways to improve your reading experience, many of which are not obvious. Creators of PDF files can similarly do much more than just "print to PDF"; they can generate files with custom content or create forms for two-way communications.

PDF Hacks shows you PDF's rich possibilities and helping you to use it in new ways.

How to Use This Book

You can read this book from cover to cover if you like, but each hack stands on its own, so feel free to browse and jump to the different sections that interest you most. If there's a prerequisite you need to know about, a cross-reference will guide you to the right hack. If you're looking for something specific, the index might help you as well.

A Note on Software

Although PDF still is closely associated with Adobe's Acrobat family of tools, you don't always need Acrobat to do useful work. And even though many of the hacks are specific to particular commercial tools (Acrobat 5, Acrobat 6 Standard, or Acrobat 6 Professional) or are bound to a particular operating system, overall the book tries to stay as environment-agnostic as possible. Whether you're running Windows, Mac OS X, or Linux, there should be a way to do most of the things described here. Some hacks are specific to a particular operating system, in which case they will say so.

Using Code Examples

This book is here to help you get your job done. In general, you can use the code in this book in your programs and documentation (all the code is available for download in a zip archive from *http://examples.oreilly.com/pdfhks/*; most of the hacks assume these example files are in place in a working directory). You do not need to contact us for permission unless you're reproducing a significant portion of the code. For example, writing a program that uses several chunks of code from this book does not require permission. However, selling or distributing a CD-ROM of examples from this book does require permission. Answering a question by citing this book and quoting an example does not require permission, but incorporating a significant number of examples from this book into your product's documentation does require permission.

We appreciate, but do not require, attribution when using code. An attribution usually includes the title, author, publisher, and ISBN. For example: "*PDF Hacks* by Sid Steward. Copyright 2004 O'Reilly Media, Inc., 0-596-00655-1."

If you feel your use of code examples falls outside fair use or the permission given here, feel free to contact us at *permissions@oreilly.com*.

How This Book Is Organized

This book is divided into seven chapters, each of which is described briefly here:

Chapter 1, *Consuming PDF*
> This chapter discusses various tools for reading PDF files and teaches you how to make these tools more convenient to use. It also describes ways in which you can get the information you want out of Acrobat and into other applications.

Chapter 2, *Managing a Collection*
> Reading and working with individual PDF files often leads to having a collection of files. This chapter provides tools and techniques for keeping track of what's in all those files and for presenting them to users looking for information.

Chapter 3, *Authoring and Self-Publishing: Hacking Outside the PDF*
> Most PDFs aren't created directly as PDFs; they start in other formats and then are converted to PDF. PDFs also feed into a lot of other processes, from printing to e-book distribution. This chapter examines techniques for creating rich sources of PDF content and looks at things you can do with PDF files outside of the usual viewing and printing contexts.

Chapter 4, *Creating PDF and Other Editions*

There are lots of different ways to create PDF files and useful ways to supplement your PDFs with the same information in different formats. This chapter looks at a variety of tools and techniques you can use to create your own PDFs.

Chapter 5, *Manipulating PDF Files*

Once you have PDF files, you might want to do more to them. This chapter shows you how to perform such techniques as splitting PDF files, encrypting documents, attaching data, reducing file sizes, building indexes, and working with bookmarks.

Chapter 6, *Dynamic PDF*

PDF files don't have to be static representations of documents created once. This chapter shows you how to make PDF itself more active through its forms capabilities and teaches you how to use a variety of different tools to generate PDFs from your data on the fly.

Chapter 7, *Scripting and Programming Acrobat*

Adobe's Acrobat family of applications remains at the heart of much PDF creation and processing. This chapter includes techniques for automating common tasks and stretching these applications in new and different ways.

Conventions Used in This Book

The following is a list of typographical conventions used in this book:

Italic

Used to indicate new terms, URLs, filenames, file extensions, directories, and program names, and to highlight comments in examples. For instance, a path in the filesystem will appear as *C:\Hacks\examples* or */usr/sid/hacks/examples*.

Constant width

Used to show code examples, XML markup, Java™ package or C# namespace names, commands and options, or output from commands.

Constant width bold

Used in examples to show emphasis or commands and other text that should be typed literally.

Constant width italic

Used in examples and tables to show text that should be replaced with user-supplied values.

Color

The second color used in the book indicates a cross-reference to other hacks within the book.

You should pay special attention to notes set apart from the text with the following icons:

This is a tip, a suggestion, or a general note. It contains useful supplementary information about the topic at hand.

This is a warning or a note of caution.

The thermometer icons, found next to each hack, indicate the relative complexity of the hack:

 beginner   moderate   expert

How to Contact Us

We have tested and verified the information in this book to the best of our ability, but you might find that some software features have changed over time or even that we have made some mistakes. As a reader, you can help us to improve future editions of this book by sending us your feedback. Let us know about any errors, inaccuracies, bugs, misleading or confusing statements, and typos that you find anywhere in this book.

Also, please let us know what we can do to make this book more useful to you. We take your comments seriously and will try to incorporate reasonable suggestions into future editions. You can write to us at:

O'Reilly Media, Inc.
1005 Gravenstein Hwy. N.
Sebastopol, CA 95472
(800) 998-9938 (in the U.S. or Canada)
(707) 829-0515 (international/local)
(707) 829-0104 (fax)

To ask technical questions or to comment on the book, send email to:

bookquestions@oreilly.com

The O'Reilly web site for *PDF Hacks* offers a zip archive of example files, errata, a place to write reader reviews, and much more. You can find this page at:

http://www.oreilly.com/catalog/pdfhks/

You can also find information about this book at:

http://www.pdfhacks.com

For more information about this and other books, see the O'Reilly web site:

http://www.oreilly.com

Got a Hack?

To explore other books in the Hacks series or to contribute a hack online, visit the O'Reilly hacks web site at:

http://hacks.oreilly.com

Consuming PDF
Hacks 1–14

Most people experience PDF as a document they must read or print. Adobe Reader and Adobe Acrobat are the most common tools for consuming PDF, but other tools provide their own distinctive features. First, we will look into the most popular PDF readers, and then we will discuss ways you can improve your PDF reading experience.

HACK #1 Read PDFs with the Adobe Reader

Use Adobe's Acrobat Reader, renamed Adobe Reader in its latest release, to read PDF files on the Web and elsewhere.

Lots of web sites that use PDF files include a Get Adobe Reader icon along with the PDF files. Whether you're running Windows, Mac OS X, Mac OS 7.5.3 or later, Linux, Solaris, AIX, HP-UX, OS/2, Symbian OS, Palm OS, or a Pocket PC, Adobe has a reader for your platform. (Different platforms are frequently at different versions and have different capabilities, but they all can provide basic PDF-reading functionality.)

To get your free reader, visit *http://www.adobe.com/products/acrobat/ readstep2.html*. You'll need to choose a language, platform, and connection speed, and then a second field showing your download options will appear. Each version has slightly different installation instructions, but when you're done you'll have either the Adobe Reader or Adobe Acrobat Reader installed. The installer will also integrate Reader with your web browser or browsers, if appropriate.

> Depending on your needs, newer isn't always better. If you want an older version of Acrobat Reader, visit *http://www. adobe.com/products/acrobat/reader_archive.html*.

Once Reader is installed, clicking web site links to PDFs will bring up a reader that enables you to view the PDFs, typically inside the browser window itself. You can also open PDFs on your local filesystem by selecting File → Open..., or by opening them through your GUI environment as usual, typically by double-clicking. Figure 1-1 shows a document as seen through Acrobat Reader running in a web browser, and Figure 1-2 shows the same document through Acrobat Reader running as a separate application.

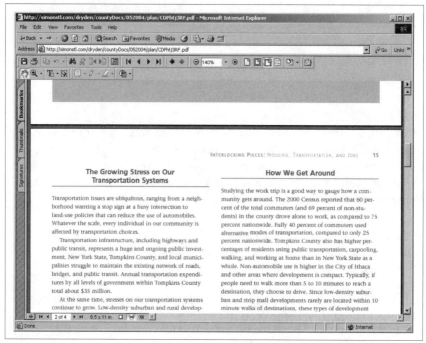

Figure 1-1. Viewing a PDF document through Acrobat Reader in the browser

As with any GUI application, you can scroll around the document, and Acrobat provides zoom options (the magnifying glass and the zoom percentage box in the toolbar), print options (the printer), search options (the binoculars), and navigation options (the arrows in the toolbar, as well as the Show/Hide Navigation Pane button to the left of the arrows that enables you to see bookmarks, if any are provided by the document's creator). Unlike the commercial Acrobat applications, Reader doesn't provide means for creating or modifying PDF documents.

After installing Reader, adjust its program properties to ensure you get the best reading experience. In Reader 5 or 6, access these properties by selecting Edit → Preferences → General from the main menu. For example, I always set the default page layout to Single Page and the default zoom to Fit Page (Reader 6) or Fit in Window (Reader 5). You can access these properties from the Page Display (Reader 6) or Display (Reader 5) sections of the Preferences dialog.

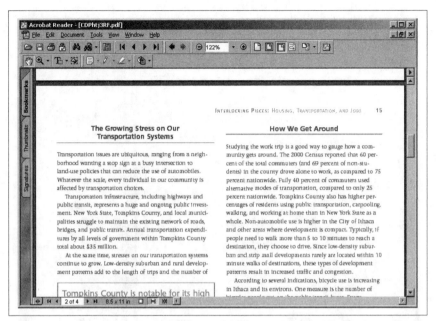

Figure 1-2. Viewing a PDF document through Acrobat Reader running as a separate application

HACK #2 Read PDFs with Mac OS X's Preview

If you have a Macintosh running OS X, the operating system includes a Preview application that enables you to look at PDFs without downloading Acrobat Reader.

Apple's latest operating system, Mac OS X, uses PDF all over. Icons and other pieces of applications are PDFs, the rendering system is tied closely to the data model used by PDFs, and any application that can print can also produce PDFs. Given this fondness for PDF, it makes sense that the Preview application Apple provides for examining the contents many different file types also supports PDF.

The Preview application is installed on Macs at *Macintosh HD:Applications: Preview*. It reads a variety of graphics formats, including JPEG, TIFF, and GIF, as well as (of course) PDF. You can open PDFs in Preview by selecting File → Open…, by dragging their icons to the Preview application, or (if Acrobat isn't installed) by double-clicking. An open PDF in Preview looks like Figure 1-3.

Preview's overall interface is much simpler than the Acrobat Reader's interface, though the options are friendly and clear. Preview also creates thumbnail images of pages, which is convenient for quick navigation. Preview also supports the PDF-creation functionality built into Mac OS X [Hack #40].

Figure 1-3. Viewing a PDF document through Mac OS X's Preview application

Also, Preview's File → Export… command enables you to save the PDFs or graphics you're examining in any of a variety of PDF formats. If you need to convert a JPEG to a PDF file, or a PDF to a TIFF file, it's a convenient option. (It's also worth noting that screenshots taken using Mac OS X's Command-Shift-3 or Command-Shift-4 options are saved to the desktop as PDFs. Those PDFs contain bitmaps, much as if they were created as TIFFs and exported to PDF through Preview.)

Read PDFs with Ghostscript's GSview

The Ghostscript toolkit for working with PostScript and PDF supports a number of simple viewers, including GSview.

The Ghostscript set of tools (*http://www.cs.wisc.edu/~ghost/*) is an alternative to a number of Adobe products. At its heart is a PostScript processor, which also works on PDF files.

> PostScript is both an ancestor of PDF and a complement to it. PostScript is a programming language focused on describing how pages should be printed, while PDF is more descriptive. You can convert from PostScript to PDF and back. Many printers and typesetting systems handle PostScript, while PDF is more commonly used as a format for exchange between computers.

Although typically you run Ghostscript from the command line or you integrate it with other processes, you can also use it as the rendering engine inside a number of viewers. Ghostview and GV support Unix and VMS, while MacGSview is a viewer for the Macintosh and GSview supports Windows, OS/2, and Linux. You'll need to install Ghostscript [Hack #39] before you install GSview. Once GSview is installed, it can open PostScript, Encapsulated PostScript (EPS), and, of course, PDF, as shown in Figure 1-4.

GSview doesn't provide a lot of bells and whistles. The toolbar across the top offers basic navigation, zoom, and search (the eyes). If you explore the menus, however, you'll find lots of PostScript-oriented utility functions. GSView is a useful tool if you need to work with PostScript and EPS files generally, because it lets you explore these files just as if they were PDFs. GSView is also a useful tool if you have a file that's misbehaving, because it provides a fair amount of detail about errors in PostScript and PDF handling. For many users, it's too stripped down to be useful, but what it lacks in chrome it has in power.

Speed Up Acrobat Startup

Move the plug-ins you don't need out of your way.

Both Adobe Acrobat and Reader implement several standard features as modular application *plug-ins*. These plug-ins are loaded when Acrobat starts up. You can speed up Acrobat startup and clean up its menus by telling Acrobat to load only the features you desire.

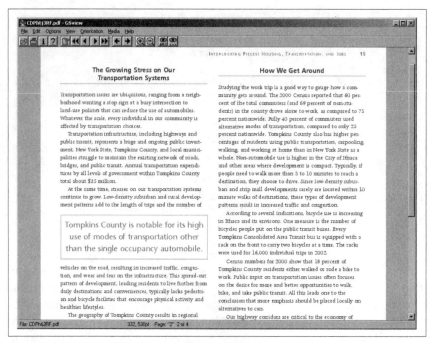

Figure 1-4. Viewing a PDF document through GSview

One simple technique is to hold down the Shift key when launching Acrobat; this prevents all plug-ins from loading. A longer-term solution is to move unwanted plug-ins to another, inert directory where the startup loader won't find them. Another solution is to create plug-in profiles [Hack #5] that are switched using a batch file gateway. This latter solution becomes really useful when combined with context menu hacks [Hack #6].

> Keep in mind that omitting plug-ins will alter how some PDFs interact with you. If a PDF seems to be malfunctioning, try viewing it with the full complement of Adobe's stock plug-ins installed.

Unplugging Plug-Ins

Acrobat (or Reader) loads its plug-ins only once, when the application starts. On Windows, it scans a specific directory and tries to interface with specific files, recursing into subdirectories as it goes. This directory is named *plug_ins* and it usually lives someplace such as:

```
C:\Program Files\Adobe\Acrobat 6.0\Acrobat\plug_ins\
```

or:

```
C:\Program Files\Adobe\Acrobat 6.0\Reader\plug_ins\
```

On Windows, plug-in files are named *.api, but they are really DLLs [Hack #97].

On the Macintosh, plug-ins are stored inside the Acrobat package. Control-click (or right-click, if you have a two-button mouse) the icon for Acrobat, and choose Show Package Contents from the menu. A window with a folder named *Contents* will appear. Inside that folder is another folder called *Plug-ins*, which contains the Macintosh version of the same plug-ins. These have names like *Checkers.acroplugin*.

Create a directory called *plug_ins.unplugged* in the same directory or folder where *plug_ins* (or *Plug-ins*) lives so that they are siblings. To prevent a plug-in from being loaded, simply move it from *plug_ins* to *plug_ins.unplugged*. When a plug-in is located in a subdirectory, such as *preflight*, move the entire subdirectory.

"But how can I tell which plug-in files do what?" Read on, friend.

Which Plug-Ins Do What?

Acrobat and Reader Versions 5 and 6 describe your installed Adobe plug-ins in the Help → About Adobe Plug-Ins dialog (Acrobat → About Adobe Plug-Ins on the Mac). Human-readable plug-in names are on the left side, as shown in Figure 1-5. Click one of these and the right side gives you the plug-in filename, a basic description, and the plug-in's dependencies. It is a good read, as it provides a straightforward laundry list of Acrobat's features.

Go through this list and write down the filenames of plug-ins you don't need. Close Acrobat and use your file manager to move these files (or directories) from *plug_ins* into *plug_ins.unplugged*. Open Acrobat and test the new configuration.

Examples of Acrobat 5 plug-ins that I rarely use include Accessibility Checker, Catalog, Database Connectivity, Highlight Server, Infusium, Movie Player, MSAA, Reflow, SaveAsRTF, Spelling, and Web-Hosted Service. Plug-ins I would never omit include Comments, Forms, ECMAScript (a.k.a. JavaScript), and Weblink.

HACK #5 Manage Acrobat Plug-Ins with Profiles on Windows

If you use Acrobat for several purposes, create several profiles.

If you use Acrobat for many different tasks, you probably need different plug-ins at different times. If you use third-party or custom plug-ins [Hack #97], it can become essential to distinguish the "production workflow" Acrobat from the "plug-in beta testing" Acrobat from the "on-screen reading" Acrobat. We can do that.

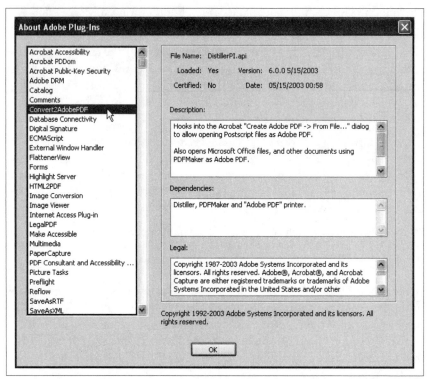

Figure 1-5. About Adobe Plug-Ins explaining Acrobat's stock plug-ins

In the same directory as your *plug_ins* folder [Hack #4], create one folder for each profile, naming it like this: plug_ins.*profile_name*. For example, a production profile might have the folder name *plug_ins.production*. Copy the desired plug-ins into each profile folder; you can copy a plug-in into one or more folders. The *plug_ins* folder will be your default profile.

Copy the following code into a text file called *C:\switchboard.bat*. Edit its path to *Acrobat.exe* to suit your configuration. This batch file takes two arguments: the name of the desired profile and, optionally, a PDF filename. Following our previous example, launch Acrobat under the production profile by invoking C:\switchboard.bat production.

```
:: switchboard.bat, version 1.0
:: visit: http://www.pdfhacks.com/switchboard/
::
:: switch the Acrobat plug_ins directory according to the first argument;
:: the second argument can be a PDF filename to open; we assume that the
:: second argument has been quoted for us, if necessary
::
:: change into the directory with Acrobat.exe and plug_ins
```

```
@echo off
echo Acrobat Plug-In Switchboard Activated
echo  ~ ~ ~ ~ ~ ~ ~ ~ ~ ~ ~ ~ ~ ~ ~ ~ ~ ~
echo Do not close this command session;
echo it will close automatically after Acrobat is closed.
cd /D "c:\program files\adobe\acrobat 6.0\acrobat\"
if exist plug_ins.on_hold goto BUSY
if not exist "plug_ins.%1" goto NOSUCHNUMBER
:: make the switch
rename plug_ins plug_ins.on_hold
rename "plug_ins.%1" plug_ins
Acrobat.exe %2
:: switch back
rename plug_ins "plug_ins.%1"
rename plug_ins.on_hold plug_ins
goto DONE
:BUSY
@echo off
echo NOTE-
echo Acrobat is already running with a switched plug_ins directory.
Acrobat.exe %2
goto DONE
:NOSUCHNUMBER
@echo off
echo ERROR-
echo The argument you passed to switchboard.bat does not match
echo a custom plug_ins directory, at least not where I am looking.
Acrobat.exe %2
:DONE
```

Now, create a shortcut to *switchboard.bat* by right-clicking it and selecting Create Shortcut. Right-click the new shortcut, select Properties → Shortcut, and add a profile name after the *switchboard.bat* target—e.g., C:\ switchboard.bat *production*. Set the shortcut to run minimized. Change its icon to the Acrobat icon by selecting Change Icon... → Browse..., opening *Acrobat.exe*, and double-clicking an icon. Click OK to close the Shortcut Properties dialog when you are done. Your result will look like Figure 1-6.

Double-click your new shortcut to see that it works as expected. As you add profiles, copy this model shortcut and then edit its target to reflect the new profile's name. Copy these shortcuts to your desktop or your Start button for easy access.

If your production shortcut is named Acrobat Production and it is located in C:\, you can use it to open a PDF from the command line by running:

```
"C:\Acrobat Production.lnk" C:\mydoc.pdf
```

To integrate these profiles with the Windows File Explorer, see "Open PDF Files Your Way on Windows" [Hack #6].

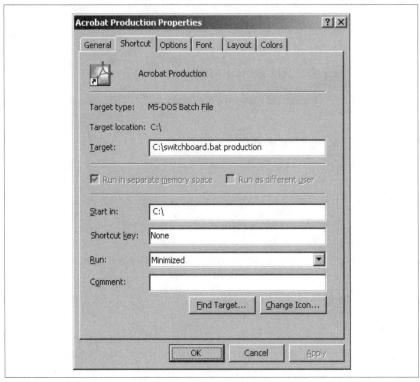

Figure 1-6. Creating a shortcut to switchboard.bat and passing in the name of a profile

 **HACK
#6** ## Open PDF Files Your Way on Windows

Multipurpose PDF defies the double-click, so make a right-click compromise.
Impose your will on Internet Explorer or Mozilla with a registry hack.

In Windows, you double-click to open a PDF in the default viewer. But what
if you have a couple of different Acrobat profiles from "Manage Acrobat
Plug-Ins with Profiles on Windows" **[Hack #5]**? Or maybe you want a quick
way to open a PDF inside your web browser **[Hack #9]**? Add these file-open
options to the context menu that appears when you right-click a PDF file.
You can even configure Windows to use one of these options when double-
clicking a PDF file. Convincing web browsers to open PDFs your way takes
a little more work.

 Windows XP and 2000 offer a convenient way to open a PDF
file using an alternative application. Right-click your PDF file
and select Open With from the context menu. A submenu
will open with a variety of alternatives. Your options might
include Illustrator and Photoshop, for example.

Add an "Open with Acrobat Profile..." Option to PDF Context Menus

In "Manage Acrobat Plug-Ins with Profiles on Windows" [Hack #5] we used a batch program to switch between named Acrobat profiles. You can add these profiles to your PDF context menu, too. In the steps that follow, substitute your profile's name for *production*.

Windows XP and 2000:

1. In the Windows File Explorer menu, select Tools → Folder Options... and click the File Types tab. Select the Adobe Acrobat Document (PDF) file type and click the Advanced button.

2. Click the New... button and a New Action dialog appears. Give the new action a name: Acrobat: *production*.

3. Give the action an application to open by clicking the Browse... button and selecting *cmd.exe*, which lives somewhere such as *C:\windows\ system32* or *C:\winnt\system32*.

4. Add these arguments after cmd.exe, changing the paths to suit, so it looks like this:

   `C:\windows\system32\cmd.exe /C c:\switchboard.bat production "%1"`

5. Click OK, OK, OK and you are done.

Windows 98:

1. In the Windows File Explorer menu, select Tools → Folder Options... and click the File Types tab. Select the Adobe Acrobat Document (PDF) file type and click the Edit... button.

2. Click the New... button and a New Action dialog appears. Give the new action the name Acrobat: *production*.

3. Give the action an application to open by clicking the *Browse...* button and selecting *command.com*, which lives somewhere such as *C:\windows*.

4. Add these arguments after command.com, changing the paths to suit, so it looks like this:

   `C:\windows\command.com /C c:\switchboard.bat production "%1"`

5. Click OK, OK, OK and you are done.

Add an "Open in Browser" Option to PDF Context Menus

This procedure adds an Open in Browser option to PDF context menus, but you can adapt it easily to use any program that opens PDFs. Viewing a PDF from inside a web browser enables you to spawn numerous views [Hack #9] into the same PDF, which can be handy. Opening a PDF in a web browser requires Adobe Acrobat or Reader [Hack #1].

Windows XP, 2000, and 98:

1. In the Windows File Explorer menu, select Tools → Folder Options... and click the File Types tab. Select the PDF file type and click the Advanced button (Windows XP and 2000) or the Edit... button (Windows 98).

2. Click the New... button and a New Action dialog appears. Give the new action a name: Open in Browser.

3. Give the action an application to open by clicking the Browse... button and selecting your favorite browser. Explorer fans select *iexplore.exe*, which lives somewhere such as *C:\Program Files\Internet Explorer*. Mozilla fans select *mozilla.exe*, which lives somewhere such as *C:\ Program Files\mozilla.org\Mozilla*.

4. Add "%1" to the end, so it looks like this:

   ```
   "C:\Program Files\Internet Explorer\iexplore.exe" "%1"
   ```

5. Click OK, OK, OK and you are done.

> If you want to use an application such as Illustrator or Photoshop, it probably has its own entry in the File Explorer's Tools → Folder Options → File Types dialog. If it does, use its native Open action as a model for your new PDF Open action.

You can set the action that Windows performs when you double-click a PDF by opening the Edit File Type dialog (Tools → Folder Options... → File Types → PDF → Advanced), selecting the action, and then clicking Set Default.

Open Online PDFs Using Reader, Even When You Have Full Acrobat

The previous instructions enable you to set the default application Windows uses when you double-click a PDF file. This default setting does not affect your browser, however, when you click a PDF hyperlink. Sometimes, for example, you would rather have online PDFs automatically open in Reader instead of Acrobat.

The trick is to make a change to the Windows registry. After installing Acrobat or Reader, Explorer and Mozilla both consult the *HKEY_CLASSES_ ROOT\Software\Adobe\Acrobat\Exe* registry key to find the path to a PDF viewer. You could change the default for this key to *C:\Program Files\Adobe\ Acrobat 6.0\Reader\AcroRd32.exe*, for example, and your browser would open online PDFs with Reader instead of Acrobat.

If you have Acrobat or Reader already running when you open an online PDF, the browser will use this open viewer instead of the viewer given in the registry key.

HACK #7 Copy Data from PDF Pages

Extract data from PDF files and use it in your own documents or spreadsheets.

Copying data from one electronic document to paste into another should be painless and predictable, such as the process depicted in Figure 1-7. Trying to copy data from a PDF, however, can be frustrating. The solution for Acrobat 6 and Adobe Reader users (on Windows, anyway) comes from an unlikely source: Acrobat 5.

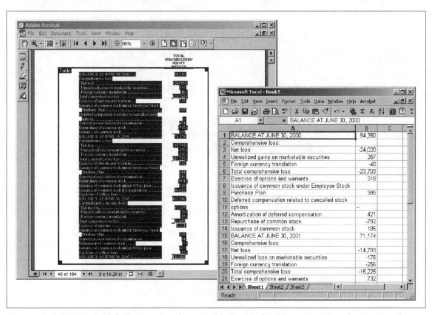

Figure 1-7. TAPS faithfully copying formatted text and tables using Acrobat or Reader

Acrobat 5 includes the excellent TAPS text/table selection plug-in. Acrobat 6 does not. Because Acrobat plug-ins are modular, you can copy the TAPS folder (named *Table*) from the Acrobat 5 *plug_ins* folder [Hack #4] and paste it into the Acrobat 6 *plug_ins* folder. Voilà! Don't have Acrobat 5? The TAPS license permits liberal distribution, so visit *http://www.pdfhacks.com/TAPS/* to view the license and download a copy. Don't have Acrobat 6, either? Use Adobe Reader instead. TAPS works in both Acrobat and Reader. Who would have guessed?

Adobe Reader 5 and 6

Adobe Reader gives you a single, simple Text Select tool that works well on single lines of text but not on tables or paragraphs. Sometimes it selects more text than you want. For greater control, hold down the Alt key (Version 6) or the Ctrl key (Version 5) and drag out a selection rectangle. Multi-line paragraphs copied with this tool do not preserve their flow. Pasted into Word, each line is a single paragraph. Yuck!

You need the TAPS plug-in, which copies paragraphs and tables with fidelity. Copy the entire *Table* folder from your Acrobat 5 plug-ins directory (e.g., *C:\Program Files\Adobe\Acrobat 5.0\Acrobat\plug_ins\Table*) into your Reader plug-ins directory (e.g., *C:\Program Files\Adobe\Acrobat 6.0\Reader\plug_ins*). Restart Reader.

If you don't have Acrobat 5, visit *http://www.pdfhacks.com/TAPS/* and download *Acrobat_5_TAPS.zip*. Unzip, and then move the resulting *TAPS* folder into your Reader *plug_ins* directory. Restart Reader. You'll now have the Table/Formatted Text Select Tool, as shown in Figure 1-8.

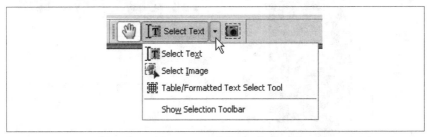

Figure 1-8. TAPS adding the Table/Formatted Text Select Tool under your Select Text button

The next section provides tips on how to use TAPS.

Acrobat 5

Acrobat 5 provides the same simple Text Select tool that Reader has. Use this basic tool for copying small amounts of unformatted text, as described previously in this hack.

For copying large amounts of formatted text, use the Table/Formatted Text Select (a.k.a. TAPS) tool. You can use it on paragraphs, columns, and tables.

It preserves paragraph flow and text styles. Check its preferences (Edit → Preferences → Table/Formatted Text...) to be sure you are getting the best performance for your purposes.

Activate the TAPS tool, then click and drag a rectangle around the text you want copied. Release the mouse and your rectangle turns into a resizable zone. There are two types of zones: Table (blue) and Text (green). If the tool's autodetection creates the wrong type of zone, right-click the zone and a context menu opens where you can configure it manually.

Copy the selection to the clipboard or drag-and-drop it into your target program.

Acrobat 6

Something went wrong with Acrobat 6 text selection. Adobe dropped the Table/Formatted Text Select tool (a.k.a. TAPS) and added the Select Table tool (a.k.a. TablePicker). This new tool is slow and performs poorly on many PDFs.

The solution is to get a copy of TAPS and install it into Acrobat 6. The preceding "Adobe Reader 5 and 6" section explains how to find and install TAPS. The preceding "Acrobat 5" section explains how to use TAPS.

 A PDF owner can secure his document to prevent others from copying the document's text. In such cases, the text selection tools will be disabled. See "Encrypt and Decrypt PDF (Even Without Acrobat)" **[Hack #52]** for a discussion on PDF security.

Selecting Text from Scanned Pages

If your document pages are bitmap images instead of text, try using Acrobat's Paper Capture OCR tool. It will convert page images into live text, though the quality of the conversion varies with the clarity of the bitmap image. You can tell when a page is a bitmap image by activating the Text Select tool and then selecting all text (Edit → Select All). If the page has any text on it, the tool will highlight it. If nothing gets highlighted, yet the page appears to contain text, it is probably a bitmap image.

Sometimes, page text is created using vector drawings. This kind of text is not live text (so you can't copy it) and it also does not respond to OCR.

Acrobat 6 users can begin capturing a PDF by selecting Document → Paper Capture → Start Capture.... Unlike Acrobat 5, Acrobat 6 has no built-in limit on the number of pages you can OCR.

Acrobat 5 users (on Windows) must download the Paper Capture plug-in from Adobe. Select Tools → Download Paper Capture Plug-in, and a web page will open with instructions and a download link. Or, download it directly from *http://www.adobe.com/support/downloads/detail.jsp?ftpID=1907*. This plug-in will OCR only 50 pages per PDF document.

HACK #8 Convert PDF Documents to Word

Automatically scrape clipboard data into a new Word document.

In general, PDFs aren't as smart as they appear. Unless they are tagged [Hack #34], they have no concept of *paragraph*, *table*, or *column*. This becomes a problem only when you must create a new document using material from an old document. Ideally, you would use the old document's source file, or maybe even its HTML edition. This isn't always possible, however. Sometimes you have only a PDF to work with.

Save As... DOC, RTF, HTML

Adobe Acrobat 6 enables you to convert your PDF to many different formats with the Save As... dialog. These filters work best when the PDF is tagged. Try one to see if it suits your requirements. Adobe Reader enables you to convert your PDF to text by selecting File → Save As Text....

If your PDF is not tagged, Acrobat uses an inference engine to assemble the letters into words and the words into paragraphs. It tries to detect and create tables. It works best on documents with very simple formatting. Tables and formatted pages generally don't survive.

The Human Touch

Fully automatic conversion of PDF to a structured format such as Word's DOC is not generally possible because the problem is too big. One workaround is to break the problem down to the point where the automation has a chance. The TAPS tool [Hack #7] works well because you meet the automation halfway. You tell it where the table is and it creates a table from the given data. This approach can be scaled to fit the larger problem of converting entire documents.

Scrape the Clipboard into a New Document with AutoPasteLoop

Copy/Paste works fine for a few items, but it grows cumbersome when processing several pages of data. *AutoPasteLoop* is a Word macro that watches the clipboard for new data and then immediately pastes it into your new document. Instead of copy/paste, copy/paste, copy/paste, you can just copy, copy, copy. Word automatically pastes, pastes, pastes.

 Scott Tupaj has ported *AutoPasteLoop* to OpenOffice. Download the code from *http://www.pdfhacks.com/ autopaste/*.

Create a new Word macro named *AutoPasteLoop* in *Normal.dot* and program it like this:

```
'AutoPasteLoop, version 1.0
'Visit: http://www.pdfhacks.com/autopaste/
'
'Start AutoPasteLoop from MS Word and switch to Adobe Reader or Acrobat.
'Copy the material you want, and AutoPasteLoop will automatically
'paste it into the target Word document.  When you are done, switch back
'to MS Word and AutoPasteLoop will stop.

Option Explicit

' declare Win32 API functions that we need
Declare Function Sleep Lib "kernel32" (ByVal insdf As Long) As Long
Declare Function GetForegroundWindow Lib "user32" () As Long
Declare Function GetOpenClipboardWindow Lib "user32" () As Long
Declare Function GetClipboardOwner Lib "user32" () As Long

Sub AutoPasteLoop()
    'the HWND of the application we're pasting into (MS Word)
    Dim AppHwnd As Long
    'assume that we are executed from the target app.
    AppHwnd = GetForegroundWindow()

    'keep track of whether the user switches out
    'of the target application (MS Word).
    Dim SwitchedApp As Boolean
    SwitchedApp = False

    'reset this to stop looping
    Dim KeepLooping As Boolean
    KeepLooping = True

    'the HWND of our target document; GetClipboardOwner returns the
    'HWND of the app. that most recently owned the clipboard;
    'changing the clipboard's contents (Cut) makes us the "owner"
    '
    'note that "owning" the clipboard doesn't mean that it's locked
    '
    Dim DocHwnd As Long
    Selection.TypeText Text:="abc"
    Selection.MoveLeft Unit:=wdCharacter, Count:=3, Extend:=wdExtend
    Selection.Cut
    DocHwnd = GetClipboardOwner()
```

```
        Do While KeepLooping
            Sleep 200 'milliseconds; 100 msec == 1/10 sec

            'if the user switches away from the target
            'application and then switches back, stop looping
            '
            Dim ActiveHwnd As Long
            ActiveHwnd = GetForegroundWindow( )
            If ActiveHwnd = AppHwnd Then
                If SwitchedApp Then KeepLooping = False
            Else
                SwitchedApp = True
            End If

            'if the clipboard owner has changed, then somebody else
            'has put something on it; if the clipboard resource isn't
            'locked (GetOpenClipboardWindow), then paste its contents
            'into our document; use Copy to change the clipboard owner
            'back to DocHwnd
            '
            If GetClipboardOwner( ) <> DocHwnd And _
            GetOpenClipboardWindow( ) = 0 Then
                Selection.Paste
                Selection.MoveLeft Unit:=wdCharacter, Count:=1, Extend:=wdExtend
                Selection.Copy
                Selection.Collapse wdCollapseEnd
            End If
        Loop
    End Sub
```

Running AutoPasteLoop

Open a new Word document. Start *AutoPasteLoop* by opening the Macros dialog box (Tools → Macros → Macros...), selecting the macro name *Auto-PasteLoop,* and clicking Run. When your loop is running, you are not able to interact with Word. Stop the loop by switching to another application and then switching back to Word.

Start the loop. Switch to Acrobat (or Reader) and use its tools to individually select and copy its columns, tables, paragraphs, and images. Switch back to Word and you should find all of your selections pasted into the new document. Start *AutoPasteLoop* again if you want to copy more material.

Hacking AutoPasteLoop

Add content filters or your own inference logic to the *AutoPasteLoop* macro. Use your knowledge of the input documents to tailor the loop, so it creates documents that require less postprocessing.

AutoPasteLoop isn't just a PDF hack. It works with any program that can copy content to the clipboard.

Browse One PDF in Multiple Windows

Tear off pages and leave them on your desktop for reference as you continue reading.

Both Adobe Reader and Acrobat confine us to a linear view of documents. Often, for instance, page 17 of a file contains a table I would like to consult as I read page 19, and Acrobat makes this difficult. Here are a couple ways to open one PDF document in many windows, as shown in Figure 1-9. These tricks work with both Acrobat and the free Reader.

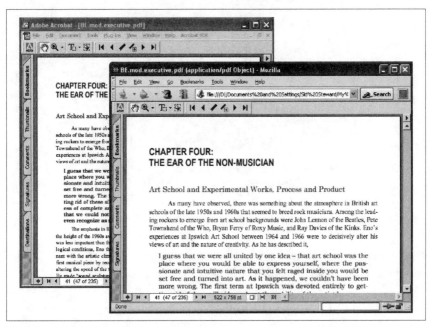

Figure 1-9. Using your favorite web browser to open one PDF document in many windows

Read PDF with Your Web Browser

One quick solution is to read the PDF from within your web browser. When you open a new browser window (or Mozilla tab), it will duplicate your current PDF view, giving you two views of the same document.

This works in Internet Explorer by default. Mozilla requires a little configuration. In Mozilla, select Edit → Preferences... → Navigator. On the right, find the Display On section and note its adjacent drop-down box. Set Display on New Window and Display on New Tab to Last Page Visited, as shown in Figure 1-10. Click OK. You must restart Mozilla before these changes take effect.

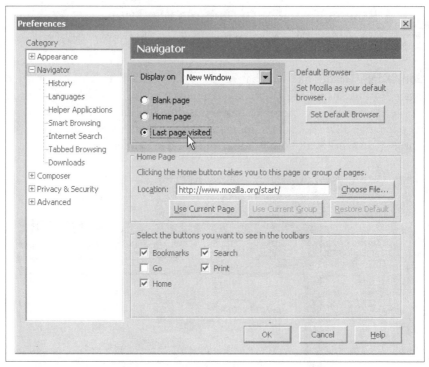

Figure 1-10. Configuring Mozilla to show the current document in newly opened windows and tabs

Drag-and-drop a PDF into your browser to open the PDF. Acrobat/Reader should display the PDF inside the browser. Select File → New... → Window (or File → New... → Tab) from the browser menu and you'll have two views into your one PDF.

> While you're viewing a PDF file in your browser, the browser hot keys won't work if Acrobat has the input focus. You will need to create new windows or tabs using the browser menu.

If trying to open a PDF inside your browser causes it to open inside of Acrobat/Reader instead, check these settings (Windows only):

Acrobat/Reader 6
Select Edit → Preferences... → Internet. Under Web Browser Options, check the Display PDF in Browser checkbox.

Acrobat/Reader 5
Select Edit → Preferences... → General... → Options. Under Web Browser Options, check the Display PDF in Browser checkbox.

If you use Acrobat instead of Reader, you will find that many Acrobat-specific features are not available from inside the browser. And, Acrobat won't allow you to save changes to a PDF file, as long as it is also visible in a browser. Close the other, browser-based views to unlock the file before saving.

To get a good blend of both Acrobat features and browser-based PDF viewing, we have a simple Acrobat/Reader JavaScript plug-in that enables you to invoke this "browser view" as needed from Acrobat or Reader. Also look into adding an "Open with Browser" option [Hack #6] to the PDF context menu.

Open a New PDF View from Acrobat or Reader

The following little JavaScript adds a menu item to Acrobat/Reader that opens your current PDF inside a browser window, giving you two views of the same document. To use this hack with Acrobat, you will need to disable Acrobat's web capture functionality by unplugging [Hack #4] its Web2PDF (*WebPDF.api*) plug-in.

Configure Mozilla. If Mozilla is your default browser and you're using Windows, read this section for possible configuration changes.

When Java is disabled, Mozilla often fails to display PDF inside the browser window; it tries to open PDF using an external program, instead. Select Edit → Preferences → Advanced, check the Enable Java checkbox, and click OK. This is a general problem with Mozilla and is not specific to this hack.

To run this hack with Acrobat 5, you will need to trick Mozilla into keeping its DDE ears open for Acrobat's calls. Mozilla activates DDE when it opens, then deactivates it when it closes. We'll open Mozilla and then alter the Windows *http* handler. This tricks Mozilla into thinking it is no longer the default browser. Under this illusion, Mozilla won't remove the DDE registry entries it created on startup.

1. Open Mozilla.
2. In the Windows File Explorer menu, select Tools → Folder Options… and click the File Types tab. Select the URL: HyperText Transfer Protocol file type and click the Advanced button (Windows XP and 2000) or the Edit… button (Windows 98).
3. Double-click the Open action to edit its settings.
4. Add -nostomp to the very end of the Application Used to Perform Action entry, so it looks like this:

```
...\MOZILLA.EXE -url "%1" -nostomp
```

5. Click OK, OK, OK.

6. Close and reopen Mozilla. It will probably complain (erroneously) that it is no longer the default browser. Uncheck the box and click No to keep it from harassing you in the future. If you click Yes, or if you ever change the default browser, your previous changes will be overwritten.

The -nostomp argument is not really a Mozilla parameter. By simply adding this text to the Open action, you trick Mozilla into thinking it is no longer the default browser.

The Code

Copy one of the following scripts into a file called *open_new_view.js* and put it in your Acrobat or Reader *JavaScripts* directory. Choose the code block that suits your default browser. "Customize Acrobat Using JavaScript" [Hack #96] explains where to find the *JavaScripts* directory on your platform. Restart Acrobat/Reader, and *open_new_view.js* will add a new item to your View menu.

The script in Example 1-1 is for Mozilla users and opens the PDF to the current page. The script in Example 1-2 is for Internet Explorer users and opens the PDF to the first page.

Example 1-1. open_new_view.moz.js

```
// open_new_view.moz.js ver. 1.0 (for Mozilla users)
//
app.addMenuItem( {
cName: "-",                 // menu divider
cParent: "View",            // append to the View menu
cExec: "void(0);" } );
//
app.addMenuItem( {
cName: "Open New View &3",  // shortcut will be: ALT-V, 3
cParent: "View",
cExec: "this.getURL( this.URL+ '#page='+ (this.pageNum+1), false );",
cEnable: "event.rc= (event.target != null);" } );
```

Example 1-2. open_new_view.ie.js

```
// open_new_view.ie.js ver 1.0 (for Internet Explorer users)
//
app.addMenuItem( {
cName: "-",                 // menu divider
cParent: "View",            // append to the View menu
cExec: "void(0);" } );
//
app.addMenuItem( {
cName: "Open New View &3",  // shortcut will be: ALT-V, 3
```

Example 1-2. open_new_view.ie.js (continued)

```
cParent: "View",
cExec: "this.getURL( this.URL, false );",
cEnable: "event.rc= (event.target != null);" } );
```

You can download these JavaScripts from *http://www.pdfhacks.com/open_new_view/*.

Running the Hack

After you restart Acrobat, open a PDF document. From the View menu, select Open New View. Your default browser should open and display the PDF, giving you two views of the same PDF.

Pace Your Reading or Present a Slideshow in Acrobat or Reader

HACK #10

You can make Acrobat or Reader advance a document at a preset interval, making it easy to maintain a given reading pace or to present slides.

If you are sitting down for a long, on-screen read, consider adding this "cruise control" feature to Acrobat/Reader. It turns PDF pages at an adjustable pace. Acrobat and Reader already have a similar "slideshow" feature, but it works only when viewing PDFs in Full Screen mode.

In Acrobat or Reader 6.0, also try the View → Automatically Scroll feature. It smoothly scrolls the pages across the screen.

Acrobat/Reader Full-Screen Slideshow

If you have a PDF photo album [Hack #48] or slideshow presentation, you can configure Acrobat/Reader to automatically advance through the pages at a timed pace. Select Edit → Preferences... → General... → Full Screen (Acrobat/Reader 6 Windows) or Edit → Preferences... → Full Screen (Acrobat/Reader 5 Windows) or Acrobat → Preferences... → Full Screen (Acrobat/Reader 6 Macintosh). Set the page advance, looping, and navigation options as shown in Figure 1-11, and click OK. Open your PDF, select Window → Full Screen View (Acrobat/Reader 6 for Windows or Macintosh) or View → Full Screen (Acrobat/Reader 5), and the slideshow begins. To exit Full Screen mode, press Ctrl-L (Windows) or Command-L (Mac).

You can also use this slideshow feature as a "cruise control" for on-screen reading. However, the Full Screen mode hides document bookmarks and application menus, and adjusting its timing is a multistep burden.

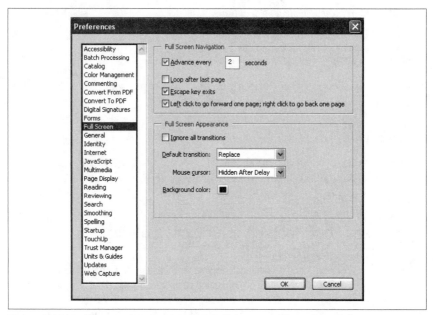

Figure 1-11. Configuring Acrobat/Reader's Full Screen mode to show slides

JavaScript Page Turner

The following JavaScript for Acrobat and Reader provides a more flexible page turner. You can run it outside of Full Screen mode, and its timing is easier to adjust.

Visit *http://www.pdfhacks.com/page_turner/* to download the JavaScript in Example 1-3. Unzip it, and then copy it into your Acrobat or Reader *JavaScripts* directory. "Customize Acrobat Using JavaScript" [Hack #96] explains where to find this directory on your platform. Restart Acrobat/Reader, and *page_turner.js* will add new items to your View menu.

Example 1-3. JavaScript for turning pages

```
// page_turner.js, version 1.0
// visit: http://www.pdfhacks.com/page_turner/

var pt_wait= 3000; // three seconds; set to taste
var pt_step= 1000; // adjust speed in steps of one second
var pt_timeout= 0;
var pt_our_doc= 0;
var pt_our_path= 0;

function PT_Stop( ) {
  if( pt_timeout!= 0 ) {
    // stop turning pages
    app.clearInterval( pt_timeout );
```

Example 1-3. JavaScript for turning pages (continued)

```
        pt_timeout= 0;
        pt_our_doc= 0;
        pt_our_path= 0;
    }
}

function PT_TurnPage( ) {
    if( this!= pt_our_doc ||
        this.path!= pt_our_path )
    { // Acrobat's state has changed; stop turning pages
        PT_Stop( );
    }
    else if( 0< this.pageNum &&
            this.pageNum== this.numPages- 1 )
    {
        app.execMenuItem("FirstPage"); // return to the beginning
    }
    else {
        // this works better than this.pageNum++ when
        // using 'continuous facing pages' viewing mode
        app.execMenuItem("NextPage");
    }
}

function PT_Start( wait ) {
    if( pt_timeout== 0 ) {
        // start turning pages
        pt_our_path= this.path;
        pt_our_doc= this;
        pt_timeout= app.setInterval( 'PT_TurnPage( )', wait );
    }
}

////
// add menu items to the Acrobat/Reader View menu

app.addMenuItem( {
cName: "-",                 // menu divider
cParent: "View",            // append to the View menu
cExec: "void(0);"
} );

app.addMenuItem( {
cName: "Start Page Turner &4",
cParent: "View",
cExec: "PT_Start( pt_wait );",
//
// "event" is an object passed to us upon execution;
// in this context, event.target is the currently active document;
// event.rc is the return code: success <==> show menu item
cEnable: "event.rc= ( event.target!= null && pt_timeout== 0 );"
} );
```

Example 1-3. JavaScript for turning pages (continued)

```
app.addMenuItem( {
cName: "Slower",
cParent: "View",
cExec: "PT_Stop( ); pt_wait+= pt_step; PT_Start( pt_wait );",
cEnable: "event.rc= ( event.target!= null && pt_timeout!= 0 );"
} );

app.addMenuItem( {
cName: "Faster",
cParent: "View",
cExec: "if(pt_step< pt_wait) { PT_Stop( ); pt_wait-= pt_step; PT_Start(pt_wait);
}",
cEnable: "event.rc= (event.target != null && pt_timeout!= 0 && pt_step< pt_
wait);"
} );

app.addMenuItem( {
cName: "Stop Page Turner",
cParent: "View",
cExec: "PT_Stop( );",
cEnable: "event.rc= ( event.target != null && pt_timeout!= 0 );"
} );
```

Running the Hack

After you restart Acrobat, open a PDF document. Select View → Start Page Turner and it will begin to advance the PDF pages at the pace set in the script's pt_wait variable. Adjust this pace by selecting View → Faster or View → Slower. As the script runs, use the Page Down and Page Up keys to fast-forward or rewind the PDF. Stop the script by selecting View → Stop Page Turner.

After starting the page turner and setting its speed, activate Acrobat/Reader's Full Screen mode for maximum page visibility. Select Window → Full Screen View (Acrobat/Reader 6) or View → Full Screen (Acrobat/Reader 5). The Page Down and Page Up keys still work as expected. Press Ctrl-L (Windows) or Command-L (Mac) to exit Full Screen mode.

HACK #11 Pace Your Reading or Present a Slideshow in Mac OS X Preview

Turn your Mac into a big, beautiful e-book reader, thanks to the wonders of Preview.

It likely comes as no big news to you that you can open images of various flavors and PDFs in Preview (Applications → Preview). But it never fails to surprise people that they've somehow managed to overlook the fact that you can hop into Full Screen mode (View → Full Screen) and view these images and pages without all the clutter of anything else you happen to have open to distract you from their stunning Quartz-rendered visage.

Just as iDVD's Full Screen mode transforms a Mac into a little movie theater, so too does Preview's Full Screen view turn your 23-inch Apple Cinema Display—or, more likely, your iBook's 12-inch screen—into a rather nice e-book, as shown in Figure 1-12.

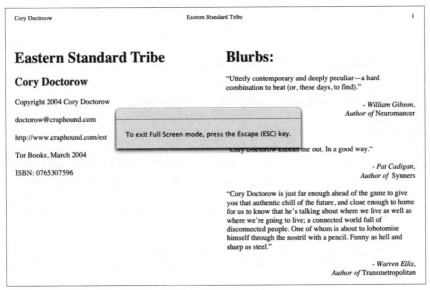

Figure 1-12. Cory Doctorow's Eastern Standard Tribe (available from http://craphound. com/est/ under a Creative Commons License), viewed in Full Screen mode in Preview

Flip forward page by page with a click of your mouse or rap on your spacebar. The Page Up, Page Down, and arrow keys move you forward and backward, while Home takes you to the first page and End to (surprise!) the end of the document.

If you switch to another application by using the basic Application Switcher (Command-Tab) and then switch back to Preview, you'll be right back in Full Screen mode. Hit the Esc key to return to normal, fully cluttered view.

It gets even better for iBook and PowerBook owners. This newfound ability to use your Mac as an electronic book means being able to tote about the Library of Alexandria—or at least what's available in Project Gutenberg (http://www.gutenberg.net)—without adding an ounce to your load.

If your PDF is formatted (as most are) in standard page layout, rotate it left or right (View → Rotate Left or View → Rotate Right) just before going full screen and hold your laptop on its side as if it were actually a book—a book with a keyboard, admittedly. Sit back, take a sip of tea, and catch up with Ms. Austen and life at Mansfield Park.

Be sure to keep tabs on where you are in your reading, as Preview doesn't yet have any sort of bookmark functionality. I suggest using a Sticky (Applications → Stickies) with a "Current Read" list of PDFs with associated page numbers.

—*C. K. Sample III*

HACK #12 Unpack PDF Attachments (Even Without Acrobat)

Save attachments to your disk, where you can use them.

Authors sometimes supplement their documents with additional electronic resources. For example, a document that displays large tables of data might also provide the reader with a matching Excel spreadsheet to work with. PDF's file attachment feature is an open-ended mechanism for packing any electronic file into a PDF like this. As discussed in "Add Attachments to Your PDF (Even Without Acrobat)" **[Hack #54]**, these attachments can be associated with the overall document or with individual pages. You can unpack PDF attachments to your disk using Acrobat, Reader, or our pdftk **[Hack #79]**. After unpacking an attachment, you can view and manipulate it independently from the PDF document.

Unpack Attachments with Acrobat or Reader

In Acrobat/Reader 6, you can view and access all PDF attachments by selecting Document → File Attachments…. Select the desired attachment and click Export… to save it to disk.

In Acrobat 5, you can view and access a document's *page* attachments using the Comments tab. Open this tab by selecting Window → Comments. Select the attachments you desire to unpack, click the Comments button, and choose Export Selected… from the drop-down menu. View and access *document* attachments in Acrobat 5 by selecting File → Document Properties → Embedded Data Objects….

Reader 5 and earlier versions do not enable you to unpack attachments.

Unpack Attachments with pdftk

pdftk simply unpacks all PDF attachments into the current directory. Future versions might introduce more control. For now, invoke it like this:

```
pdftk mydoc.pdf unpack_files
```

If the PDF is encrypted, you must supply a password, too:

```
pdftk mydoc.pdf input_pw bazpass unpack_files
```

Unpacking a PDF's attachments does not remove them from the PDF. You can always unpack them again later.

Hacking the Hack

Dispense with the command line [Hack #56] to create a quick right-click action for unpacking a PDF with pdftk on Windows.

HACK #13 Jump to the Next or Previous Heading

Use PDF bookmark information to stride from section to section in Acrobat on Windows.

PDF bookmarks greatly improve document navigation, but they also have their annoyances. When I click a bookmark in Acrobat, shown in Figure 1-13, the document loses input focus. Pressing arrow keys or Page Up and Page Down has no effect on the document until I click the document page. That makes two clicks, and clicking two times to visit one book-marked page is annoying.

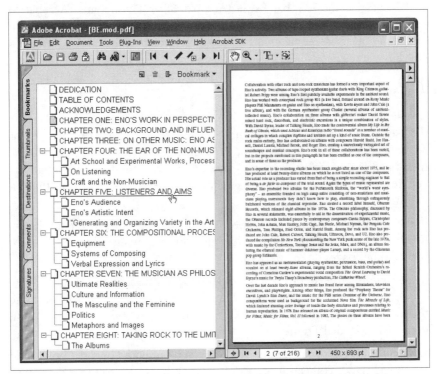

Figure 1-13. A no-click solution to annoying bookmark behavior

So, I created a "no-click" solution for navigating bookmarks. After installing this Acrobat plug-in, you can jump from bookmarked page to bookmarked page by holding down the Shift key and pressing the left and right arrow keys.

Visit *http://www.pdfhacks.com/jumpsection/* and download *jumpsection-1.0.zip*. Unzip, and then move *jumpsection.api* to your Adobe Acrobat plug-ins directory. This directory is located somewhere such as *C:\Program Files\Adobe\Acrobat 5.0\Acrobat\plug_ins*.

Restart Acrobat, open a bookmarked PDF, and give it a try. Hold down the Shift key and press the right and left arrow keys to jump forward and back.

"Tool Up for Acrobat Plug-In Development" [Hack #97] uses *jumpsection* as an example of customizing Acrobat with plug-ins. *jumpsection* does not work with the free Adobe Reader.

Navigate and Manipulate PDF Using Page Thumbnails

Acrobat's thumbnail view pane has some useful, unexpected features for reorganizing or jumping through your documents.

At first glance, the Acrobat Pages (Acrobat 6) or Thumbnails (Acrobat 5) pane might seem like a cute but unnecessary view into your PDF files. In fact, it is not a passive view, but an interactive easel with features not available anywhere else.

Tune the Thumbnail View

As you widen this pane, more thumbnails become visible and they organize themselves into rows and columns. The nearby Options (Acrobat 6) or Thumbnail (Acrobat 5) button opens a menu where you can change the thumbnail size. Acrobat 6 enables you to enlarge or reduce thumbnails as you desire. Acrobat 5 enables you to choose between small and large thumbnail sizes.

If the Acrobat 6 thumbnails appear grainy as you enlarge them, choose Remove Embedded Thumbnails from the Options menu. This forces Acrobat to render pages on the fly, as shown in Figure 1-14.

If the thumbnails seem to display too slowly, try selecting Embed All Page Thumbnails from the Options (or Thumbnail) menu. Acrobat will store the thumbnail images into the PDF file. You can always undo this by selecting Remove Embedded Thumbnails.

Your current PDF page view, on the right, is represented by a red box in the thumbnail pane. You can resize this box or grab its edge to move it around.

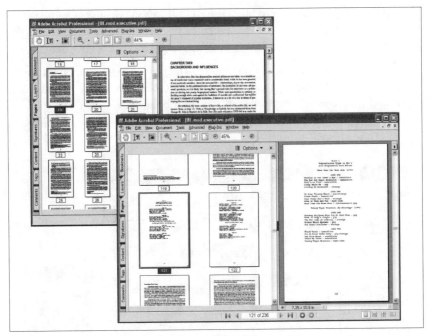

Figure 1-14. Large thumbnails showing more detail

Manipulate this box to manipulate the current PDF page view. Click any thumbnail to view that page.

Print, Modify, Move, or Copy Selected Pages

Invoked from the menu, most Acrobat features operate on one page or a contiguous range of pages. In the thumbnail pane, you can select the exact pages you want to print or modify. Click and drag out a rectangle to select a group of pages. Hold down the Ctrl key (Shift on the Macintosh) while clicking single pages to add or remove them to your selection. When your selection is complete, right-click one of your selected pages to see a menu of possible page operations.

 To select all pages in the thumbnail view, you must first select one page, then click Select All.

To move the pages you selected to a new location within the document, click-and-drag the selection. A cursor will appear between page thumbnails as you continue dragging. Dropping the selection will move the pages, inserting them where the cursor is.

To copy the pages you selected to a different location within the same document, hold down the Ctrl key and then click-and-drag the selection to the desired location. Acrobat will copy your pages instead of moving them.

To copy the pages you selected to another document, open the target document so that both documents are visible in Acrobat (Window → Cascade). Click-and-drag the selection over to the thumbnail view of the target document. Navigate the cursor to the desired location and drop, as shown in Figure 1-15.

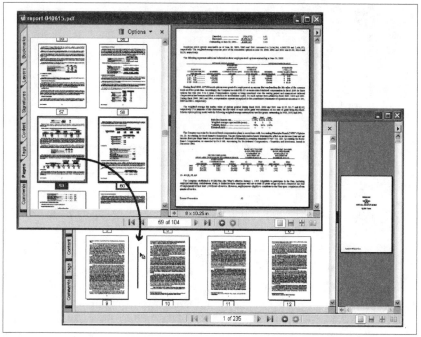

Figure 1-15. Quickly copying pages from one PDF to another via drag-and-drop

To move the pages you selected to another document, hold down the Ctrl key before you click-and-drag the selection over to the target document. Acrobat will remove your selection from the source document and add it to the target.

Managing a Collection

Hacks 15–23

While you'll often work with individual PDF files, documents have a way of accumulating. As your collection of PDF files grows, finding things in that collection often becomes more difficult. These hacks will show you ways to work with groups of documents, adding features and creating supporting frameworks for managing multiple documents.

HACK #15 Bookmark PDF Pages in Reader

Create and maintain a list of PDF pages for rapid access.

Web browsers enable you to bookmark HTML pages, so why doesn't Adobe Reader enable you to bookmark PDF pages? Here is a JavaScript that extends Reader so that it can create bookmarks to specific PDF pages. It works on Windows, Mac, and Linux.

 The bookmarks created by this JavaScript aren't PDF bookmarks that get saved with the document. They behave more like web browser bookmarks in that they enable you to quickly return to a specific PDF page.

Bookmark JavaScript for Acrobat and Reader

Visit *http://www.pdfhacks.com/bookmark_page/* to download the JavaScript in Example 2-1. Unzip it, and then copy it into your Acrobat or Reader *Java-Scripts* directory. "Customize Acrobat Using JavaScript" **[Hack #96]** explains where to find this directory on your platform. Restart Acrobat/Reader, and *bookmark_page.js* will add new items to your View menu.

Example 2-1. Adding bookmark functionality to Acrobat and Adobe Reader

```
// bookmark_page.js, ver. 1.0
// visit: http://www.pdfhacks.com/bookmark_page/
```

Example 2-1. Adding bookmark functionality to Acrobat and Adobe Reader (continued)

```
// use this delimiter for serializing our array
var bp_delim= '%#%#';

function SaveData( data ) {
  // data is an array of arrays that needs
  // to be serialized and stored into a persistent
  // global string
  var ds= '';
  for( ii= 0; ii< data.length; ++ii ) {
    for( jj= 0; jj< 3; ++jj ) {
      if( ii!= 0 || jj!= 0 )
        ds+= bp_delim;
      ds+= data[ii][jj];
    }
  }
  global.pdf_hacks_js_bookmarks= ds;
  global.setPersistent( "pdf_hacks_js_bookmarks", true );
}

function GetData( ) {
  // reverse of SaveData; return an array of arrays
  if( global.pdf_hacks_js_bookmarks== null ) {
    return new Array(0);
  }

  var flat= global.pdf_hacks_js_bookmarks.split( bp_delim );
  var data= new Array( );
  for( ii= 0; ii< flat.length; ) {
    var record= new Array( );
    for( jj= 0; jj< 3 && ii< flat.length; ++ii, ++jj ) {
      record.push( flat[ii] );
    }
    if( record.length== 3 ) {
      data.push( record );
    }
  }
  return data;
}

function AddBookmark( ) {
  // query the user for a name, and then combine it with
  // the current PDF page to create a record; store this record
  var label=
    app.response( "Bookmark Name:",
                  "Bookmark Name",
                  "",
                  false );
  if( label!= null ) {
    var record= new Array(3);
    record[0]= label;
    record[1]= this.path;
    record[2]= this.pageNum;
```

Example 2-1. Adding bookmark functionality to Acrobat and Adobe Reader (continued)

```
    data= GetData( );
    data.push( record );
    SaveData( data );
  }
}

function ShowBookmarks( ) {
  // show a pop-up menu; this seems to work only when
  // a PDF is already in the viewer;
  var data= GetData( );
  var items= '';
  for( ii= 0; ii< data.length; ++ii ) {
    if( ii!= 0 )
      items+= ', ';
    items+= '"'+ ii+ ': '+ data[ii][0]+ '"';
  }
  // assemble the command and then execute it with eval( )
  var command= 'app.popUpMenu( '+ items+ ' );';
  var selection= eval( command );
  if( selection== null ) {
    return; // exit
  }

  // the user made a selection; parse out its index and use it
  // to access the bookmark record
  var index= 0;
  // toString( ) converts the String object to a string literal
  // eval( ) converts the string literal to a number
  index= eval( selection.substring( 0, selection.indexOf(':') ).toString( ) );
  if( index< data.length ) {
    try {
      // the document must be 'disclosed' for us to have any access
      // to its properties, so we use these FirstPage NextPage calls
      //
      app.openDoc( data[index][1] );
      app.execMenuItem( "FirstPage" );
      for( ii= 0; ii< data[index][2]; ++ii ) {
        app.execMenuItem( "NextPage" );
      }
    }
    catch( ee ) {
      var response=
        app.alert("Error trying to open the requested document.\nShould I remove
this bookmark?", 2, 2);
      if( response== 4 && index< data.length ) {
        data.splice( index, 1 );
        SaveData( data );
      }
    }
  }
}
```

Example 2-1. Adding bookmark functionality to Acrobat and Adobe Reader (continued)

```
function DropBookmark( ) {
  // modeled after ShowBookmarks( )
  var data= GetData( );
  var items= '';
  for( ii= 0; ii< data.length; ++ii ) {
    if( ii!= 0 )
      items+= ', ';
    items+= '"'+ ii+ ': '+ data[ii][0]+ '"';
  }
  var command= 'app.popUpMenu( '+ items+ ' );';
  var selection= eval( command );
  if( selection== null ) {
    return; // exit
  }

  var index= 0;
  index= eval( selection.substring( 0, selection.indexOf(':') ).toString( ) );
  if( index< data.length ) {
    data.splice( index, 1 );
    SaveData( data );
  }
}

function ClearBookmarks( ) {
  if( app.alert("Are you sure you want to erase all bookmarks?", 2, 2 )== 4 ) {
    SaveData( new Array(0) );
  }
}

app.addMenuItem( {
cName: "-",                // menu divider
cParent: "View",           // append to the View menu
cExec: "void(0);" } );

app.addMenuItem( {
cName: "Bookmark This Page &5",
cParent: "View",
cExec: "AddBookmark( );",
cEnable: "event.rc= (event.target != null);" } );

app.addMenuItem( {
cName: "Go To Bookmark &6",
cParent: "View",
cExec: "ShowBookmarks( );",
cEnable: "event.rc= (event.target != null);" } );

app.addMenuItem( {
cName: "Remove a Bookmark",
cParent: "View",
cExec: "DropBookmark( );",
cEnable: "event.rc= (event.target != null);" } );
```

Example 2-1. Adding bookmark functionality to Acrobat and Adobe Reader (continued)

```
app.addMenuItem( {
cName: "Clear Bookmarks",
cParent: "View",
cExec: "ClearBookmarks( );",
cEnable: "event.rc= true;" } );
```

Running the Hack

When you find a PDF page you want to bookmark, select View → Book-mark This Page, or use the Windows key combination Alt-V, 5. A dialog will ask you for the bookmark's name. Enter a title and click OK.

> The bookmarks you create persist across Acrobat/Reader sessions because the data is stored in a persistent, global JavaScript variable. Acrobat/Reader stores persistent data in a text file named *glob.js* in the *JavaScripts* directory.

To activate a bookmark, some PDF document (*any* PDF document) must already be open in the viewer. This is due to a quirk in Acrobat's JavaScript pop-up menu. Select View → Go To Bookmark, or use the Windows key combination Alt-V, 6. A pop-up menu appears, showing your bookmark titles. Select a title, and that PDF will open in the viewer and then advance to the bookmarked page.

Remove a bookmark by selecting View → Remove a Bookmark. A pop-up menu will show all of your current bookmarks. Select a bookmark, and it will be removed permanently.

> The pop-up menu of bookmarks appears as a floating menu next to where the View menu was. That floating menu does work. Also, you'll need to have a PDF file open for the book-mark choices on the View menu to be active.

HACK #16 Create Windows Shortcuts to Online PDF Pages with Acrobat

Quickly return to the particular page of an online PDF, and manage these shortcuts with your other Favorites.

Web browsers don't enable you to bookmark online PDF pages as precisely as you can bookmark HTML web pages. Sure, you can bookmark the PDF *document*, but if that document is 300 pages long, your bookmark isn't help-ing you very much. The problem is that the browser doesn't know which PDF page you are viewing; it leaves those details to Acrobat or Reader. The solution is to have Acrobat/Reader create the shortcut for you. This little plug-in for Acrobat does the trick by creating page-specific Internet shortcuts in your *Favorites* folder, as shown in Figure 2-1.

> Our Shortcuts plug-in does not work with Reader. Visit *http://www.pdfhacks.com/shortcuts/* to see the status of Reader support.

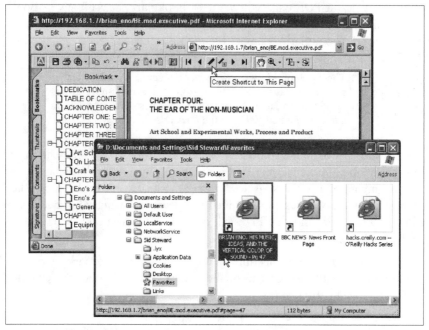

Figure 2-1. Creating a PDF page shortcut that you can manage with your other Favorites

Visit *http://www.pdfhacks.com/shortcuts/* and download *shortcuts-1.0.zip*. Unzip, and then copy *shortcuts.api* to your Acrobat *plug_ins* folder. This folder is usually located somewhere such as *C:\Program Files\Adobe\Acrobat 5.0\Acrobat\plug_ins*.

Restart Acrobat. Our Shortcuts plug-in adds a PDF Hacks → Shortcuts submenu to the Acrobat Plug-Ins menu. It also adds this Create Shortcut to This Page button to the navigation toolbar:

When viewing an online PDF, click this button and an Internet shortcut will appear in your personal *Favorites* folder. This shortcut is visible immediately from the Favorites menu in Internet Explorer. You can organize shortcuts into subfolders, rename them, or move them. When you activate one of these shortcuts, your default browser opens to the given URL, in this case to the PDF page you were viewing.

> You can convert the shortcuts in your *Favorites* folder into Mozilla bookmarks by using the Internet Explorer Import/ Export Wizard. Start the wizard from Internet Explorer by selecting File → Import and Export....

Examine one of these shortcut URLs and you will see our trick for opening an online PDF to a specific page. It is simply a matter of appending information to the PDF's URL. For example, *http://www.pdfhacks.com/eno/BE. pdf#page=44* takes the reader to page 44. "Hyperlink HTML to PDF Pages" [Hack #69] explains this technique in detail.

> If your browser fails to refresh its display after you activate one of our PDF shortcuts, try one of these tips.
>
> On Internet Explorer, configure your browser to open short-cuts in new windows by opening Tools → Internet Options... → Advanced and then removing the checkmark next to the "Reuse windows for launching shortcuts" option.
>
> On Mozilla, click the Reload button or select View → Reload after you activate a shortcut.

Our Shortcuts plug-in also works on local PDF files, but this requires some additional configuration. So read on, friend!

HACK #17 Create Windows Shortcuts to Local PDF Pages

Pinpoint and organize the essential data in your local PDF collection.

PDF files can hold so much information, yet Acrobat provides no conve-nient way to reference an individual PDF page outside of Acrobat. This makes it harder to organize a collection. To solve this problem, I developed an Acrobat plug-in that can create Windows shortcuts that open specific PDF pages. However, it works only after you add some special Dynamic Data Exchange (DDE) messages to the PDF Open action. Use this plug-in to create Windows shortcuts to the PDF pages, sections, or chapters most use-ful to you. Name these shortcuts and organize them in folders just like Inter-net shortcuts.

Adobe Reader users should use "Bookmark PDF Pages in Reader" [Hack #15] instead of this hack.

Configure the Shell to Open PDF to a Given Page

First, we must have Acrobat open PDF files to a particular page, when a page number is given. The Windows *shell* is responsible for opening Acrobat when you double-click a PDF file or shortcut. You can view and edit this association from the Windows Explorer File Manager.

In the Windows File Explorer menu, select Tools → Folder Options... and click the File Types tab. Select the Adobe Acrobat Document (PDF) file type and click the Advanced button (Windows XP and 2000) or the Edit... button (Windows 98). Double-click the Open action to change its configuration.

Now you should be looking at the Edit Action dialog for the Adobe Acrobat Document file type. Check the Use DDE checkbox and then add/change the DDE fields like so:

Field name	Field value
DDE Message	[DocOpen("%1")] [DocGoTo("%1",%2=0)]
Application	acroview
DDE Application Not Running	
Topic	control

This DDE message tells Acrobat to open the PDF file given in the first argument (%1) and then to go to the page given in the second argument (%2). If %2 is not given, Acrobat opens the PDF to the first page (page zero).

> Sometimes the Application field is filled with a different name. It must be acroview for our DDE message to work properly.

When you are done, the PDF Open action should look like Figure 2-2.

Click OK, OK, and Close, and you are done.

> This could change how you open PDF files from the command line. You will need to supply the full path to the PDF file, even if the PDF file is in your current directory. So, for example, instead of typing AcroRd32 mydoc.pdf you would need to type AcroRd32 C:\myfolder\mydoc.pdf.

Acrobat Shortcuts Plug-In

Follow the directions in "Create Windows Shortcuts to Online PDF Pages with Acrobat" [Hack #16] to install and use our Shortcuts Acrobat plug-in. Internet shortcuts are a little different from shortcuts to local files, but for our purposes they behave the same way.

Figure 2-2. Adding an Acrobat command to the PDF Open action using DDE

Hacking the Hack

Acrobat and Reader recognize more than 30 DDE messages. They are documented in the Acrobat Interapplication Communication Reference, which comes with the Acrobat SDK [Hack #98]. Its filename is *IACReference.pdf*. Use DDE messages to program your own Acrobat context menu actions.

Also, look into the PDF Open Parameters document from Adobe, which you can find at *http://partners.adobe.com/asn/acrobat/sdk/public/docs/ PDFOpenParams.pdf*.

 HACK #18 Turn PDF Bookmarks into Windows Shortcuts

Turn your PDF inside out.

We've talked about creating a shortcut to a single PDF page [Hack #17]. Now let's create a complete tree of shortcuts, each representing a PDF bookmark, such as those in Figure 2-3. Organize them in folders and use the Windows File Explorer to navigate your PDF collection. It works with local and online PDF files.

Install the Shortcuts plug-in [Hack #16] and then configure your computer for local shortcuts [Hack #17]. Open a bookmarked PDF and press the ⊞ button. Or, select Plug-Ins → PDF Hacks → Shortcuts → Create Shortcuts to All Document Bookmarks. A set of shortcuts will appear in your *Favorites* folder. Create a new folder and move the new shortcuts to a convenient location.

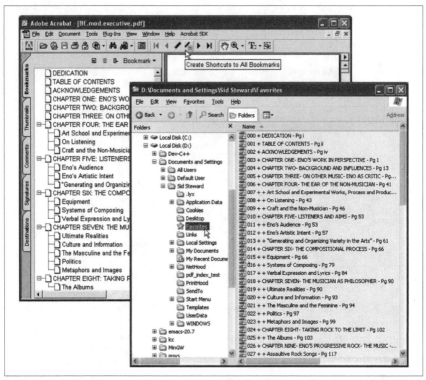

Figure 2-3. Converting a PDF's bookmarks into desktop shortcuts, which can then be organized using the File Explorer

Generate Document Keywords

Complement your search strategy with document keywords.

Lost information is no use to anybody, and the difference between lost and found is a good collection search strategy. Keywords can play a valuable role in your strategy by giving you insight into a document's topics. Of course, a document's headings, listed in its Table of Contents, provide an outline of its topics. Keywords are different. Derived from the document's full text, they fill in the gaps between the formal, outlined topics and their actual treatments. This hack explains how to find a PDF's keywords using our kw_catcher program.

How the kw_catcher Keyword Generator Works

Finding keywords automatically is a hard problem. To simplify the problem, we are going to make a couple of assumptions. First, the document in question is large—50 pages or longer. Second, the document title is known—i.e., we aren't trying to discover the document's global topic, represented by its title. Rather, we are trying to discover subtopics that emerge throughout the document.

Stopwords, noise, and signal. *Stopwords* are the words that appear most frequently in almost any document, such as *the*, *of*, *and*, *to*, and so on. Stopwords do not help us identify topics because they are used in *all* topics. Words that are used with uniform frequency throughout a document are called *noise*. Stopwords are the best example of noise. For any given document, dozens of other words add to the noise.

We are trying to find a document's *signal*, which is the set of words that communicate a topic. Automatically separating signal from noise is tricky.

Recall our assumption that the document title, or global topic, is known. This is because a book's global topic tends to come up consistently throughout the document. For example, the word *PDF* occurs so regularly throughout this book, it looks like noise.

Identifying local topics. Document word frequency is the number of times a word occurs in a document. By itself, it does not help us because noise words and signal words can occur with any frequency.

Instead, we will look at the word frequency in a given *window* of pages and compare it to the document's global word frequency. For example, *frequency* occurs ten times in this book, and nine of those occurrences are clustered within these few pages. That certainly distinguishes it from the document's constant noise, so it must be a keyword.

This is the central idea of kw_catcher. The program uses a few other tricks to ensure good keyword selection. kw_catcher is free software.

Installing and Using pdftotext

We must convert a PDF into a plain-text file before we can analyze its text for keywords. The Xpdf project (*http://www.foolabs.com/xpdf/*) includes the command-line utility pdftotext, which does a good job of converting a PDF document into a plain-text file. Xpdf is free software.

Windows users can download *xpdf-3.00-win32.zip* from *http://www.foolabs. com/xpdf/download.html*. Unzip, and copy *pdftotext.exe* to a folder in your *PATH*, such as *C:\Windows\system32*. Macintosh OS X users can download a pdftotext installer from *http://www.carsten-bluem.de/downloads/pdftotext_en/*.

Run pdftotext from the command line, like so:

```
pdftotext input.pdf output.txt
```

In general, kw_catcher can take any plain-text file that uses the formfeed character (0x0C) to mark the end of each page.

Installing and Using kw_catcher

Visit *http://www.pdfhacks.com/kw_index/* and download *kw_index-1.0.zip*. This archive contains Windows executables and C++ source code. Unzip, and move *kw_catcher.exe* and *page_refs.exe* to a folder in your *PATH*, such as *C:\Windows\system32*. Or, compile the source to suit your platform.

Run kw_catcher from the command line, like so:

```
kw_catcher <window size> <report style> <text input filename>
```

where the arguments are given as follows:

`<window size>`
> This is the number of sequential pages used to identify peaks in word frequency. If most of a word's occurrences occupy a window of this size, it is a keyword. A large window admits more noise, whereas a small window misses signal. Try starting with a size of 12 and then adjust.

`<report style>`
> How do you want the data presented?

> `keywords_only`
>> Yields a basic list of keywords.

> `frequency`
>> Organizes keywords according to the number of times they occur in the document.

> `reading_order`
>> Outputs every keyword only once, in the order they first appear in the original text.

> `reading_order_repeat`
>> Outputs keywords as they appear in the original text. These last two preserve a sense of the keywords' contexts.

`<text input filename>`
> This is the filename for the plain-text input. Typically, this input is created with pdftotext.

If all goes well, you'll get results such as those shown in Figure 2-4.

For example, creating a keyword list named *mydoc.kw.txt* from *mydoc.pdf* would look something like this:

```
pdftotext mydoc.pdf mydoc.txt
kw_catcher 12 keywords_only mydoc.txt > mydoc.kw.txt
```

See "Create a Traditional Index Section from Keywords" [Hack #57] for an example of how you can put these keywords to use.

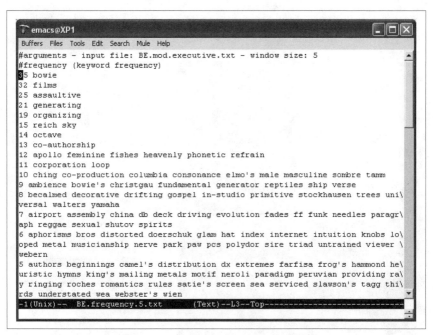

Figure 2-4. The frequency report, which orders keywords by the number of times they appear in the document

HACK #20 Index and Search Local PDF Collections on Windows

Teach Windows XP or 2000 how to search the full text of your PDF along with your other documents. Or, use Adobe Reader to search PDF only.

Search is essential for utilizing document archives. Search can also find things where you might not have thought to look. The problem is that Windows search doesn't know how to read PDF files, by default. We present a couple of solutions.

Search PDF with Adobe Reader

The free Adobe Reader 6.0 provides the easiest solution. It enables you to perform searches across your entire PDF collection (Edit → Search). Its detailed query results include links to individual PDF pages and snippets of the text surrounding your query, as shown in Figure 2-5. Its Fast Find setting, enabled by default, caches the results of your searches, so subsequent searches go much faster. View or change the Reader search preferences by selecting Edit → Preferences → Search.

The downside to Adobe Reader search is that it searches PDF documents only.

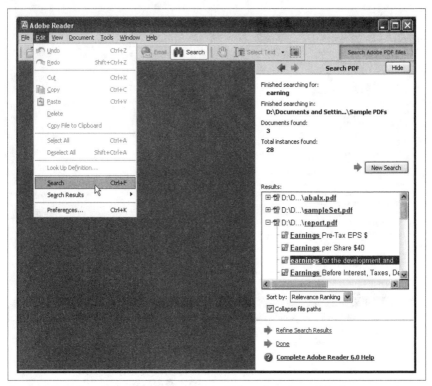

Figure 2-5. Collection search results in Reader linking directly into the documents

Index and Search PDF with Windows XP and 2000

It makes sense to search across all file types from a single interface. Newer versions of Windows enable you to extend its built-in search feature to include PDF documents. With Windows 2000, all you need to do is install the freely available PDF IFilter from Adobe. With Windows XP, you must also apply a couple of workarounds. In both cases, you can use the Windows Indexing Service to speed up searches.

The Windows Indexing Service is powerful but needs to be configured for best performance. The next section introduces you to the Indexing Service. We then discuss installing and troubleshooting Adobe's PDF IFilter.

Windows Indexing Service: Installation, Configuration, and Documentation

You don't need Indexing Service to search your computer, but it can be handy. Queries run much faster, and you can use advanced search features such as Boolean operators (e.g., *AND*, *OR*, and *NOT*), metadata searches (e.g., @DocTitle Contains "pdf"), and pattern matching. The downside is that the Indexing Service always runs in the background, using resources to index new or updated documents. A little configuration ensures that you get the best performance.

First off, do you have Indexing Service? If not, how do you install it? Both questions are answered in the Windows Components Wizard window. In Windows XP or 2000, open this wizard by selecting Start → Settings → Control Panel → Add or Remove Programs and clicking the Add/Remove Windows Components button on the left. Find the Indexing Service component and place a check in its box, if it is empty, as shown in Figure 2-6. Click Next and proceed through the wizard.

Figure 2-6. Adding the Indexing Service component to XP or 2000

Access Indexing Service configuration and documentation from the Computer Management window, shown in Figure 2-7. Right-click My Computer and select Manage. In the left pane, unroll Services and Applications and then Indexing Service.

Sometimes you must stop or start the Indexing Service. Right-click the Indexing Service node and select Stop or Start from the context menu.

Under the Indexing Service node you'll find index *catalogs*, such as System. Add, delete, and configure these catalogs so that they index only the directories you need. For details on how to do this, I highly recommend the

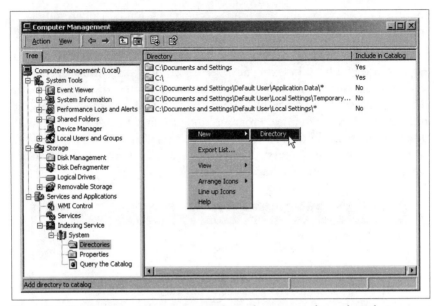

Figure 2-7. *The Computer Management window, where you configure the Indexing Service*

documentation under Help → Help Topics → Indexing Service. This document also details the advanced query language.

> You can fine-tune your Indexing Service with the registry entries located at *HKEY_LOCAL_MACHINE\SYSTEM\CurrentControlSet\Control\ContentIndex*. These are documented at *http://msdn.microsoft.com/library/default.asp?url=/library/en-us/indexsrv/html/ixrefreg_192r.asp*.

You still can search the directories you do not index by selecting Start → Search → For Files or Folders, so don't feel compelled to index your entire computer.

Before installing the PDF IFilter, create a special catalog for testing purposes. Put a few PDFs in its directory. Disable indexing on all other catalog directories by double-clicking these directories and selecting "Include in Index? No." This will simplify testing because indexing many documents can take a long time.

> Download our indexing test PDF from *http://www.pdfhacks.com/ifilter/*. During testing, search this PDF for *guidelines*.

Prepare to Install PDF IFilter 5.0

On Windows XP and 2000, you have two kinds of searches: *indexed* and *unindexed*. An indexed search relies on the Indexing Service, as we have discussed. An unindexed search takes a brute-force approach, scanning all files for your queried text, as shown in Figure 2-8. In both cases, the system uses filters to handle the numerous file types. These filters use the IFilter API to interface with the system.

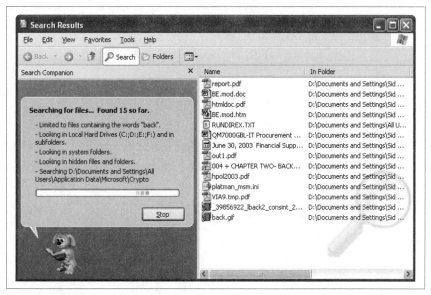

Figure 2-8. An unindexed search

A PDF IFilter is freely available from Adobe. Visit *http://www.adobe.com/support/salesdocs/1043a.htm* and download *ifilter50.exe*. Adobe's web page states that this PDF IFilter works only on servers. In fact, it works on XP Home Edition, too.

If you run Windows 2000, you can install the PDF IFilter and it will work for both indexed and unindexed PDF searching.

If you run Windows XP Home Edition and install the PDF IFilter (Version 5.0), you might need to disable the PDF IFilter for unindexed PDF searches. Unindexed searching of PDFs on XP Home Edition with the PDF IFilter can leave open file handles lying around, which will cause all sorts of problems. Visit *http://www.pdfhacks.com/ifilter/* and download *PDFFilt_FileHandleLeakFix.reg*. We will use it in our installation instructions, later in this hack. This registry hack ensures that only the Indexing Service uses the PDF IFilter. After you apply this hack, PDFs will be treated like plain-text files during unindexed searches. You can undo this registry hack with *PDFFilt_FileHandleLeakFix.uninstall.reg*.

Unindexed searching of PDFs on XP with the PDF IFilter can leave open file handles lying around.

If you perform an unindexed search in a folder of PDFs and then find you can't move or delete these PDFs, you have open file handles. Reboot Windows to close them.

Download Process Explorer from *http://www.sysinternals.com* and follow the *explorer.exe* process to see these open file handles. Use our *PDFFilt_FileHandleLeakFix.reg* registry hack as a workaround, as we describe next.

Install and Troubleshoot Adobe PDF IFilter 5.0

On XP, installing the PDF IFilter might require a couple of registry hacks. First we'll install it, then we'll troubleshoot.

1. In the Computer Management window (right-click My Computer and select Manage), right-click Services and Applications → Indexing Service and select Stop.

2. Run the Adobe PDF IFilter installer through to completion.

3. Windows XP Home users: install *PDFFilt_FileHandleLeakFix.reg* by double-clicking it and selecting Yes to confirm installation. (If you need to undo this registry hack, run *PDFFilt_FileHandleLeakFix.uninstall.reg*.)

4. Start Indexing Service back up again (right-click Services and Applications → Indexing Service and select Start).

5. Rescan your test catalog. Do this by selecting the catalog's Directories node, right-clicking your test directory, and selecting All Tasks → Rescan (Full).

6. Wait for the rescan to complete.

Follow the Indexing Service's progress by selecting Services and Applications → Indexing Service in the Computer Management window. Watch the pane on the right. It is done indexing a catalog when Docs to Index goes to zero.

If a PDF is open in Acrobat, it won't get indexed. Be sure your test document is closed.

To test your index, don't select Start → Search. Instead, in the Computer Management window, select the Query Catalog node listed under your test catalog. Submit a few queries that would work only on the full text of your PDFs. Avoid using document headings or titles. Did it work? If so, you're done! If you get no results, as shown in Figure 2-9, work through the next section, which explains a common workaround for Windows XP.

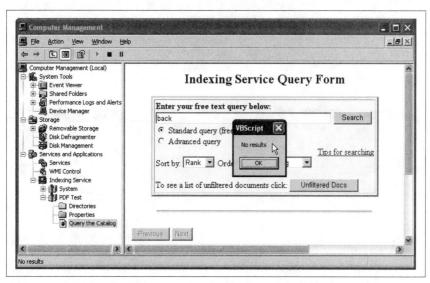

Figure 2-9. Testing your index with negative results

PDF IFilter doesn't work with XP Indexing Service—workaround. PDF IFilter and Indexing Service don't see eye to eye on Windows XP. If querying indexed PDF yields empty sets, give this a try:

1. In the Computer Management window (right-click My Computer and select Manage), right-click Services and Applications → Indexing Service and select Stop.

2. Open the Registry Editor (Start → Run... → Open: regedit → OK).

3. Select *HKEY_CLASSES_ROOT* and then search for *pdffilt.dll* in the registry data (Edit → Find... → Find what: pdffilt.dll → Look at: Data → Find Next).

4. You should hit upon an *InprocServer32* key that references *pdffilt.dll* and specifies its ThreadingModel. Double-click the ThreadingModel and change it from Apartment to Both.

5. Select *HKEY_LOCAL_MACHINE\SYSTEM\CurrentControlSet\Control\ContentIndex* and double-click the *DLLsToRegister* key to edit it.

6. In the list of DLLs, delete the following line:

   ```
   C:\Program Files\Adobe\PDF IFilter 5.0\PDFFilt.dll
   ```

7. Click OK, and then close the Registry Editor.

8. Start the Indexing Service back up (right-click Services and Applications → Indexing Service and select Start).

9. Rescan your test catalog. Do this by opening the catalog's Directories node, right-clicking your test directory, and selecting All Tasks → Rescan (Full).

10. Wait for rescan to complete.

Your test query should now work, as shown in Figure 2-10.

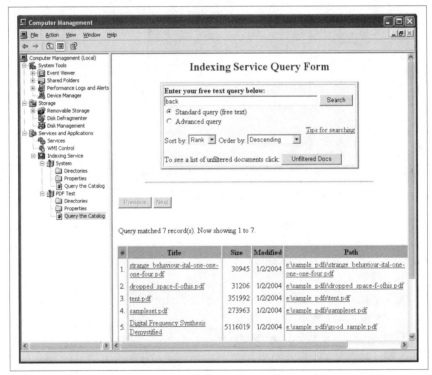

Figure 2-10. PDF indexed search success

Adobe documents this workaround on its web site at *http://www.adobe.com/support/techdocs/333ae.htm*.

Using Start → Search → For Files and Folders

When searching PDFs by selecting Start → Search → For Files and Folders, don't search for Documents. Search All Files and Folders instead. The Documents search overlooks PDFs.

If you indexed a specific folder instead of an entire drive, that folder (or one of its subfolders) must be given in the Look In: field when using Start → Search → For Files and Folders. Otherwise, the index won't be consulted; an unindexed search will be performed instead, even within the indexed folder. Set the Look In: field to a specific folder by clicking the drop-down box and selecting Browse…, as demonstrated in Figure 2-11.

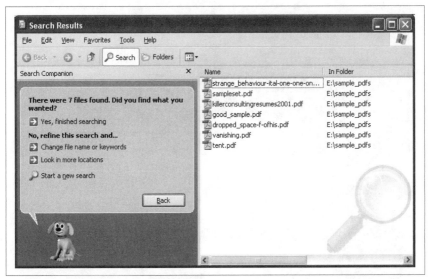

Figure 2-11. Similar results produced by the traditional Start → Search → For Files and Folders interface when searching within indexed folders

When searching within an indexed folder, you can use advanced search terms (e.g., @DocTitle Contains "earnings"). Consult the Indexing Service online documentation, described earlier, for details.

Searching PDF Using Windows 98 and NT System Tools

Using the older Windows search tool on PDF still can be useful, even if it doesn't access the full text of your document. If the PDF documents are not encrypted, their metadata (Title, Author, etc.) and bookmarks are visible to the search tool as plain text. PDF shortcut titles [Hack #17] also are searched.

Spinning Document Portals

Help readers navigate your PDF documents with an HTML front-end. Let them search your PDF's full text, and then link search hits directly to PDF pages.

An HTML portal into a PDF document should describe the document, and it should link readers directly to the sections they might need. This hack uses the information locked in a PDF to create its portal page, as shown in Figure 2-12. We automate the process with PHP, so portals are created on demand. An optional search feature enables readers to drill down into the PDF's full text. Visit *http://www.pdfhacks.com/eno/* to see an online example.

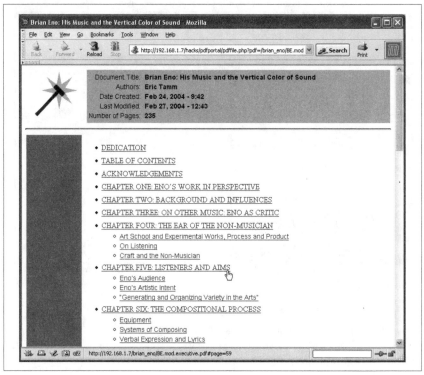

Figure 2-12. Our automatic HTML portals linking readers directly to PDF sections

In "Create an HTML Table of Contents from PDF Bookmarks" **[Hack #70]**, we discussed how to extract document information from a PDF using pdftk **[Hack #79]**. Here, we automate the process with PHP, casting the PDF information into a friendly, dynamic web page. Pass a PDF's path into the script and it yields an HTML portal. If the PDF has no bookmarks or metadata (Title, Author, etc.), this portal will look pretty lean. Even so, the search feature will help readers find what they want.

Tool Up

We'll need pdftk [Hack #79] and pdfportal (*http://www.pdfhacks.com/pdfportal/*). pdftk can extract information from PDF documents, like metadata and bookmarks. pdfportal is a set of PHP scripts that use this document data to create hyperlinked HTML pages.

To install pdfportal, visit *http://www.pdfhacks.com/pdfportal/* and download *pdfportal-1.0.zip*. Unpack the archive and copy its files to a location on your PHP-enabled web server where it can read and execute them. Edit *pdfportal.config.php* to reflect the location of pdftk on your web server.

If you want to use the pdfportal search feature, you must also have pdftotext [Hack #19]. Pdftotext converts PDF documents into plain text. Edit *pdfportal. config.php* to reflect the location of pdftotext on your web server.

 If you can't install pdftk or pdftotext on your web server, use pdftk and pdftotext on your local machine to create the necessary data files and then upload these data files to your web server. Read *pdfportal.config.php* for details.

Windows users without access to a PHP-enabled web server can download and install IndigoPerl from *http://www.indigostar.com*. IndigoPerl is an Apache installer for Windows that includes PHP and Perl support.

Open the Portal

Let's say you copied the pdfportal files to *http://localhost/pdfportal/* and you have a PDF named *http://localhost/collection/mydoc.pdf*. To view this PDF using the portal, pass its path to *pdffile.php* like so:

```
http://localhost/pdfportal/pdffile.php?pdf=/collection/mydoc.pdf
```

pdffile.php calls pdftk to create *http://localhost/collection/mydoc.pdf.info*, if it doesn't already exist. *pdffile.php* then uses this plain-text *info* file to create an HTML page. An info file is simply the output from pdftk's dump_data operation [Hack #64].

Search the PDF's Full Text

Open your PDF's document portal. If *pdffile.php* can find pdftotext on your computer (see *pdfportal.config.php*), it does two things. It uses pdftotext to convert your PDF into a plain-text file, and it activates its search interface. It stores the plain-text file in the same directory as the PDF file.

When you submit a search, *pdffile.php* scans this text file to discover which PDF pages contain your search terms. It reports search hits in reading order, as shown in Figure 2-13. If the PDF has bookmarks, these are used to organize the results. Click a link and the PDF opens to that page.

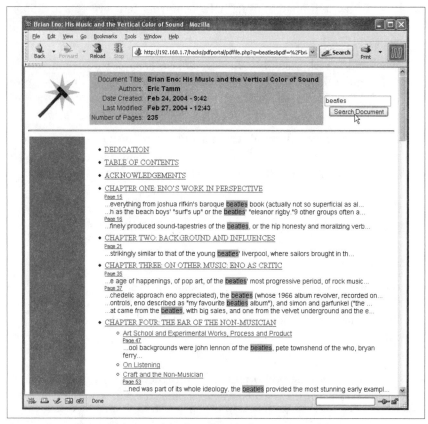

Figure 2-13. pdfportal's document bookmarks, which organize search results

Spinning Collection Portals

HACK #22

Convert directories full of secretive PDFs into inviting HTML portals, automatically.

You can create portals that enable readers to comfortably navigate entire directories of PDF documents. These *directory portals* list document titles, authors, and modification dates, a layer up from the document portals created in "Spinning Document Portals" **[Hack #21]**. They offer hyperlinks to each PDF's document portal and to neighboring directories. Written in PHP, these portals, shown in Figure 2-14, are easy to adapt to your requirements.

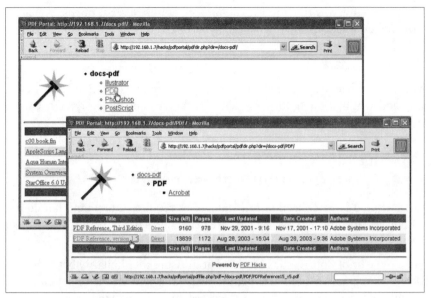

Figure 2-14. Our collection portals reporting PDF information to the reader

Tool Up

You'll need pdftk **[Hack #79]** and pdfportal. To install pdfportal, visit *http://www.pdfhacks.com/pdfportal/* and download *pdfportal-1.0.zip*. Unpack the archive and copy its files to a location on your PHP-enabled web server where it can read and execute them. Edit *pdfportal.config.php* to reflect the location of pdftk on your system.

Windows users without access to a PHP-enabled web server can download and install IndigoPerl from *http://www.indigostar.com*. IndigoPerl is an Apache installer for Windows that includes PHP and Perl support.

Running pdfdir.php

Let's say you copied the pdfportal files to *http://localhost/pdfportal/* and you have a directory named *http://localhost/collection/*. To view this directory using the portal, pass it to *pdfdir.php* like so:

```
http://localhost/pdfportal/pdfdir.php?dir=/collection/
```

pdfdir.php calls pdftk's dump_data operation to create info files for every PDF in this directory, as needed. It then uses these plain-text info files to create an informative HTML summary page. As noted earlier, an info file is simply the output from pdftk's dump_data operation **[Hack #64]**.

Click a document's title, and its document portal [Hack #21] opens. Navigate from directory to directory using the hyperlinked tree at the top of the page.

Hacking the Hack

You can easily expand this portal framework in many directions. For example, add features for uploading PDFs to the current directory. Or, enable users to move a PDF from one directory to another.

Identify Related PDFs
#23   Analyze word frequency to find relationships between PDFs.

Organizing a large collection into categories requires a firsthand familiarity with every document. This level of care generally is not possible. In any case, some documents inevitably get filed into the wrong categories.

Here is a pair of Bourne shell scripts that measure the similarity between two PDF documents. You can use them to help categorize PDFs, to help identify misfiled documents, or to suggest related material to your readers. Their logic is easy to reproduce using any scripting language. To install the Bourne shell on Windows, see "Tool Up for Acrobat Plug-In Development" [Hack #97].

They use the following command-line tools: pdftotext [Hack #19], sed (Windows users visit *http://gnuwin32.sf.net/packages/sed.htm*), sort, uniq, cat, and wc (Windows users visit *http://gnuwin32.sf.net/packages/textutils.htm*). These tools are available on most platforms. Here are some brief descriptions of what the tools do:

pdftotext
    Converts PDF to plain text

sed
    Filters text and makes substitutions

sort
    Sorts lines of text files

uniq
    Removes duplicate lines from a sorted file

cat
    Concatenates files

wc
    Prints the number of bytes, words, and lines in a file

The first script, *wordlist.sh*, takes the filename of a PDF and creates a text file that contains a sorted list of each word that occurs at least twice in the document. Save this script to your disk as *wordlist.sh* and then apply chmod 700 to it, if necessary:

```
#!/bin/sh
pdftotext $1 - | \
sed 's/ /\n/g' | \
sed 's/[^A-Za-z]//g' | \
sed '/^$/d' | \
sed 'y/ABCDEFGHIJKLMNOPQRSTUVWXYZ/abcdefghijklmnopqrstuvwxyz/' | \
sort | \
uniq -d > $1.words.txt
```

First, it converts the PDF to text. Next, it puts each word on its own line. Then, it removes any nonalphabetic characters, so *you'll* becomes *youll*. It removes all blank lines and then converts all characters to lowercase. It sorts the words and then creates a list of individual words that appear at least twice. The output filename is the same as the input filename, except the extension *.words.txt* is added.

If you call *wordlist.sh* like this:

wordlist.sh *mydoc1.pdf*

it creates a text file named *mydoc1.pdf.words.txt*. For example, the word list for *Brian Eno: His Music and the Vertical Color of Sound* (*http://www. pdfhacks.com/eno/*) includes:

```
anything
anyway
anywhere
apart
aperiodic
aphorisms
apollo
apparatus
apparent
apparently
appeal
appear
```

The second script, *percent_overlap.sh*, compares two word lists and reports what percentage of words they share. If you compare a document to itself, its overlap is 100%. The percentage is calculated using the length of the shorter word list, so if you were to take a chapter from a long document and compare it to the entire, long document, it would report a 100% overlap as well.

Given any two, totally unrelated documents, their overlap still might be 35%. This also makes sense, because all documents of the same language use many of the same words. Two unrelated fiction novels might have considerable overlap. Two unrelated technical documents would not.

In this next Bourne shell script, note that we use backtick
characters (`` ` ``), not apostrophes ('). The backtick character
usually shares its key with the tilde (~) on your keyboard.

Save this script to your disk as *percent_overlap.sh* and then apply chmod 700
to it, if necessary:

```
#!/bin/sh
num_words_1=`cat $1 | wc -l`
num_words_2=`cat $2 | wc -l`
num_common_words=`sort $1 $2 | uniq -d | wc -l`

if [ $num_words_1 -lt $num_words_2 ]
then echo $(( 100 * $num_common_words/$num_words_1 ))
else echo $(( 100 * $num_common_words/$num_words_2 ))
fi
```

Run *percent_overlap.sh* like this, and it returns the overlap between the two
documents as a single number (in this example, the overlap is 38%):

```
$ percent_overlap.sh mydoc1.pdf.words.txt mydoc2.pdf.words.txt
38
```

If you do this on multiple documents, you can see a variety of relationships
emerge. For example, Table 2-1 shows the overall overlaps between various
documents on my computer.

Table 2-1. The results of comparing various documents with percent_overlap.sh

	A	B	C	D	E	F	G
A=PDF Reference, 1.4	100	98	65	36	48	50	35
B=PDF Reference, 1.5	98	100	67	37	51	52	34
C=PostScript Reference, Third Edition	65	67	100	38	47	49	36
D=The ANSI C++ Specification	36	37	38	100	38	40	25
E=Corporate Annual Report #1	48	51	47	38	100	62	49
F=Corporate Annual Report #2	50	52	49	40	62	100	52
G=Brian Eno Book by Eric Tamm	35	34	36	25	49	52	100

Authoring and Self-Publishing: Hacking Outside the PDF

Hacks 24–31

Publishing documents involves a lot more than creating PDF files. The next few chapters will take a look at the details involved in publishing with PDF, but the hacks here will make that work easier and perhaps even more profitable for you.

HACK #24 Keep Your Source Smart

Cherish and maintain your source document; dumb PDF is no substitute.

PDF has grown to be a very capable file format. Starting out as *dumb* "electronic paper," PDF is now also used as a *smart* authoring file format by many Adobe products. By *smart*, I mean that it perfectly preserves a document's structure. For example, you can create artwork in Adobe Illustrator and then save it as a PDF without any loss of information (File → Save As... → Save as Type: PDF). Open this smart PDF in Illustrator and continue editing; it functions just like Illustrator's native AI file format. Smart PDFs have beauty *and* brains.

> Smart PDFs aren't suited for general, online distribution. They are packed with application data and are much larger than their optimized, dumb derivatives. Some authoring programs give you the option to create dumb PDF. In Illustrator, for example, you can disable Preserve Illustrator Editing Capabilities when you choose to create a PDF (File → Save a Copy... → Save as Type: PDF). Or, dumb down a smart PDF with refrying [Hack #60] before releasing it for wide distribution.

Between *smart* and *dumb*, you have *clever* (or *tagged*) PDFs, which retain a loose sense of the original document's structure [Hack #34]. Screen readers and downstream filters can use this information to extract document text and tables from the PDF. The *PDFMaker* macro, which ships with Adobe Acrobat and integrates with Microsoft Word, can create clever PDFs [Hack #32].

Smart, clever, and dumb PDFs have different advantages, but they all share the same, beautiful face. Each kind can represent your document with excellent visual fidelity. This makes it hard to tell them apart by sight and leads to some confusion.

Only a few applications can create smart PDFs. Adobe Acrobat is not one of them. Acrobat can create dumb or clever PDF, but it can't create a PDF that is clever enough to replace your source document. When using popular word processors like Microsoft Word, Sun StarOffice/OpenOffice, or Corel WordPerfect, PDF is not a substitute for the program's native file format.

> When making corrections to a PDF, remember to update the source file, too. Ideally, you would make all changes to your source document first, and then re-create the PDF edition. Depending on your workflow, this might not be practical.

So, cherish and maintain your source document. Dumb (or even clever) PDF is not a substitute. A good source document will reward you with HTML, handheld, and full-featured PDF editions. Process it to create derivative material, or easily apply new styles. As we shall see, your smart source document is pure content and should give you good service.

Meanwhile, dumb PDF remains perfectly suited for its original purpose: easy creation and distribution of great-looking electronic documents.

Authoring a Smart Source Document

A smart source document promises great rewards. Creating smart source documents takes discipline. The trick is to separate the document's *content* from its *presentation*. We accomplish this by introducing *styles*, such as Heading 1, Body Text, and List Number. Styles separate content and presentation like so:

Content → Style → Presentation

For example:

"Chapter One: Eno's Work in Perspective" → Heading 1 → Arial Narrow, Bold, 18 pts.

When you create a new paragraph, tag it with a style. In this case, we used Heading 1. The Heading 1 style, in turn, describes how all such paragraphs should appear. If you set the Heading 1 style to use the Bold, Arial Narrow font, all Heading 1 paragraphs in your document will be rendered using Bold, Arial Narrow. Without styles, changing the Heading 1 font from Arial

Narrow to Times could involve selecting and changing every single heading paragraph by hand. Ugh!

The benefits of styles go well beyond rapidly changing fonts. You can also:

- Create a dynamic table of contents
- Create a full-featured PDF edition [Hack #32]
- Create an HTML edition [Hack #35]
- Create a handheld edition [Hack #36]
- Generate derivative documents [Hack #55]

How? Styles give your content intelligence. When creating the full-featured PDF, Heading 1 paragraphs also become level-1 bookmarks. When creating the HTML edition, Heading 1 paragraphs are appropriately tagged <h1>. Styles give your content meaning, so downstream filters can interpret it properly.

Styles in Microsoft Word 2002, Word 2000, and Word:Mac v.X

When you create a new document in Word, you inherit a collection of styles from the document's *template*. If you did not specify a template, the *normal.dot* template is used as your document's template. How do you access these styles?

In Word 2002, select Format → Styles and Formatting..., and a task pane opens on the right. If the list of styles looks too short, go to the bottom of this pane and set Show: All Styles to show everything. The list should grow to include dozens of paragraph, character, list, and table styles. At the top, as shown in Figure 3-1, it shows the style of your current selection. Change your current selection's style by simply clicking one of the alternative styles in the list.

In Word 2000 or Word:Mac, select Format → Style to open a dialog that shows a list of available paragraph and character styles. Set List: All Styles to see everything. You can also use this dialog, shown in Figure 3-2, to change the current selection's style. After you change a style, the dialog closes. This is a cumbersome way to apply styles.

A better way to view and change paragraph styles in Word 2000 and Word: Mac is with the Style Area, shown in Figure 3-3. In Word 2000, select Tools → Options → View. In Word:Mac, select Word → Preferences and select the View option. Set the Style Area Width, near the bottom of the dialog box, to 1" and click OK. Now, select View → Normal or View → Outline, and a column on the left will show you the style of each paragraph. Double-click a style name and the *Style* dialog box opens, enabling you to change the paragraph's style.

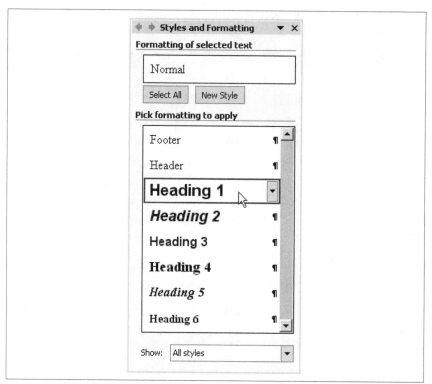

Figure 3-1. Quickly changing styles using the Styles and Formatting task pane

Writing a document using only styles takes discipline. Word makes it very easy to apply paragraph formatting outside of styles, so reduce temptation by closing the Formatting toolbar (View → Toolbars → Formatting), which is shown in Figure 3-4. After closing the Formatting toolbar, you can easily open the *Style* dialog by pressing Ctrl-Shift-S (Windows) or Command-Shift-S (Mac).

In most cases, you should change a paragraph's formatting by changing its style (e.g., from Normal to List Bullet) or by modifying the style's formatting (e.g., adding an indent to all Normal paragraphs). You can modify a style's formatting with the Modify Style dialog, which you can access in many ways.

From the Styles and Formatting task pane, available in Word XP and 2003 and shown in Figure 3-5, you can open the Modify Style dialog by selecting Modify... from the current style's drop-down menu. Or, in any version of Word, select the paragraph, open the Style dialog by pressing Ctrl-Shift-S (Windows) or Command-Shift-S (Mac), and then click Modify.... When using the Style Area, you can open the Style dialog by double-clicking the paragraph's style name. Then click Modify... to open the Modify Style dialog.

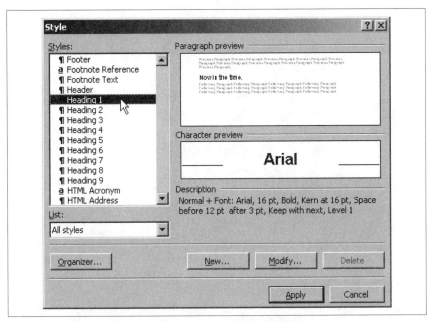

Figure 3-2. Changing a paragraph's style using the Style dialog

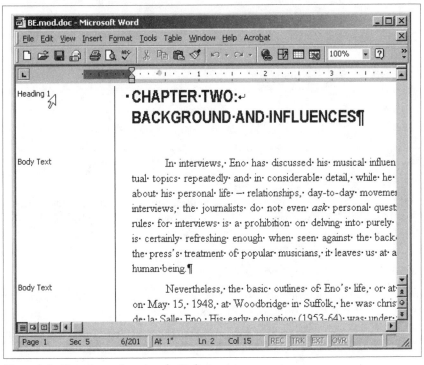

Figure 3-3. Changing styles using the Style Area

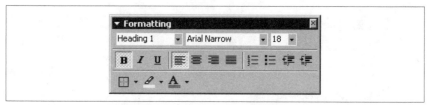

Figure 3-4. The Formatting toolbar: a dangerous temptation

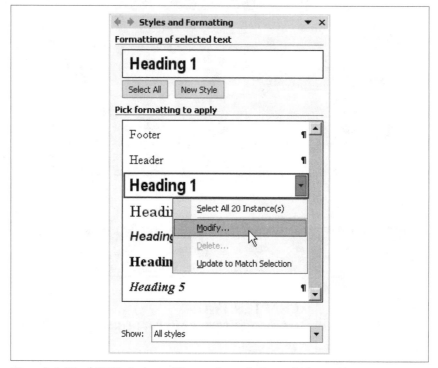

Figure 3-5. Word 2002's Styles and Formatting task pane, which provides easy access to a style's format settings

Finally, avoid using tabs, repeated spaces, or repeated carriage returns (empty paragraphs) to format your content. Instead, update the style's paragraph indents and spacing to suit your taste. Use tables for tabular data.

Creating an Automatic Table of Contents in Word

To create an automatic table of contents from your document's Heading styles, select Insert → Reference → Index and Tables... → Table of Contents (Word 2002), or Insert → Index and Tables... → Table of Contents (Word 2000/Word:Mac).

Convey Your Document's Value with Good Design

Ensure that your document looks good and reads well.

Although content is king, presentation must not be overlooked. Just as you would dress up for a business interview or date, you should take care to dress your content according to its purpose. This should include practical as well as aesthetic considerations.

Your document's design should convey the value and care you have invested in its content. It should complement your content and help the reader understand your work. So, design your document with the same eye you used to craft your content. Research and consult, and consider working with a professional whose work you admire. Once you establish your document's design, apply it consistently.

A highly recommended book on the subject is Marshall Lee's *Bookmaking: Editing, Design, Production* (W.W. Norton).

> For online tips about hyphenating words, punctuating sentences, and capitalizing titles, visit the New York University Editing Workshop Syllabus (*http://www.nyu.edu/classes/copyXediting/syllabus.html*).

Every genre uses established styles that you are expected to follow, so you may already have guidelines to use. Some guidelines are strict (e.g., patent applications), but most leave room for personality and branding (e.g., *The Wall Street Journal* versus *USA Today*). Study established works in your genre to learn what your readers generally expect. This is also a good way to find the particular styles you prefer. Think of it as window-shopping for your document's outfit.

I'll Take That Font

Once you have spotted a font you want to use, identifying it can be tricky. If you found it in a book, check the back of the book for a *colophon*. If you found it in a PDF, check its font properties (File → Document Properties... → Fonts).

An online, intelligent assistant can help identify your font (it is also a fun way to browse fonts):

http://www.fonts.com/findfonts/identifontframe.asp?FONTNAME=identifont

Or, try the optical font recognition engine at:

http://www.myfonts.com/WhatTheFont/

Thousands of professional fonts are on the market, so it might be impossible to precisely identify your font sample. Or, if you do identify your font, it might turn out to be too expensive for your budget. In these cases, you often can discover a good substitute. Later, we discuss some convenient and economical sources for fonts.

 See some fonts that other people use by visiting the Best Sellers page at *http://www.myfonts.com/fonts/bestsellers.html.*

To install fonts on Windows, open *C:\Windows\Fonts* or *C:\WINNT\Fonts* in the File Explorer. Select File → Install New Font… and a dialog opens. Navigate over to the folder where your new fonts are, and their names should appear in the List of Fonts. Select the fonts you want to install and click OK.

Installing Type 1 or OpenType fonts on older Windows systems (NT, 98, or 95) or older Macintosh systems (pre–OS X) requires that you install one of Adobe's ATM products first. ATM Light is freely available from *http://www.adobe.com/products/atmlight/main.html.*

Free Fonts

The Internet seems awash with free or cheap fonts. Crafting a good font takes hard work, and a bad font can actually create production problems. I advocate using professional fonts from reputable designers and foundries. Consider buying a *font pack* to bootstrap your font collection economically.

One source for good, free fonts is the Base 35 font package that comes with Ghostscript [Hack #39]. If you installed Ghostscript to *C:\gs\gs8.14*, these fonts will be unpacked to *C:\gs\fonts*. Another free, professional font family is Bitstream's Vera (*http://www.bitstream.com/categories/products/fonts/vera/*).

Microsoft made its core TrueType fonts freely distributable. If you don't have them already, you can fetch them from *http://corefonts.sf.net.*

 The venerable Computer Modern fonts are freely available from *http://www.ams.org/tex/type1-fonts.html.* However, they don't work as expected with popular word processors such as Microsoft Word. Consider purchasing European Modern (*http://www.yandy.com/em.htm*) instead.

System Fonts

Computer systems come with dozens of useful fonts. However, some might have licensing restrictions that could prevent you from embedding them into your PDF. When you create your PDF and try to embed such a font, Distiller will report the error in its log file. The resulting PDF might use a poor substitute font instead, such as Courier.

> TrueType font files include built-in license restriction information; Type 1 font files do not. You mustn't rely on Distiller to enforce restrictions; read the license.

> If you want to minimize your PDF's file size, consider using common fonts that you don't need to embed. The Base 14 fonts and some system fonts are available on most computers, so you don't need to pack them into your PDF. See "Embed and Subset Fonts to Your Advantage" [Hack #43] to learn more.

Bundled Fonts

Some authoring products come with fonts. For example, my Adobe Illustrator 9.0.1 CD has 213 fonts located in its *Fonts & ATM\Fonts* directory. Even though I asked the Illustrator installer to install fonts, it overlooked these. This same disc includes other goodies, such as clip art and stock photos.

Discover font files on your hard drives and CDs by searching for *.ttf* (TrueType or OpenType), *.pfa*, *.pfb* (Adobe Type 1), or *.otf* (OpenType) font files.

Font Packs

The different type foundries offer bulk discounts when you purchase *collections* of fonts. For example, Adobe offers the Type Basics collection of 65 fonts for $99 (*http://www.adobe.com/type/*). Visit *http://fonts.com* and *http://www.myfonts.com* to learn about the various font packs and CDs on the market.

Typography Tips

Here are some suggestions for formatting your document's text and pages. There are no hard-and-fast rules for good design, so apply these tips judiciously.

- When using two font families in one document, select one *serif* family and one *sans-serif* family, as shown in Figure 3-6. Avoid using more than two font families in one document. Some font families include dozens of fonts; Helvetica has 35 (*http://www.myfonts.com/fonts/linotype/helvetica/*).

Serif Fonts are Easier to Read on Paper	Sans-serif Fonts are Easier to Read On-Screen

Figure 3-6. One serif family (left) and one sans-serif family (right)

- Serif body text is easier to read on paper; sans-serif body text is easier to read on-screen. Select a conservative font for long paragraphs so that they are comfortable to read. Headings can be more fanciful.

- Text size is not the height of any specific letter. Rather, it is a loose measurement of the horizontal space used by a line of text. It is measured in *points*, and there are 72 points per inch.

  A typical size for body text is 9 or 10 points. For an older audience, 11- or 12-point text is better because it is easier to read. Use 12-point body text in wide columns so that the words-per-line ratio remains reasonable.

- Activate automatic kerning for your styles, particularly heading styles. Kerning tweaks the spaces between letters so that they look their best as shown in Figure 3-7.

  In Word, add automatic kerning to a style by opening its Modify Style dialog and selecting Format → Font... → Character Spacing. Check the Kerning for Fonts checkbox and click OK.

Wove Keys Together

Kerning off

Wove Keys Together

Kerning on

Figure 3-7. Activating automatic kerning to make text look better

- Adjust column width and font size so that your body text averages 10 to 14 words per line. For example, text using a 9-point font might fit nicely in a 4-inch-wide column. The same text and font at 10 points might require a 4.5-inch-wide column. Long lines slow down the reader.

- When you must scale a paragraph to fit into a given, vertical space, adjust its line spacing, as illustrated in Figure 3-8, before adjusting its font size. For example, 11- or 12-point line spacing looks good with a 9-point font. 13-point line spacing looks good with a 10-point font.

In Word, open your style's Paragraph dialog, set Line Spacing: to Exactly, and enter your desired line point size.

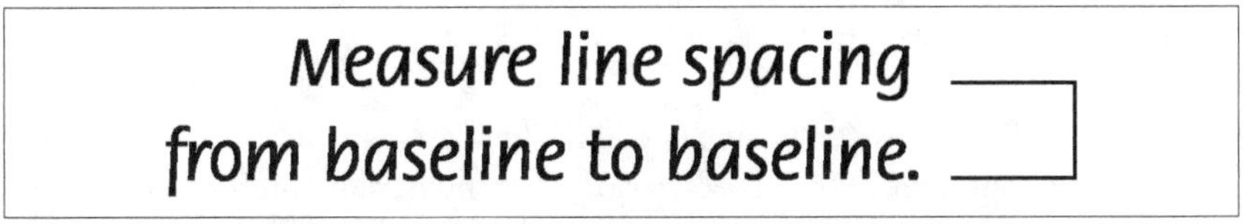

Measure line spacing *from baseline to baseline.*

Figure 3-8. Line spacing measured from baseline to baseline

- When using narrow columns (nine words or fewer per line), consider aligning text to the left instead of using justified alignment. Otherwise, words can end up spaced too far apart, as shown in Figure 3-9.

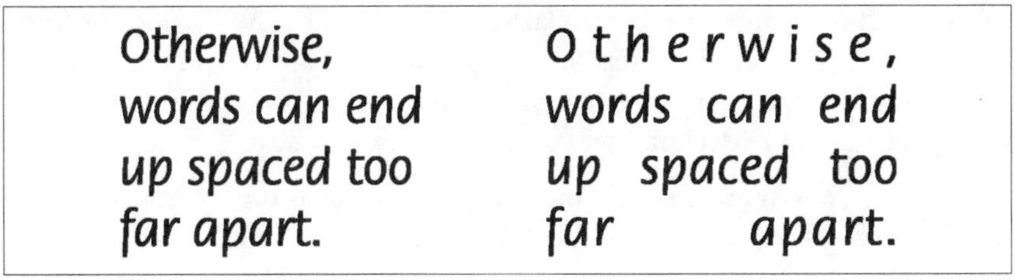

Otherwise,	*O t h e r w i s e ,*
words can end	*words can end*
up spaced too	*up spaced too*
far apart.	*far apart.*

Figure 3-9. Narrow columns left-aligned (left) and justified (right)

- Avoid using all-caps or underlines for emphasis; use italic or bold instead. When using a light font, emphasize text using light italic or regular, not bold.

  When you desire an all-caps style, try to find a font designed for that purpose, as shown in Figure 3-10.

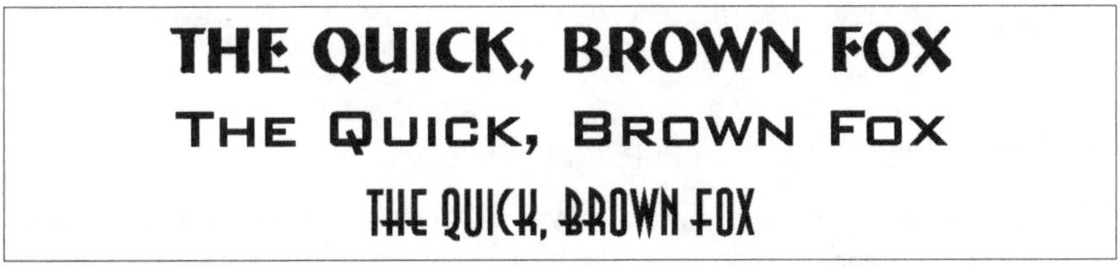

THE QUICK, BROWN FOX
THE QUICK, BROWN FOX
THE QUICK, BROWN FOX

Figure 3-10. All-caps or small-caps fonts, which provide good-looking, all-caps styles

Handling Long URLs

Placing URLs in a paragraph can leave you with awkward line lengths. Microsoft Word won't break a URL over two lines, so the preceding line can end up looking too short. Here are some ideas for improving URL formatting.

Use page footnotes for URLs. A URL usually references related material and does not contribute to the paragraph's narrative. So, place it in a page footnote, where references traditionally belong. This also makes it easier for readers to quickly find the URL later.

Insert Zero-Width Spaces to cue line breaks. The *Zero-Width Space* (ZWS) is a nonprinting character that tells Microsoft Word where it can break the URL. A natural location for the ZWS is after each slash that follows the domain name. Style the URL text a little differently than the body text, so readers aren't confused by URLs broken over two or more lines.

In Word 2002, insert a ZWS by typing 200b (the Unicode for ZWS) at the insertion point and then pressing Alt-X.

In Word 2000, you can replace slashes with slashes+ZWS using the Find and Replace dialog (Edit → Replace…). Set Find What: to /. Enter a slash in Replace With: and then append a ZWS by holding down the Alt key and typing 8203 (200b in decimal) on your keypad.

For handy ZWS Word macros and more information on ZWS, visit *http://word.mvps.org/FAQs/Formatting/NoWidthSpace.htm*. If you're using a Macintosh, unfortunately this is a much more complicated process. Visit *http://word.mvps.org/FAQs/WordMac/Unicode.htm* for more information.

HACK #26   Create Charts and Graphs from Raw Data

Put a friendly face on your data before turning it into PDF.

Instead of chilling readers with tables of raw data, invite them to understand your numbers by displaying them in charts or graphs. Popular word processors can create charts for you, or you can use free software to create graphs.

Microsoft Word 2002, Word 2000, and Word:Mac v.X

Select and copy your table data. In Word, select Insert → Picture → Chart and a little spreadsheet opens. The first row and first column of this Datasheet are reserved for your data's row and column headings. Select the upper-left cell and paste your table's data. The chart will change to reflect your data. Activate/deactivate rows and columns by double-clicking the Datasheet's row and column labels.

When you first create a chart, Word enters a special state called Microsoft Graph. Exit this state by clicking the document page outside the chart. Re-enter this state by double-clicking the chart. Within this state, you can update the chart's Datasheet, change the chart type (Chart → Chart Type…), or tailor the chart's styling (to change a chart component's color or style, double-click it). You can also resize or scale the chart by clicking its borders and dragging them around.

Corel WordPerfect

WordPerfect's charts behave much like Word's. In WordPerfect, you can select a table's data, right-click, and choose Chart to rapidly create a chart. WP's chart gallery (right-click and choose Gallery...) offers dozens of chart types (as does Word's). I find WP's charts the easiest to style.

Sun StarOffice and OpenOffice

Sun's word processor includes chart features that resemble those in Microsoft Word. Select Insert → Object → Chart... to start its wizard. Select your table's data (step 1), select the chart type (steps 2 and 3), set the title (step 4), and you're done. Double-click the chart to enter a special chart-editing state.

Create Standalone Plots with gnuplot

You can also create standalone plots using gnuplot. Easily create basic 2D or 3D plots from input data, or program gnuplot to precisely style the output. Preview plots on-screen, and then render them as PostScript, PNG, or one of the many other supported formats. Visit *http://www.gnuplot.info* for downloads, documentation, and examples. gnuplot is free software.

Store your two-dimensional data points in a text file like so (from *DEMO/ 1.DAT*):

```
-20.000000 -3.041676
-19.000000 -3.036427
-18.000000 -3.030596
...
```

Store your three-dimensional data points in a text file like so (from *DEMO/ GLASS.DAT*):

```
0.568000 0.000000 -0.911000
0.518894 0.231026 -0.911000
0.380066 0.422106 -0.911000
...
```

Launch gnuplot and an interactive shell opens. By default, gnuplot renders plots on-screen. View a basic 2D plot of *DEMO/1.DAT* like so:

```
gnuplot> plot 'DEMO/1.DAT'
```

View a basic 3D plot of *DEMO/GLASS.DAT* like so:

```
gnuplot> splot 'DEMO/GLASS.DAT'
```

Create a PostScript file from your plot like so (the second set output releases the output file handle):

```
gnuplot> set term postscript enhanced color solid
gnuplot> set output 'DEMO/1.ps'
gnuplot> plot 'DEMO/1.DAT'
gnuplot> set output
```

Run one of the DEMO scripts that come with the Windows distribution like so:

```
gnuplot> cd 'DEMO'
gnuplot> load 'WORLD.DEM'
```

gnuplot has a good interactive help system. To learn about a keyword, type help *keyword* (e.g., help term). The gnuplot newsgroup, *comp.graphics.apps.gnuplot*, can also help you.

Show Relationships with Graphviz

A *graph* illustrates relationships between *nodes* by connecting them with *edges*. A *directed graph* uses one-way edges, indicated by arrowheads. An *undirected graph* does not. Use directed graphs to illustrate hierarchies or workflows.

Graphviz is a set of open source tools for creating graphs from input data. Visit *http://www.research.att.com/sw/tools/graphviz/* for documentation, downloads, and examples.

The Graphviz program we'll use is called *dot*. Here is a basic example taken from the *dot* user's manual. Label nodes and describe their relationships using a text file:

```
// example_graph.dot
digraph G {
    main -> parse;
    main -> execute;
    main -> init;
    main -> cleanup;
    parse -> execute;
    execute -> make_string;
    execute -> printf;
    init -> make_string;
    main -> printf;
    execute -> compare;
}
```

Pass this text file to *dot* and specify an output file format. We use Post-Script, but you can also use PNG, SVG, or one of more than two dozen other formats:

```
dot -Tps example_graph.dot -o example_graph.ps
```

The results in Figure 3-11 look good and make sense.

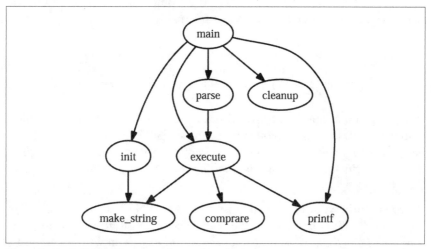

Figure 3-11. Graphviz illustrating hierarchies nicely

Graphviz can also create elaborate, colorful graphs. Visit the Graphviz web site to see some examples.

 HACK
#27

Become a Publisher

Purchase your book's ISBN and become a publisher.

Whoever registers your book's ISBN is given credit for publishing your book. By purchasing your own ISBN, you also inherit the privileges of a publisher. *ISBN* stands for *International Standard Book Number*. It is a ten-digit number, and every published book has a unique ISBN. Your book must have one, such as the one in Figure 3-12, if you desire distributors and retailers to carry it. This ISBN must be printed on the book, so get one before going to press.

Figure 3-12. A book's ISBN in barcode

Think of a name for your publishing house, get out your credit card, and visit *http://www.isbn.org* to apply for an ISBN *publisher prefix*. This prefix will be used in all your ISBNs. At the same time, you must purchase a block of 10, 100, 1,000, or 10,000 ISBN numbers. As of this writing, 10 ISBNs cost $244.95, and 100 ISBNs cost $853.95. After completing the application, you should receive your numbers in about 10 days.

> Publishing a book involves coordinating many resources. Assume that each step will require twice as much time as you would expect and you might have your book ready on time.

When your ISBN numbers arrive, you will also receive online account information. Use this online account to assign an ISBN to your book. Remember: you cannot reuse an ISBN. After assigning your book's ISBN, go to Books in Print at *http://www.bowkerlink.com* and list your book free of charge.

When you print your book, you must print the ISBN on the inside copyright page and the ISBN barcode on the outside cover. Visit *http://www.isbn.org/ standards/home/isbn/us/major.asp* for details on exactly how to use an ISBN number. Using it incorrectly can cause fulfillment problems.

> You can create your ISBN barcode free of charge using this Lightning Source web page: *http://www.lightningsource.com/ LSISecure/PubResources/CoverSpecsEntry.asp*. After submitting your ISBN, you will receive a PDF template for your book's cover via email. This template is designed for use by Lightning's system, but you can use Illustrator, Acrobat, or Photoshop to copy the barcode graphic from the given PDF template and paste it onto your book's cover.

Now that you are a publisher, you can talk to distributors about carrying your book. Lightning Source is a wholesale distributor that also provides print-on-demand (POD) production and secure e-book fulfillment [Hack #29]. If you decide to print your own book, consider using Amazon's Advantage program [Hack #30].

Or, Consider a For-Fee Publisher

If self-publishing your book sounds like too much trouble, consider using a service provider that will publish your book for a fee. View a list of providers at *https://www.lightningsource.com/ResourcesLinks.htm#AuthorServicesLinks*. They offer various programs and à la carte features.

One example is the iUniverse Select program (*http://www.iuniverse.com*). For $459, iUniverse takes your electronic document and creates two editions: the POD paperback edition and the PDF e-book edition. iUniverse registers ISBNs, creates cover graphics, and lists your book with Amazon and Barnes & Noble. iUniverse pays you a 20% royalty on the money it receives (as opposed to the retail price) minus book shipping and handling charges.

Given this royalty formula, it is impossible to know how much you might receive for each book sold. Let's make some guesses. If iUniverse gives your book a $25 suggested retail price, a sale through Amazon might pay iUniverse 50% ($12.50). Let's guess that shipping and handling costs $1.50, which leaves $11. From that, you receive 20%, or $2.20. As I say, this is just a guess. For a broader discussion of royalty voodoo, visit *http://www.booksandtales.com/pod/rword.htm*.

> Every book has a publisher, and every publisher has a reputation. This reputation can help or hinder your book's sales. Before choosing a for-fee publisher, look at other books the company has published to make sure your work fits in.

Consult the newsgroups (*http://groups.google.com*) for opinions and testimonials on these various services. Perform an advanced search on Amazon to locate books by publisher, and check out their best-selling books.

Print at Home, at the Office, or at Kinko's
HACK #28

Copy shops pick up where your laser printer leaves off.

Your electronic document's shortest path to paper is probably a laser printer. You have one, or somebody you know has one, and its fidelity is remarkable. Your local office supply store has aisles of specialty papers and binding devices that help turn your printout into a publication.

When you need to quickly print and bind dozens of documents, your next stop might be the local copy shop. They are equipped with commercial-strength laser printers, copiers, paper trimmers, collators, and bindery equipment. A print shop with copying services might have better equipment, a greater selection of papers, and a more knowledgeable staff. They can also advise you when to upgrade from high-volume copying to offset printing. Shop around, and seek recommendations.

> A *trimmer* is a powerful guillotine that can make a clean cut through inches of paper. A *collator* is a device for getting your document's pages into the proper order. *Binding* is the process of attaching your pages together into a single document.

Selecting the Paper

Tasteful use of specialty or colored papers can improve your document's appeal and make it stand out. However, different types of paper are used for different purposes. *Bond* paper generally is used in office copiers. *Book* paper is formulated for offset printing. If you want to use a special paper, ask a professional printer for advice. Naturally, a copy shop will stock only the papers they can use on-site.

A paper's thickness, or *weight*, is measured differently for different types of paper. So, a 20-pound bond paper is not comparable to a 20-pound book paper. An introduction to paper choices is available online at *http://depts. washington.edu/bsc/general_PDF's/Choosing_Paper.pdf*.

Copying Photographs

Photographs are difficult to reproduce using a common copier. When detail or color is important, consider grouping this artwork together onto a few, select pages. Use the more expensive color laser printing or color copying on just those few pages, and then insert these color pages into your document before binding.

Binding

A staple or paperclip might serve to hold your document together, but a proper spine and covers dress up your work. And, they make your document easier to navigate. Some binding mechanisms, such as a plastic comb, allow your pages to lie flat. Other techniques, such as glue binding, do not.

If your finished document won't be lying flat, consider using your word processor to add gutters to your document pages. Gutters keep your page text from getting lost in the spine's fold. In Word, select File → Page Setup... → Margins and increase the Gutter setting as needed.

> Kinko's has combined online document hosting with POD to create its DocStore service. Visit *http://www.fedex.com/us/officeprint/commsols/solutions/docstore.html* to learn more about this interesting hybrid.

 HACK **Publish POD and E-books**

#29   Partner with Lightning Source and plug your book into the system.

Lightning Source works with publishers (that's you [Hack #27]) to print and distribute books and e-books. Its POD facilities create paper books only when orders arrive, sparing you the trouble, risk, and expense of a large print run. Its secure e-book fulfillment service gives your readers more options and minimizes production costs. Distributing your book through Lightning Source will get it into the catalogs of Amazon, Barnes & Noble, and other retailers worldwide. Lightning Source is a subsidiary of Ingram Industries, which ties it to the awesome Ingram Book Group, so Lightning Source has firm footings and a broad network.

 Wholesale distributors supply books to retailers, who then sell books to the public. Publishers rely heavily on wholesale distributors to get their books into readers' hands.

Lightning Source is not for everybody. It does not provide the many services you get from a for-fee publisher. Lightning Source simply takes your finished book, prints it, and distributes it. You are responsible for everything else, which includes registering an ISBN [Hack #27], typesetting your book to fit Lightning Source's specifications, and creating a suitable cover graphic. Not following Lightning Source's guidelines can cause frustration and additional expense. Guidelines and templates are available from *http://www.lightningsource.com/ResourcesBookDesigner.htm*.

To start, you must apply for an account at *http://www.lightningsource.com*. Upon acceptance, log in to upload your print-ready book and its cover art. This online account also enables you to order printed books, track your orders, and read sales reports.

Entering your book into the system requires a setup fee, which varies according to your book. For a 300-page book, your setup fee might be $100. Maintaining one book on Lightning Source's servers costs $12 per year.

A few days after entering your book into the system, you will receive a printed *proof* to examine and approve. Iron out any problems you discover with the proof, and then your book will be ready for printing. When using Lightning Source's distribution service, it could take two weeks or so for retailers to add your book to their catalogs. Meanwhile, you can order books directly from Lightning Source.

As the publisher, you control the suggested retail price of your book. You then sell your books to the wholesale distributor at a discounted, wholesale price. By giving Lightning Source a 55% discount, you leave room for them to extend an attractive discount to retailers. When you sell a book, Lightning Source charges you for printing, but not for shipping and handling. The price for printing a 300-page book is around $5 per book.

 For a discussion on discount arithmetic, visit: *http://julieduffy.com/writing/econo_discount.htm*.

So, if we gave our hypothetical 300-page book a suggested retail price of $25, each sale through Lightning Source would pay 45% ($11.25) minus the $5 printing charge, or $6.25.

You can also sell e-book editions of your book through Lightning Source. There is no printing charge for these electronic editions.

HACK #30   Sell Through Amazon

Partner with Amazon and let them handle the transaction.

You have written, edited, and typeset your content. You have registered an ISBN and printed your book. Now, you must sell your book and ship it to your readers. If you are in North America and have worldwide distribution rights, consider applying for the Amazon Advantage program.

Upon approval, Amazon adds your title to its catalog and puts a few of your books in its warehouse. When customers purchase your book, Amazon processes and ships the orders. In exchange, you give Amazon a 55% discount from the suggested retail price that you set. Amazon also charges you a $29.95 annual membership fee.

So, if you gave your book a suggested retail price of $25, each sale through Amazon would pay 45%, or $11.25.

In addition to books, you can also sell CD music or VHS/DVD videos that you created, but not e-books. For more details on how to join the Amazon Advantage program, see *http://www.amazon.com/exec/obidos/subst/partners/direct/advantage/home.html*.

For a different perspective on the Amazon Advantage program, see *http://julieduffy.com/writing/amazon_a.htm*.

HACK #31   Sell Your Book, Sell Yourself

What are you selling? Who's going to buy it?

Convincing people to buy your book is your greatest challenge. It helps if you think of your book as one part of a larger selling strategy. This larger strategy has to do with selling yourself. After people begin to see you as a trusted source of information or entertainment, they will also buy your book, attend your seminar, purchase your consulting, visit your site, read your blog, and refer friends. OK, maybe they'll do just two of these things, but it all helps to move your strategy forward.

Here are some ideas on how to complement your career with publishing.

Target a Niche

Common topics are pretty well buttoned up by hundreds of popular books. A new book on Photoshop must compete with the 800 other books about Photoshop currently available. Consider aiming at a niche market instead. For example, an Amazon search suggests that only a handful of books are dedicated to *scripting* Photoshop. A shopper who wants to read about scripting Photoshop certainly would investigate these conspicuous titles.

As a professional, you probably have a specialty. It makes sense to highlight your specialty using a specialized, niche publication. It will be easier to write, and it will enjoy a distinctive profile in the market.

Explore Timely Topics

Write about an emerging technology or trend. Or, write about a recent event. Such publications might look more like reports than books, but shoppers will appreciate your timeliness. A related service has sprung up at *http://www.LJBook.com*. It creates a printable PDF from your LiveJournal blog.

Complement Your Consulting

If you are a consultant, publish a book that discusses the most common problems you encounter in your field. Think of it as a consumer-grade product that complements your high-caliber practice. Your status as a consultant will fuel book sales and your status as an author will fuel your practice. For example, the folks at *http://www.irwebreport.com* use a combination of gratis online articles, for-fee reports, and consulting services to advance their industry profile.

> Track the sales of all your products, so you can measure the cost-effectiveness of your sales strategy. When you test a new strategy (e.g., place an ad in one journal instead of another), compare the results with your historical records.

Seminar Swag

If seminars are your specialty, publish a book to sell to your students, fans, and peers. Selling a tangible book will complement your intangible seminar product.

In short, publish a book as part of your larger strategy to sell yourself. Sell yourself by participating in and contributing to your community.

## CHAPTER FOUR

Creating PDF and Other Editions

Hacks 32–50

There are lots of different ways to create PDF files, from simple printing to PDF, to macros, to tools built into various applications. After putting the effort into creating your source document, choose a pathway to PDF that produces exactly what you expect. Some ways of creating PDF are simple, and some are more involved.

> Some applications, including many applications from Adobe, let you save files as PDF directly. This doesn't require much hacking and so isn't covered here, but it might be worth checking to see if there's an easy path to PDF built into your application (e.g., File → Save a Copy... → Save as Type: PDF in Adobe Illustrator).

HACK #32 **Create Interactive PDF with Your Word Processor**

Interactive PDFs take advantage of the information in word processing documents to create navigation features such as bookmarks and hyperlinks.

Printing a document to create its PDF edition is common practice. It works beautifully, but it also leaves much behind. Document headings could have been turned into an outline of PDF bookmarks, and document links could have become live PDF links. Adding these features, shown in Figure 4-1, will help ensure that your readers have the best possible reading experience.

The trick to creating an interactive PDF from your source document is to use PDF tools that understand your document's styles [Hack #24]. Such tools typically integrate with your word processor.

> On Mac OS X, you can Save As PDF [Hack #40] from any application. That's a quick way to get PDF, but it doesn't create PDF navigation features that the methods described in this hack produce.

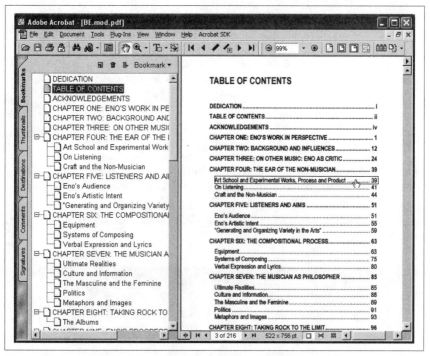

Figure 4-1. Automatically adding PDF navigation features from your document's styles

Microsoft Word and Adobe Acrobat's PDFMaker

During setup, Adobe Acrobat gives you the option to install its *PDFMaker* macro for Word. *PDFMaker* adds a menu to Word called Adobe PDF (Acrobat 6) or Acrobat (Acrobat 5). It also adds a toolbar with buttons that activate items from this menu. Select Adobe PDF → Convert to Adobe PDF or click the toolbar button (🔃) to create your PDF. On the Macintosh, Acrobat installs only the toolbar, with no extra menus, providing very little control over its operation.

On Windows, configure *PDFMaker* by selecting Adobe PDF → Change Conversion Settings… from inside Word. The Conversion Settings drop-down box enables you to select a Distiller profile [Hack #38], just as you would if you were printing a PDF. The remaining tabs enable you to add encryption, links, metadata, bookmarks, and other nifty features to your PDF. One feature I specifically *dis*able is Enable Accessibility and Reflow with Tagged PDF (Acrobat 6) or Embed Tags in PDF (Acrobat 5). This feature allows PDF to behave somewhat like HTML, but it can double (or more!) your PDF's file size. If you require HTML-like features, I recommend distributing an HTML edition [Hack #35] alongside your PDF edition.

When creating a PDF with a custom page size using *PDF-Maker*, your links might end up in the wrong place on the page. As a workaround, try using a larger, standard page size with larger page margins. Create your PDF and then crop it down [Hack #59] to your custom page size in Acrobat.

Adobe offers various solutions for shifted PDF links at *http://www.adobe.com/support/techdocs/19702.htm*.

Microsoft Word and GhostWord on Windows

GhostWord is a Ghostscript interface that integrates with Word. It adds a toolbar button to Word that launches the GhostWord GUI, shown in Figure 4-2. Use the GUI to convert the currently active Word document to full-featured PDF. You can also run the GUI outside of Word. GhostWord even has a command-line interface.

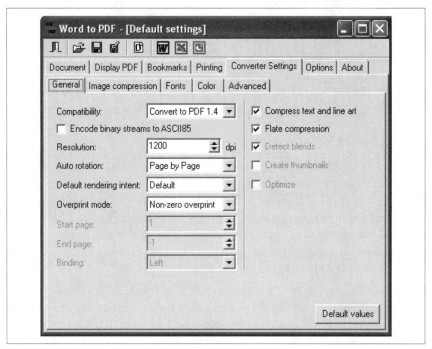

Figure 4-2. Managing PDF feature settings and Ghostscript PDF creation settings from the GhostWord GUI

GhostWord can add bookmarks, links, metadata, and display settings to your PDF. It also manages your Ghostscript settings. Select a hardcoded Ghostscript profile from the Document → Optimize PDF for: drop-down box, or tweak Ghostscript settings individually under the Converter Settings tab. Save these settings to a configuration file for later retrieval.

GhostWord is distributed free of charge from *http://www.et.dtu.dk/software/ ghostword/*.

> GhostWord, along with the *Gs4Word*, *PDF Tweaker*, and *extendedPDF* macros, all require Ghostscript, a free program that works like Adobe's Distiller. To install Ghostscript, see "Print to PDF with Ghostscript and RedMon on Windows" [Hack #39].

Microsoft Word and Gs4Word on Windows

Gs4Word is a Word macro that interfaces with Ghostscript. It adds a menu to Word called PDF and a shortcut button to Word's Standard toolbar. It can add bookmarks, metadata, and display setting to your PDF. Its configuration dialog enables you to manage a set of Ghostscript profiles. Set your desired profile with the PDF → Configure… → PDF File → Output Medium drop-down box.

The *Gs4Word* home page (*http://www.schmitz-huebsch.net/gs4word/*) is in German, but you can configure the program's interface to use English.

Sun StarOffice, OpenOffice, and extendedPDF

Newer versions of OpenOffice can create PDFs directly from your document with the File → Export as PDF feature. However, the resulting PDF lacks interactive features.To create a PDF with bookmarks, metadata, and hyperlinks, you must use the *extendedPDF* macro in combination with Ghostscript or Distiller. Visit *http://www.jdisoftware.co.uk/pages/epdf-home.php* to learn more about *extendedPDF*.

Corel WordPerfect and PDF Tweaker

Newer versions of Corel WordPerfect have a File → Publish To → PDF feature that gives you options for adding PDF features. Or, you can use the *PDF Tweaker* macro for WordPerfect, which also adds links and bookmarks to your PDF. In addition to *PDF Tweaker*, you must also have Acrobat Distiller or Ghostscript. *PDF Tweaker* does not actually create the PDF; it just adds pdfmarks to the print job.

Visit *http://www.wpuniverse.com/vb/showthread.php?threadid=6136* to learn more about *PDF Tweaker*.

Create a Printable, On-Screen Edition from Word

Change a few page settings to yield two-column, screen-oriented pages.

Most documents are configured to print letter-size pages with a vertical, portrait orientation. Yet computer screens have a horizontal, landscape orientation. Accommodate on-screen reading *and* paper printing by setting your document's layout to two-column, landscape-oriented pages, producing the result in Figure 4-3. Sadly, Acrobat's *PDFMaker* can't create accurate bookmarks and hyperlinks in this kind of document.

CHAPTER SIX:
THE COMPOSITIONAL PROCESS

Equipment

Composer/non-musician Brian Eno's domain or arena of operation has always been that of the recording studio and tape recorder, both of which he has referred to as his "real instruments." As we have seen, many of his comments on other pieces of music hinge not on what a musicologist might be inclined to call their "purely musical" qualities – melody, harmony, rhythm, and so on – but rather on aspects of production and engineering, on how the recording studio was used to produce a particular kind of sound texture.

As Eno himself has pointed out, his musical work is so heavily dependent on technology that it could not have existed in any previous age.[1] When he speaks of himself in terms of being a painter working with light in his video pieces is identical to tape is his canvas, and he applies his sound-substances to that canvas, mixes them, blends them, determines their shape, in a specific "painterly" way. He has just enough instrumental technique to give him his "pigments" to begin with, in the previous chapter we saw how he finds it much more difficult to work with initial recorded materials that already have a complexity of their own. His claim to be not so much a composer as a sound-painter is reinforced by his statements to the effect that the way he works with light in his video pieces is identical to the way he works with sound in his music.

Eno wrote a lecture called "The Studio As Compositional Tool" which he delivered at a number of places in England and the United States in the late 1970s and which was eventually published in *Down Beat* magazine in 1983.[2] The first part of the lecture presents an informal, sketchy history of sound recording,

[1] Eno, "Pro Session – Part I," 57.
[2] Brian Eno, "Pro Session: The Studio as Compositional Tool – Part I," lecture delivered at New Music New York, the first New Music America Festival sponsored in 1979 by the Kitchen, excerpted by Howard Mandel, *Down Beat* 50 (July 1983), 56. "Part II" of this lecture appeared in the next issue of *Down Beat* (Aug. 1983).

86

while the second part presents an overview of the structure and components of the modern studio, with examples of how Eno has taken advantage of this layout in his own work. But even when Eno is talking about the nuts and bolts of history, his point of view – his interpretation of history – is clearly evident. A philosophical point on which he lays particular stress is how the act of recording has radically changed the nature of music. Before the advent of sound recording,

The piece disappeared when it was finished, so it was something that only existed in time. The effect of recording is that it takes music out of the time dimension and puts it into the space dimension. As soon as you do that, you're in a position of being able to listen again and again to a performance, to become familiar with details you most certainly had missed the first time through, and to become very fond of details that weren't intended by the composer or the musicians. The effect of this on the composer is that he can think in terms of supplying material that would actually be too subtle for a first listening.[3]

Eno's history of recording touches on other philosophical points, some of which we have already dealt with: recording makes music available to any location than has playback equipment, the early emphasis on faithful reproduction of musical performances has yielded to a realization that the medium has its own unique

[3] Eno, "Pro Session – Part I," 56. The idea that *recording* is solely responsible for the spatialization of music is debatable. A recent pointed scholarly exchange in the pages of *19th Century Music* revolved around the issue of whether or not it is valid to view the tonal structure of Verdi's operas as existing on an ideal, "spatial" plane outside the temporal plane of actual performance and perceived, heard, local modulations. Whatever side one favors in that debate, it is probably true that the debate itself could not arise with reference to music that has not been notated: in the case of the Verdi operas, it is the *score* that takes music out of the time dimension and puts it into the space dimension, or at least makes it much more susceptible to "spatial perception" and structural tonal analysis. Music notation has perhaps always had this sort of spatializing effect, but it is interesting that the linear vs. spatial debate has arisen only since the advent of sound recording. See Sigmund Levarie, "Key Relations in Verdi's *Un Ballo in Maschera*," *19th Century Music* 2 (1978), 143-7, Joseph Kerman, "Viewpoint," *19th Century Music* 2 (1978), 186-91, and Levarie's reply to Kerman, *19th Century Music* 3 (1979), 88-9.

87

Figure 4-3. A landscape orientation, which is better suited for on-screen reading

Microsoft Word 2002

Select File → Page Setup → Margins. Set Apply To: to Whole Document. Set the Multiple Pages field to 2 Pages per Sheet. Set the Orientation to Landscape. Set the page margins to:

Top: 0.75 inch   Bottom: 0.75 inch
Outside: 0.50 inch   Inside: 0.50 inch

Click the Paper tab and set the Paper Size: to Letter. Click the Layout tab and set both Header and Footer to 0.40 inch. Click OK to accept these new Page Setup settings.

When you use the print preview, it will show you only one side of your "2-up" page. Print to PDF and review the results.

Microsoft Word 2000

Select File → Page Setup → Margins. Set Apply To: to Whole Document. Check the 2 Pages per Sheet checkbox. Set both Header and Footer to 0.40 inch. Set the page margins to:

Top: 0.75 inch   Bottom: 0.75 inch
Outside: 0.50 inch   Inside: 0.50 inch

Click the Paper Size tab. Set the Paper Size: to Letter and the Orientation to Landscape. Click OK to accept these new Page Setup settings.

When you use the print preview, it will show you only one side of your "2-up" page. Print to PDF and review the results.

Microsoft Word:Mac v.X (or any Mac application)

On the Macintosh, you don't need to make changes to the document in Word, because the operating system offers a range of pages per sheet on the Layout area of the Print dialog box. Format the document as you normally would, and when you go to print to PDF, select the Layout option. You can pick from 1 to 16 pages on a sheet, though 2 is probably best if you want people to read it on-screen. Again, you won't have all the features that *PDF-Maker* provides.

Multipurpose PDF

#34   Give readers many editions in one package without tagging your PDF.

PDF makes a document portable by wrapping all its resources into a neat, single package. As people desire more features, more things get packed into the PDF. By attempting to make one file do all things for all people, that one file becomes large and unwieldy. Its portability begins to suffer.

In particular, Adobe has worked to add an information-oriented XML-ish layer on top of its presentation-oriented PDF features. The result is a single file that you can use for many purposes, such as paper printing, handheld reading, accurate text-to-speech, and accurate data extraction. However, creating these *tagged* PDFs is a slow and expensive process. The data layer is interwoven with the presentation layer, so accessing the data is difficult.

Consequently, your readers have few options for utilizing this data. Finally, a tagged PDF file can grow to more than twice the size of its untagged counterpart.

In general, I advocate distributing a separate edition for each target medium. This is much easier on your readers and on your workflow. Eating sushi requires two chopsticks. Planar geometry requires five postulates. Some things shouldn't be reduced too far; don't feel compelled to make one edition do all things for all readers.

Tools, Not Rules

With that said, sometimes it makes sense to distribute multiple editions as a single PDF. For example, you might want to use PDF features such as encryption or digital signatures across all your editions. Instead of tagging your PDF, consider packing alternative editions into your PDF as attachments [Hack #54].

> Candidates for attachments include the HTML edition [Hack #36], spreadsheet-ready document data [Hack #55], the handheld edition [Hack #36], or even the source document.

The concept of different attachments for different purposes makes more sense to readers than a single, shape-shifting (tagged) PDF. Also, they will immediately understand the benefits of each alternative edition. "HTML Edition" means reflowing text, easy data extraction, and easy text-to-speech. "Tagged PDF" means little to most people, so you might add: "…that acts like HTML sometimes. You own Acrobat, right?" You will have a struggle on your hands, assuming your reader has that much patience.

HACK #35 Create an HTML Edition from Your Word Processor

Offer readers both PDF and HTML editions of your work and they will love you.

PDF is the ideal medium for preserving your document's look. HTML is a better choice for distributing your document's data. Your source document can give you both, as shown in Figure 4-4, which is another reason to cherish your source document [Hack #24]. Offer multiple editions of your work and readers will love you. And why not? It is so easy.

PDF does have newer features for tagging document data, allowing it to behave somewhat like HTML. However, PDF tagging can double your file size. Also, only a few, proprietary programs are able to tease the tagged data

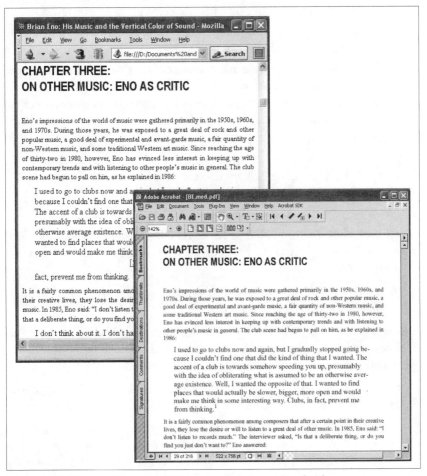

Figure 4-4. Different editions for different purposes; let readers decide

out of a PDF. Consider attaching alternative editions or even attaching the source document to your PDF [Hack #54] instead of tagging.

Create an HTML Edition from Microsoft Word 2002 and 2003

In Word 2002 and 2003 you can save your document as a *web page* or a *filtered web page*. A Word web page includes extra document information in case you want to edit it in Word later. A filtered web page omits this extra information, making it more suitable for distribution.

1. If you have been making changes, save your source document now (File → Save). Otherwise, your changes will be lost.

2. Select File → Save As....

3. In the "Save as type" drop-down box, select Web Page, Filtered.

4. A dialog will open, warning you that this format doesn't contain Word's special tags. Confirm that this is acceptable by clicking Yes.

5. The side effect of this Save As... operation is that you are no longer editing the source document in Word. Instead, you are editing the filtered HTML document you just created. Close this document, because you should make edits only to the source.

Customize HTML output options by selecting Tools → Options... → General → Web Options.... For example, you can enable old-fashioned HTML 3.2 text styling by disabling Rely on CSS for Font Formatting.

Create an HTML Edition from Microsoft Word 2000

Word 2000 does not have a built-in Save As Filtered Web Page option. You must download and install the Office 2000 HTML Filter 2.0 component from Microsoft:

> *http://www.microsoft.com/downloads/details.aspx?FamilyID=209ADBEE-3FBD-482C-83B0-96FB79B74DED*

This adds an Export to Compact HTML feature to Word 2000. It also includes a standalone program for filtering Word's special tags out of existing HTML.

From Word, select File → Export To → Compact HTML.... After you create the HTML, your source document remains open in Word (unlike using Save As... in Word 2002, as noted earlier).

Customize HTML output options by selecting Tools → Options... → General → Web Options.... For example, you can enable HTML 3.2 text styling by unchecking the Rely on CSS for Font Formatting checkbox.

Create an HTML Edition from Microsoft Word:Mac v.X

Word:Mac does not have a built-in Save As Filtered Web Page option, but it does include a Save Only Display Information option under File → Save As Web Page that accomplishes a similar result. The Web Options button on that dialog also enables you to choose how some aspects of web page creation are handled.

Convert Word Documents to HTML with wvWare

wvWare can convert Microsoft Word documents to several formats, including HTML. It is a command-line tool developed on Linux that has been

ported to Windows. It is free software and can be found at *http://wvware.
sourceforge.net*.

Create an HTML Edition from StarOffice and OpenOffice

Like Word 2002, StarOffice enables you to Save As... HTML, but it then
replaces the currently open source document with the new HTML document. Close this new document because you should edit only the source.

Customize HTML output options from Tools → Options... → Load/Save,
especially the HTML Compatibility section. I like to set the HTML Compatibility Export to HTML 3.2 when creating material for handheld reading.

HACK #36 Create a Handheld Edition from Your HTML

Deliver your content to mobile professionals and gadget geeks without PDF's
overhead.

PDF is wonderful stuff—otherwise, you wouldn't likely be reading this
book—but there are times when it's not the right tool for the job. If you
need to distribute information to readers using handheld devices such as
Palms and Pocket PCs, you should take a look at Plucker.

Palm OS Reading with Plucker

Plucker is a toolset for reading HTML documents on Palm OS devices.
Plucker Distiller prepares your HTML and packs it into a Palm PDB file.
Plucker Desktop is a graphical interface for managing Distiller. Plucker
Viewer, shown in Figure 4-5, organizes Plucker documents on your Palm so
that you can read them. Desktop and Distiller run on your host machine,
while the Viewer runs on your Palm. Plucker is free software.

Visit *http://www.plkr.org* and download the Plucker Desktop installer for
your platform. Launch the installer and it will unpack all three components.
You must supply information about your target Palm device, but do not
worry about getting locked into these preferences. You can configure document conversion settings individually later.

> If the Plucker Desktop gives you regular errors that the locale
> cannot be set, select Options → Preferences → Interface and
> uncheck the "Translate interface into the local language"
> checkbox.

Plucker Desktop organizes local files and remote web pages into *channels*.
To create a channel for your HTML file, drag-and-drop it into Plucker

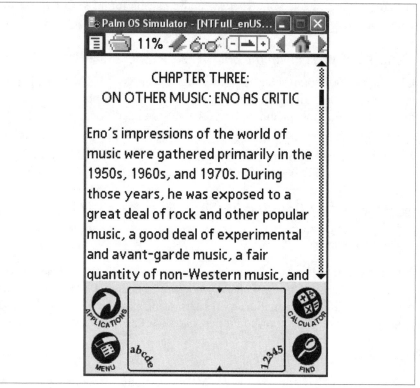

Figure 4-5. Mobilizing your document

Desktop. After you name the new channel, its configuration window opens. Here are a few items of particular interest:

Limits

For converting a traditional document (as opposed to a web site), increase the Maximum Depth to ensure that all your links get followed. Set Stay on Host to keep Plucker from following any Internet references.

Images

Images can quickly bloat your document file size. Tune these settings to match your document's requirements.

Under Advanced Image Handling you can set the maximum dimensions for image thumbnails. Any image larger than this gets downsampled to fit. Thumbnails are displayed inline with your document and can be linked to a larger image.

The original, standard Palm OS display is 160×160, so thumbnails shouldn't be wider than 150 pixels on these models (to leave room for the scrollbar). The newer, high-resolution display is 320×320, which can accommodate a 300-pixel-wide thumbnail. Using the smaller, 150-pixel width ensures your images are fully visible on all Palm OS devices. The viewer trims thumbnails that are too wide to fit on the screen. When fidelity is essential, use the other settings in this window to link the thumbnail to a larger image that the user can pan.

> High-resolution Palm OS devices should use the "hires" versions of the viewer and SysZLib library.

Output Options

ZLib compression works much better than DOC compression does. To read ZLib-compressed documents you must run Palm OS 3 or later (OS 3 premiered in 1998 on the Palm III) and have the SysZLib shared library installed on the device. SysZLib comes packaged with Plucker Desktop.

Destination

Specify the location where the output document will be put.

Create the Plucker document by selecting the channel and then selecting Update → Update Selected Channels.

> Preview your Plucker documents on your PC by installing the Palm OS 5 Simulator. Download it from *http://www. palmos.com/dev/tools/simulator/*.

For best results, the input should use old-fashioned HTML 3.2 text-styling tags (e.g., <font>) instead of CSS styling. "Create an HTML Edition from Your Word Processor" **[Hack #35]** discusses how to set your word processor for HTML 3.2 output.

Plucker for Pocket PC

As of this writing, a Pocket PC reader for Plucker files is under development at *http://vade-mecum.sourceforge.net*. Microsoft provides a Pocket PC emulator you can use to test it. Download Embedded Visual Tools (EVT) from:

> *http://www.microsoft.com/downloads/details.aspx?FamilyId=F663BF48-31EE-4CBE-AAC5-0AFFD5FB27DD*

When installing EVT, use the following CD Key, which is provided by the documentation:

```
TRT7H-KD36T-FRH8D-6QH8P-VFJHQ
```

Choose to install the Pocket PC SDK, or run the *PocketPC_2002_SDK.exe* setup program (which was unpacked by the EVT installer). Start the emulator by launching *CEFILEVW.EXE* and opening a connection.

HACK #37 Convert Documents from Tools You Don't Own to PDF

Even if you don't have the document's authoring tool, you can often convert it to a PDF file.

With the wide variety of authoring tools people use, it is easy to find yourself with a document you can't open and read. Here are some freely available document viewers. Open your trouble document and then print it to PDF.

Microsoft Office Viewers

Microsoft provides freely distributable, Windows-based document viewers for its Office suite. Download the viewer you need from:

http://office.microsoft.com/assistance/preview.
aspx?AssetID=HA010449811033

Install the viewer, open your document, and then print to Acrobat Distiller. If you don't have Acrobat, use our GS Pdf Printer [Hack #39], instead.

> OpenOffice (*http://www.openoffice.org*) is a free authoring suite that can open a variety of file formats, including Microsoft Word, Excel and PowerPoint. It also includes a built-in Export as PDF feature. Use it to convert your Microsoft Office files to PDF.

Corel WordPerfect Viewer

The Microsoft Word Viewer, referenced earlier, can also open WordPerfect files. You must first install the Microsoft Office Converter Pack.

Download the Office 2003 Resource Kit (*ork.exe*) from *http://www.microsoft.com/office/ork/2003/tools/BoxA07.htm*. Install *ork.exe*, and it will unpack the Microsoft Office Converter Pack installer (*oconvpck.exe*). While *ork.exe* does not run on Windows 98, *oconvpck.exe* (which is really all we want) does. Search your disk for *oconvpck.exe* and install it.

After installing the Office Converter Pack, the Word Viewer Open dialog still won't see WordPerfect WPD files. You'll need to drag-and-drop, type the full name, or change *WPD* file extensions to *DOC*. This last choice could end up confusing people down the road.

Once it's open, print the document to Acrobat Distiller or the GS PDF Printer [Hack #39].

Online Conversion

Adobe offers an online service for creating PDFs from your source documents. It accepts Microsoft Office and Corel WordPerfect documents. It also accepts Adobe Illustrator, InDesign, FrameMaker, PageMaker, and Photoshop files. Visit *https://createpdf.adobe.com* to learn more.

HACK #38 Acrobat Distiller and Its Profiles

Select the best Distiller profile for your purpose.

When you use Acrobat's "Print to PDF" or use the *PDFMaker* macro for Word, Adobe's Distiller is the engine that creates your PDF. What kind of PDF do you need? You can configure Distiller to create the best PDF for your purpose. The choice is usually between document fidelity and file size. File size becomes an issue only when distributing a PDF electronically. When in doubt, choose fidelity.

Changing the Distiller Profile

Acrobat Distiller comes with a few preconfigured profiles. They are also called Settings or *joboptions* files. When printing to PDF, change the profile by clicking the Print dialog's Properties button (Windows), or by selecting PDF Options from the drop-down box that starts out saying Copies & Pages (Mac). Select the Adobe PDF Settings tab and select a Distiller profile from the Default Settings: (Acrobat 6) or Conversion Settings: (Acrobat 5) drop-down box. This choice is not permanent. To change the default profile, consult the Adobe PDF (Acrobat 6) or Acrobat Distiller (Acrobat 5) printer properties.

When using *PDFMaker* on Windows, change its profile inside Word by selecting Adobe PDF → Change Conversion Settings… (Acrobat 6) or Acrobat → Change Conversion Settings… (Acrobat 5). This choice, shown in Figure 4-6, becomes the default.

When creating a PDF for a print shop or service bureau, ask them for a *joboptions* file to use. On Windows, move it to Distiller's *Settings* folder, which is located somewhere such as *C:\Program Files\Adobe\Acrobat 5.0\Distillr\Settings*. On the Macintosh, open Distiller and use the Settings → Add Adobe PDF Settings… menu option to add it to the list. Then, select the print shop or service bureau's profile when creating your PDF, as described earlier.

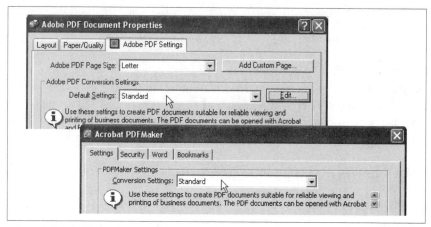

Figure 4-6. Distiller settings, which you use whenever you create PDFs using Acrobat

Stock Distiller Profiles, Side by Side

Each profile that comes with Acrobat has subtle differences. We highlight only the big differences in Tables 4-1 and 4-2 because they have the greatest effect on your PDF.

Table 4-1. Acrobat 6 Distiller profiles

	Smallest File Size	Standard	High Quality and Press Quality
Color Image Resolution (dpi)	100	150	300
Gray Image Resolution (dpi)	150	150	300
Mono Image Resolution (dpi)	300	300	1200
Compressed Image Fidelity	Low	Medium	Maximum
Embedded Fonts	None	a	All

a All fonts are embedded except Base 14 fonts and these Windows system fonts: Century Gothic, Georgia, Impact, Lucida Console, Tahoma, Trebuchet, and Verdana.

Table 4-2. Acrobat 5 Distiller profiles

	Screen	eBook	Print	Press
Color Image Resolution (dpi)	72	150	300	300
Gray Image Resolution (dpi)	72	150	300	300

Table 4-2. Acrobat 5 Distiller profiles (continued)

	Screen	eBook	Print	Press
Mono Image Resolution (dpi)	300	300	1200	1200
Compressed Image Fidelity	Medium	Medium	High	Maximum
Embedded Fonts	None	All Except Base 14	All	All

A 150 dpi image is usually appropriate for printing on a 600 dpi black-and-white laser or inkjet printer. So, the Standard profile (Acrobat 6) seems to suit most purposes. Color printers can take advantage of higher image resolutions. Visit *http://www.scantips.com/basics03.html* to discover the principles of printer arithmetic.

In Acrobat 5, the eBook profile serves most purposes; it resembles the Standard profile very closely. Who would have guessed that?

> When distilling a document containing mostly screenshot images, try using the ZIP image compression filter instead of JPEG. In Distiller 5, you can also try the 4-bit and 8-bit quality settings. Not only does this yield superior screenshot compression, but you also get superior images. See "Configure Distiller and Ghostscript for Your Purpose" [Hack #42] to learn how to alter Distiller profiles. These compression settings are under the profile's Images tab (Acrobat 6) or Compression tab (Acrobat 5)

If your readers will be downloading files from the Web or receiving them through email, using the Smallest File Size (Acrobat 6) or Screen (Acrobat 5) profile will ensure that low-bandwidth users aren't clobbered with long PDF downloads. On the other hand, if you're sending files to a printer and want the best results possible, you'll want to use the Press Quality profile, which yields the highest-fidelity PDF.

HACK #39 Print to PDF with Ghostscript and RedMon on Windows

Enjoy a convenient path to PDF, free of charge.

Any program that prints can also create PDFs. Adobe Acrobat sets the standard for PDF creation, but it can be too expensive. Ghostscript is a free PostScript interpreter that can also create PDFs, much like Acrobat's Distiller. Use RedMon to plug the power of Ghostscript into the convenience of a Windows printer, and you'll have "Print to PDF"!

> For a prepackaged Ghostscript/RedMon installer, try PDFCreator (*http://sourceforge.net/projects/pdfcreator/*) or PrimoPDF (*http://www.primopdf.com*).

Download and Install Ghostscript

The Ghostscript home page is *http://www.cs.wisc.edu/~ghost/*. As of this writing, the current version of AFPL Ghostscript is 8.14. Download and run the corresponding installer, *gs814w32.exe*. Our configuration, which follows, assumes Ghostscript is installed in the default location, *C:\gs*. If you ever need to reinstall Ghostscript, first uninstall it from the Add or Remove Programs dialog in the Windows Control Panel.

Download and Install RedMon

The RedMon home page is *http://www.cs.wisc.edu/~ghost/redmon/*. As of this writing, the current version of RedMon is 1.7. Download the corresponding zip file, *redmon17.zip*, into a new directory called *redmon17*. Unzip it and double-click *setup.exe* to install.

Download and Unpack Our Virtual Printer Kit

The *PDF Hacks* Virtual Printer Kit (VPK) has printer driver files, PPD files, and sample configuration files. Download it from *http://www.pdfhacks.com/virtual_printer/*. Unzip it into a convenient directory and note its contents. We'll call on these pieces as we need them. The *README* file might contain updates to these instructions.

> You can download a PostScript driver installer for Windows from the Adobe web site. However, its license suggests that you can use it only in conjunction with other Adobe products, such as a PostScript printer. Review this license. If it suits you, download the latest installer (currently 1.0.6) from *http://www.adobe.com/support/downloads/product.jsp?product=44&platform=Windows*
>
> You can use the *ADIST5.PPD* printer description from the Virtual Printer Kit during setup to create a GS Pdf Printer. Continue with the section "Add and configure the RedMon redirected port."

The rest of this hack is divided by platform: Windows XP or 2000, and Windows 98.

Install and Configure a PDF Printer: Windows XP, 2000

You already installed Ghostscript, RedMon, and our Virtual Printer Kit, right? All that remains is to install and configure your PDF printer.

Install a Virtual PostScript printer. Any number of PostScript (PS) printers can use the same, core PS driver. To create a complete printer driver, we must combine this core with a printer's PPD file, which describes its capabilities in detail.

Windows XP comes with an up-to-date core PS driver. Our Virtual Post-Script Printer driver is simply an INF file instructing Windows to combine this core with the (freely distributable) PPD from Adobe that describes the Acrobat 5 Distiller printer. The result is a printer that is almost ready to create a PDF.

1. From the *Printers and Faxes* folder (Start → Settings → Printers and Faxes) click Add a Printer under Printer Tasks and the wizard will open. Click Next to begin.

2. Select Local Printer, uncheck Automatically Detect, and click Next.

3. Select Create a New Port and choose the Redirected Port from the drop-down list. Click Next. A dialog will open asking for the port name. Enter RPTPDF: and click OK. When you installed RedMon, it created this Redirected Port option.

4. The wizard will present you with a list of printers and manufacturers, but we don't want these. Click Have Disk... and then Browse.... Navigate to the *driver\WinXP* directory in our Virtual Printer Kit, open *ADIST5GS.INF*, and then click OK. The wizard should now display only one printer, our Virtual PostScript Printer. Select this printer, as shown in Figure 4-7. Windows might complain that this printer driver is not signed. Click Next.

5. If the wizard remarks that a driver already is installed for this printer, select Keep Existing Driver and click Next.

6. Name the printer GS Pdf Printer and select No default printer. Click Next.

7. Select No to keep it from printing a test page and click Next.

8. Click Finish to complete the installation. Windows might complain that our driver is not Windows Logo–certified. If so, confirm that you want to install our driver.

The *GS Pdf Printer* printer should now appear in your *Printers and Faxes* folder.

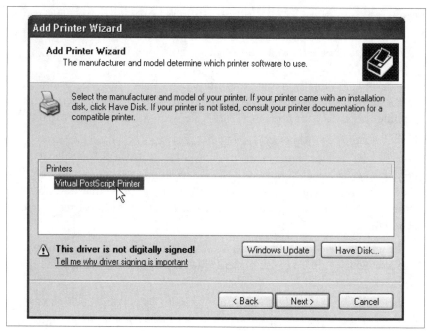

Figure 4-7. Our Virtual PostScript Printer driver, which has the exact same printer profile as Acrobat's PDF printer

Configure the RedMon redirected port to print PDF. Now, wire your new printer to the Ghostscript program by configuring the redirected port you created, *RPTPDF:*.

1. Right-click your new GS Pdf Printer printer and select Properties. Click the Ports tab.

2. Make sure the "Enable bidirectional support" checkbox is unchecked.

3. Select the Redirected Port you just created, *RPTPDF:*, and click Configure Port....

4. Set the port properties as shown in Table 4-3, changing the paths to suit your setup. Be careful not to overlook the solitary hyphen at the end of the program arguments.

Table 4-3. RedMon port properties

Field	Value
Redirect this port to the program:	C:\gs\gs8.14\bin\gswin32c.exe
Arguments for this program are:	-sOutputFile="%1" @C:\gs\pdf_printer.cfg -f -
Output:	*Prompt for Filename*
Run:	*Minimized*

5. Click the Log File button to configure the Log File Properties. Set Use Log File and enter a log filename, such as C:\gs\pdf_printer.log. Don't set Debug.

6. Click OK to close the Log File Properties. Click OK to accept the new port settings. Click Close to accept the new printer settings, as shown in Figure 4-8, and close the GS Pdf Printer Properties dialog.

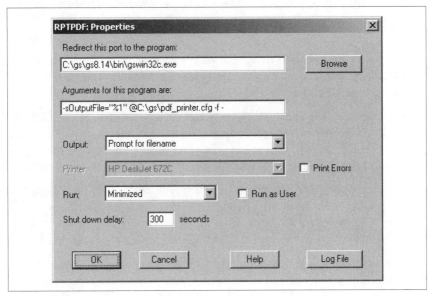

Figure 4-8. RedMon passing the PostScript created by your printer driver to Ghostscript

To complete the port configuration, you must create the file *C:\gs\pdf_printer.cfg*, referenced earlier. It is a text file of additional arguments passed to Ghostscript. An example is included with our Virtual Printer Kit. Change the paths to suit your Ghostscript and system setup.

```
-dSAFER
-dBATCH
-dNOPAUSE
-Ic:\gs\gs8.14\Resource
-Ic:\gs\fonts
-Ic:\gs\gs8.14\lib
-sFONTPATH=c:\WINDOWS\FONTS
-sDEVICE=pdfwrite
-r1200
-c save pop
```

Voilà! Now, let's test it. Jump down to the section "Test Your GS Pdf Printer," later in this hack.

Install and Configure a PDF Printer: Windows 98

You already installed Ghostscript, RedMon, and our Virtual Printer Kit, right? All that remains is to install and configure your PDF printer.

Install our Virtual PostScript printer. Any number of PostScript (PS) printers can use the same core PS driver. To create a complete printer driver, we must combine this core with a printer's PPD file, which describes its capabilities in detail.

The trouble is, we need an up-to-date PS core. Search your computer hard drive for *ADOBEPS4.DRV* to see if a recent PS core is installed. If you find it, you will be able to copy our required files, listed later in this section, from your hard drive. If you don't find it, you have a couple options.

One option is to use the Adobe PostScript driver installer, as described in the earlier note. However, its license severely restricts its use. The other option is to download a printer driver from some manufacturer, a driver that contains all the core files we need and employs a permissive license.

For this latter purpose, I like the printer driver download for the Phaser 550 (driver version 4.52) from *http://www.Xerox.com*. It is a self-extracting executable, *win9xadb.exe*, which provides all the necessary files in a neat directory. Check the Virtual Printer Kit *README* for other possible sources.

Whichever driver you use, these are the files you ultimately must collect. You should collect them all from a single source to ensure they're compatible:

> *ADOBEPS4.DRV*
> *ADOBEPS4.HLP*
> *ADFONTS.MFM*
> *ICONLIB.DLL*
> *PSMON.DLL*

Copy these files into the Virtual Printer Kit directory *driver\Win9x*. That directory already contains the final two ingredients: our Virtual PostScript Printer PPD file and the Windows INF file used by the Add Printer install wizard to tie everything together.

1. From the *Printers* folder (Start → Settings → Printers) double-click the Add Printer icon. Click Next to begin.

2. Select Local Printer and click Next.

3. The wizard will present you with a list of printers and manufacturers, but we don't want these. Click Have Disk… and then Browse…. Navigate to the *driver\Win9x* directory in our Virtual Printer Kit and click Open and then OK. The wizard should now display only one printer, our Virtual PostScript Printer. Select this printer. Click Next.

4. If the wizard remarks that a driver is installed for this printer, select Replace Existing Driver and click Next.

5. Under Available Ports, select FILE: and click Next.

6. Name the printer GS Pdf Printer and select No default printer. Click Next.

7. The wizard should be finished. If a Version Conflict dialog opens to complain that you are overwriting newer files with older files, the safest thing to do is to keep the newer files.

The GS Pdf Printer printer now should appear in your *Printers and Faxes* folder. Wire your new printer to the Ghostscript program by adding and configuring a redirected port.

Add and configure the RedMon redirected port. Let's wire your new GS Pdf Printer printer to the Ghostscript program with a RedMon redirected port.

1. Right-click your new GS Pdf Printer printer and select Properties. Click the Details tab.

2. Click Add Port… and a dialog opens. Select Other, select Redirected Port, and click OK. Name the port RPTPDF: and click OK.

3. On the Details tab, click Spool Settings…. Select "Disable bi-directional support for this printer" and click OK.

4. On the Details tab, click Port Settings…. Set the port properties as shown in Table 4-4, changing the paths to suit your Ghostscript setup. Be careful not to overlook the solitary hyphen at the end of the program arguments.

Table 4-4. RedMon port properties

Field	Value
Redirect this port to the program:	C:\gs\gs8.14\bin\gswin32c.exe
Arguments for this program are:	-sOutputFile="%1" @"C:\gs\pdf_printer.cfg" -f -
Output:	*Prompt for Filename*
Run:	*Minimized*

5. Click the Log File button to configure the Log File Properties. Set Use Log File and enter a log filename, such as C:\gs\pdf_printer.log. Don't set Debug.

6. Click OK to close the Log File Properties. Click OK to accept the new
   port settings. Click OK to accept the new printer settings and close the
   GS Pdf Printer Properties dialog.

To complete the port configuration, you must create the file *pdf_printer.cfg*,
referenced earlier. It is a text file of additional arguments passed to Ghostscript. An example is included with the Virtual Printer Kit. Change the paths
to suit your Ghostscript and system setup.

```
-dSAFER
-dBATCH
-dNOPAUSE
-I"c:\gs\gs8.14\Resource"
-I"c:\gs\fonts"
-I"c:\gs\gs8.14\lib"
-sFONTPATH=c:\WINDOWS\FONTS
-sDEVICE=pdfwrite
-r1200
-c save pop
```

Voilà! Now, let's test it.

Test Your GS Pdf Printer

Open the GS Pdf Printer properties dialog, click the General tab, and click
Print Test Page. After a pause, a dialog will open where you can enter the
PDF's filename. Select a suitable filename and click OK. Note that it will
overwrite a file without asking and that it does not automatically add the
PDF extension to the filename.

When it is done, open the PDF in Reader. How does it look? The next few
hacks discuss how to tune Ghostscript for your purposes.

If an error occurs or the PDF file isn't created, carefully double-check the
printer configuration and consult the log file:

- Is bi-directional printing disabled?

- Does the redirected port setting match those given earlier? Mind the
  separate, trailing hyphen in the program arguments.

- Is *pdf_printer.cfg* in the correct location? Do its contents match those
  given earlier?

- Have all *C:\gs* paths been updated to reflect the location of your Ghostscript installation?

Save As PDF with Mac OS X

Create PDFs quickly and easily from any Macintosh OS X program.

Apple built a "Save As PDF" capability right into the Macintosh OS X Print
dialog box. Any time you go to print a document, you can choose Save As
PDF... from the bottom of the Print dialog box. Unfortunately, this
approach provides no options and tends to produce large files, but at least it
is a quick solution to producing PDFs. This option is available at the bottom left of any Print dialog box, as shown in Figure 4-9.

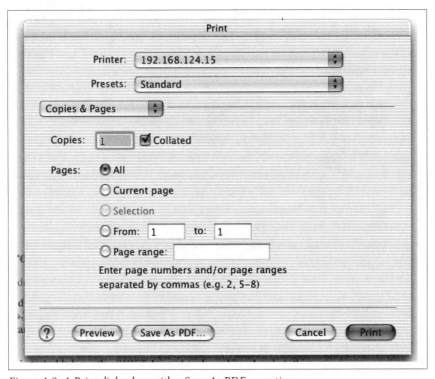

Figure 4-9. A Print dialog box with a Save As PDF... option

If you click the Save As PDF... button, a file dialog box will ask you where
to put the resulting PDF file. Select a location, click OK, and the Mac will
print to a PDF file.

The results are different from those created by Distiller. On an early draft of
Chapter 1 of this book, without figures, Mac OS X produced a 344 KB file,
while the *PDFMaker* macro produced a 144 KB file.

There aren't any obvious configuration options for Save as PDF..., but if
you have Mac OS X 10.3 or later, you can choose settings through the Fil-

ters tab of the ColorSync utility's Preferences window. (The ColorSync utility is in *Macintosh HD:Applications:Utilities*.) If you check PDF Workflow in the Domains tab, you'll be able to change your PDF options from the Print dialog box as well.

HACK #41 Maximize PDF Portability

PDF version differences can affect you and your readers.

To best serve your readers, you should ensure that your PDF is compatible with their viewers. What PDF viewers are they running? Assume that they have at least upgraded to the *previous* version of Acrobat/Reader (or another, compatible viewer). PDFs created with the *newest* Acrobat might be incompatible with previous versions. A little care can prevent inconveniences to your readers such as the one shown in Figure 4-10.

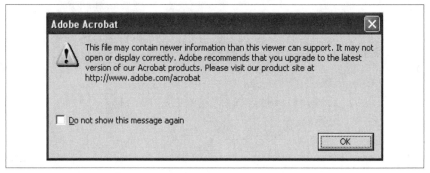

Figure 4-10. Messages that annoy readers

PDF Versions Overview

With each new version of Acrobat, Adobe introduces an updated version of the PDF specification. They go together, as shown in Table 4-5.

Table 4-5. Acrobat version information

Acrobat version	Year introduced	PDF version
3.0	1996	1.2
4.0	1999	1.3
5.0	2001	1.4
6.0	2003	1.5

In many cases, an older viewer still can read a newer-version PDF (although the viewer will complain). Its behavior depends on which new features the PDF uses. Which viewers implement newer features? Here are some highlights, selected for their bearing on mass distribution. For complete details, consult the PDF Reference, Versions 1.3, 1.4, and 1.5.

PDF 1.3 (Acrobat 4) introduced:

- Digital signatures
- File attachments
- JavaScript support
- Logical page numbering

PDF 1.4 (Acrobat 5) introduced:

- Additional 128-bit encryption option
- Additional JavaScript trigger events (document close, will save, did save, will print, did print)
- Enhanced interactive forms

PDF 1.5 (Acrobat 6) introduced:

- Additional file compression options
- Additional encryption options

An older viewer can simply ignore many of the things it doesn't understand. The showstoppers are the compression or encryption features, because the viewer can't show the document if it can't read the streams.

> If your PDF relies on newer JavaScript or forms features to work properly, prevent older viewers from opening your PDF. Determine the minimum PDF version your document requires and then apply the corresponding encryption using an empty password [Hack #52]. Older viewers simply won't be able to read it.

Create Compatible PDFs

Out of the box, Distiller or *PDFMaker* yields PDFs that are compatible with the previous version of Acrobat. No problem.

When you open a PDF in Acrobat, modify it, and then save it, your PDF's version is upgraded silently to match Acrobat's. It is no longer compatible with the previous versions of Acrobat/Reader. This happens regardless of whether your PDF uses any of the new features.

> Install older versions of Acrobat Reader and test your PDFs, if you are worried about how they'll look or function. Download old installers from *http://www.adobe.com/products/ acrobat/reader_archive.html* or *http://www.oldversion.com/ program.php?n=acrobat.*

One solution is to use the Reduce File Size feature in Acrobat 6 (File → Reduce File Size... → Compatible with: Acrobat 5.0 and later), which enables you to also set the compatibility level of the resulting PDF. Another solution is to use the PDF Optimizer feature (Advanced → PDF Optimizer...) and set the "Compatible with" field to "Acrobat 5.0 and later." A third option is to refry your PDF [Hack #60].

HACK #42 Configure Distiller and Ghostscript for Your Purpose

Unlock the secret powers of Distiller and Ghostscript.

Acrobat Distiller creates PDF based on its current profile setting [Hack #38]. On Windows, choose a profile when you print by changing the Print → Properties... → Adobe PDF Settings tab → Default Settings drop-down box, as shown in Figure 4-11. On a Macintosh, choose PDF Options from the drop-down box that starts out saying Copies & Pages instead of selecting the Adobe PDF Settings tab. When using Ghostscript, you can reference a *joboptions* file in *pdf_printer.cfg*.

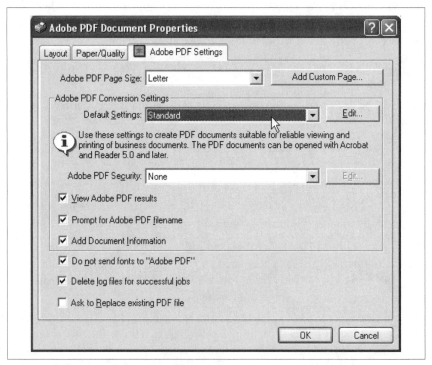

Figure 4-11. Choosing PDF printer properties

Whenever you print to an Acrobat PDF printer, you can select a profile that creates the best PDF for your purpose. You can view and edit these profiles using the graphical Distiller application. The surprise is that these profiles, or *joboptions* files, are plain-text PostScript snippets that give you more control over Distiller than the GUI does. They are also compatible with Ghostscript, although Ghostscript does not implement all the possible settings. Indeed, the *joboptions* file (and its specification) is a good place to get the straight dope on what Distiller and Ghostscript can really do.

Acrobat Distiller Parameters Tell the Full Story

To fully understand Distiller and Ghostscript features, you must read the Acrobat Distiller Parameters document from Adobe. It is also the definitive guide to *joboptions* file parameters.

If you have Acrobat on your computer, open Distiller and select Help → Distiller Parameters Guide, or search your disk for *distparm.pdf*. On the Macintosh, this file is in the *Extras* folder on the installer CD. The Acrobat 6 version of *distparm.pdf* is not available online except to paying Adobe ASN Developer Program members. The next best thing is the Acrobat 5 version, which is bundled with the freely downloadable Acrobat 5 SDK:

http://partners.adobe.com/asn/acrobat/download.jsp

Ghostscript users should also read *C:\gs\gs8.14\doc\Ps2pdf.htm* or, online:

http://www.cs.wisc.edu/~ghost/doc/cvs/Ps2pdf.htm

If you plan to deliver PDF to a service bureau, find out if they have a *joboptions* file you should use when creating your PDF.

Distiller joboptions Profiles

Acrobat Distiller's *joboptions* files are easy to view and modify using the Distiller GUI, as shown in Figure 4-12. Launch the Distiller application, and set Default Settings (Acrobat 6) or Job Options (Acrobat 5) to the profile you want to view or edit. Then, select Settings → Edit Adobe PDF Settings (Acrobat 6) or Settings → Job Options (Acrobat 5).

As noted earlier, this graphical interface does not give you access to all the settings documented in Acrobat Distiller Parameters. Because *joboptions* files are plain text, you can also view or edit them using a text editor.

Ghostscript joboptions Profiles

joboptions files are written in PostScript, so you can pass them to Ghostscript just before your input file using the -f option. Add a *joboptions* file to

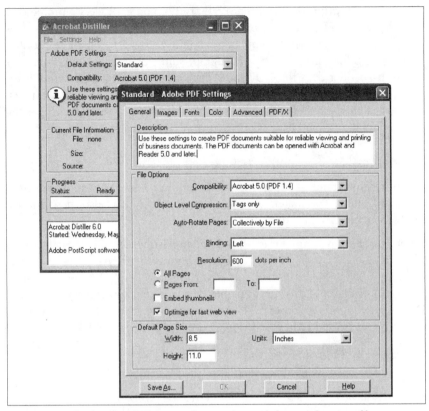

Figure 4-12. The Distiller GUI: a nice place to view and change joboptions files

your GS Pdf Printer [Hack #39] by appending it to the end of the *pdf_printer.cfg* file you created, like so:

```
-dSAFER
-dBATCH
-dNOPAUSE
-Ic:\gs\gs8.14\Resource
-Ic:\gs\fonts
-Ic:\gs\gs8.14\lib
-sFONTPATH=c:\WINDOWS\FONTS
-sDEVICE=pdfwrite
-r1200
-c save pop
-f c:\gs\pdfhacks.gs.joboptions
```

The file *pdfhacks.gs.joboptions* comes with our Virtual Printer Kit [Hack #39]. It is organized and commented to make parameters easy to read and understand. Open it in your text editor and take a look. Edit it to suit your needs. Parameters not supported by Ghostscript are commented out.

If you need to manage a collection of these profiles, consider creating one GS Pdf Printer for each profile. Each printer would have its own Redirected Port, each port using its own *cfg* file, each *cfg* file referencing its own *joboptions* file.

Embed and Subset Fonts to Your Advantage

Sometimes it makes sense to embed fonts, while other times it just costs you space.

An *embedded* font is a font that has been packed into your PDF file as a resource. Embedding ensures that your PDF text looks perfect wherever it is printed or viewed. Embedding also bulks up your PDF's file size. In this hack we discuss embedding and its alternatives, their upsides and down-sides. We also discuss font *subsetting*, which is the practice of embedding only a subset of the entire font. Subsetting was designed to reduce file size, but it can actually create bloat when misused.

> See which PDF fonts are embedded or subset in your PDF by opening the PDF in Acrobat or Reader and selecting File → Document Properties… → Fonts. Embedded fonts will describe themselves as Embedded, whereas unembedded fonts will not—likewise for subset fonts.

Embedding Fonts into PDF

For most purposes, all fonts should be embedded. If a font is not embedded in your PDF, Acrobat/Reader will try to find it on the computer. If the font isn't installed on the computer, Acrobat/Reader will try to approximate the font using its own resources, as shown in Figure 4-13. By not embedding a font, your PDF might end up looking slightly different on different machines.

Impact, Un-Embedded
Century Gothic, Un-Embedded

Impact, Un-Embedded
Century Gothic, Un-Embedded

Figure 4-13. Original fonts (top) approximated by Acrobat (bottom), when they are not embedded in the PDF and they are not available on the system

How well does Acrobat/Reader approximate fonts? Turn off Use Local Fonts in Reader or Acrobat to see how your unembedded fonts might appear on other computers. Acrobat 6: Advanced → Use Local Fonts. Reader 6: Document → Use Local Fonts. Acrobat 5: View → Use Local Fonts. Or, just Ctrl-Shift-Y.

The drawback to embedding is that each embedded font could add about 20 KB to your PDF file size. For some large PDFs this is negligible. For online PDFs of only a few pages, it can be unacceptable.

When PDF file size is critical, select some or all of your document fonts from one of the Base font collections and then configure Distiller to never embed them. The Base 14 fonts provide a solid core that is the safest to use without embedding. The Base 35 fonts provide traditional styles that are reasonably safe to use without embedding. For the fonts you must embed, prefer Type 1 fonts over TrueType fonts because embedded Type 1 fonts are much smaller.

The Base 14 Fonts

The Base 14 fonts are utilitarian fonts that you can use safely in any PDF without embedding. Their family names are Times, Helvetica, Courier, and Symbol. Times New Roman commonly is used instead of Times, and Arial commonly is used instead of Helvetica.

If your document uses Helvetica and you want to be sure your PDF is displayed using Helvetica (and not Arial), double-check to make sure it gets embedded. Some Distiller profiles **[Hack #38]** automatically exclude all Base 14 fonts from embedding.

Figure 4-14 provides samples of the Base 14 fonts, along with samples of the *Base 35* fonts.

The Base 35 Fonts

The Base 35 fonts are a superset of the Base 14 fonts. They add style, and most of them are reasonably safe to use without embedding. If your system does not have one of these font families, shown in Table 4-6, try using a *lookalike* font instead.

Times New Roman	Book Antiqua
Arial	Arial Narrow
Courier New	Bookman Old Style
Σψμβολ (Symbol)	Century Gothic
	Century Schoolbook

Figure 4-14. The Base 35 fonts: a superset of the Base 14 fonts (left column)

Table 4-6. Base 35 font families and common lookalikes that are reasonably safe to use without embedding

Font family name	Common lookalike
Times	Times New Roman
Helvetica	Arial
Helvetica Narrow	Arial Narrow
Palatino	Book Antiqua
Bookman	Bookman Old Style
Avant Garde	Century Gothic
New Century Schoolbook	Century Schoolbook
Courier	Courier New
Symbol	Symbol MT

If you use the Base 35 fonts shown in Table 4-7, you should embed them. Any decorative or stylized font always should be embedded.

Table 4-7. Base 35 font families you should embed

Font family name	Common lookalike
Zapf Dingbats	Monotype Sorts
Zapf Chancery	Monotype Corsiva

If the Base 35 fonts shown in Figure 4-14 (or their lookalikes) aren't available on your system, install the free fonts that come with Ghostscript [Hack #25].

Configure Distiller Font Embedding

The Fonts tab in your Distiller Job Options setting is the place to control font embedding, as shown in Figure 4-15. The Embed All Fonts checkbox sets the default policy. Unchecking it means Embed No Fonts. The Never Embed and Always Embed font lists are used to override the default policy on a font-by-font basis. So, if Embed All Fonts is checked, all document fonts get embedded in the PDF except those listed under Never Embed. If Embed All Fonts is unchecked, only the document fonts listed under Always Embed get embedded in the PDF.

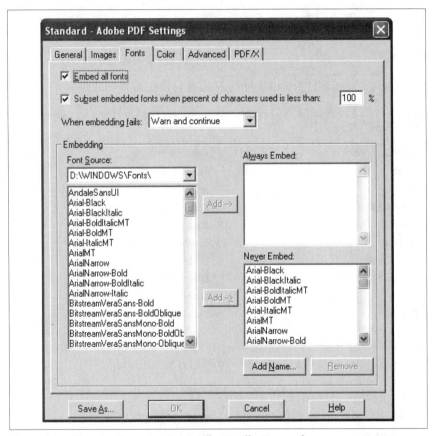

Figure 4-15. Changing font settings using the Distiller Fonts tab

Configure Distiller to never embed Base 14 fonts by putting them (and their lookalikes) on the Never Embed list. Give the Base 35 fonts (and their lookalikes) the same treatment if you desire. When using Acrobat/Distiller 5.0, the Base 14 fonts do not automatically include their lookalikes. On Windows, change the Font Source drop-down box to *C:\windows\fonts* or *C:\winnt\fonts* in order to see a list of your system fonts, which is where you'll find the lookalike fonts.

Acrobat 6 enables you to remove embedded fonts from your PDF using its PDF Optimizer feature. Select Advanced → PDF Optimizer... → Fonts to select fonts for removal.

Configure Ghostscript Font Embedding

Ghostscript must embed all fonts except the Base 14 fonts. You can embed these, too, if you choose. Asking Ghostscript to withhold embedding of any other font could yield a PDF that doesn't work properly in Acrobat and Reader. Perhaps a future version of Ghostscript will resolve this issue.

Subset Embedded Fonts

It does not make sense to pack an entire font into a PDF when only a few characters from that font are actually used. *Font subsetting* is the technique of embedding only a portion of a font. A font subset contains only the characters used in your document. The alternative is to pack the entire font into the PDF. Distiller can entirely pack only Type 1 fonts into a PDF. Distiller subsets fonts in any other format (e.g., TrueType).

For most purposes, all embedded fonts should be subset. It only becomes an issue later, when assembling many PDF pieces into a single PDF. If each PDF piece uses embedded subset fonts, the resulting final document is in danger of having a single font represented by many unnecessary subsets. This can severely bloat the final document file size.

One solution to *subset bloat* is to use Acrobat 6 for assembling your document. After assembly, Save As... to a new PDF. Acrobat 6 works to consolidate the individual subsets into a single subset. Acrobat 5 does not do this. Another solution is to refry the PDF [Hack #60] after assembly.

If you plan to edit PDF text at the source-code level using a text editor, avoid subsetting the PDF fonts. If you add text to the PDF that uses characters not present in the font subset, your text will not display.

Configure Distiller Font Subsetting

Distiller's Fonts tab is the place to control the subsetting of embedded fonts. To prevent Type 1 fonts from subsetting, uncheck the "Subset embedded fonts" checkbox. All other fonts (e.g., TrueType) are always subset.

To the right of this checkbox you can put a threshold for deciding which fonts get subset. If your document uses 95% of the characters in a font and you don't want that font subset, enter 94 into this field. Setting this to 100 means that every font will be subset.

Configure Ghostscript Font Subsetting

To prevent Type 1 font subsetting, set /SubsetFonts *false* in your *joboptions* file or add -dSubsetFonts=*false* to your command line. If you desire font subsetting, set these to *true* instead of *false*.

To change the threshold for deciding which fonts get subset, set /MaxSubsetPct *100* in your *joboptions* file or add -dMaxSubsetPct=*100* to your command line. Replace *100* with your desired setting.

HACK #44   Share a PDF Network Printer with Samba

Share a PDF printer with your entire network using Ghostscript, Samba, and Linux.

Ghostscript lets you freely print to PDF. However, maintaining Ghostscript on every client in your enterprise can be a nuisance. Consider installing it on a single Linux server instead. Then, use Samba to share it as a PDF printer to your entire network.

Before creating a PDF printer server, install a local PDF printer [Hack #39] to test Ghostscript and make sure it fits your requirements. Note that some Linux distributions provide GNU Ghostscript (Version 7) instead of the more recent AFPL Ghostscript (Version 8). Factor this into your testing. You will probably want to compile AFPL Ghostscript for your Linux server, later.

The Server

Every Linux distribution should have Samba and Ghostscript packages that you can install painlessly. Use them. Later, consider downloading and compiling the latest AFPL Ghostscript.

Samba is powerful, so its configuration requires some skill and patience. Consult man smb.conf and edit *smb.conf* to suit your network. Exercise your favorite Internet search engine, and drop by *http://us3.samba.org/samba/docs/using_samba/toc.html*. When things aren't working, consult the log files (e.g., */var/log/samba*). Don't forget to restart the samba service (e.g., */etc/init.d/samba restart*) after changing *smb.conf*.

Create the directory */home/pdf_printer/output*, and chmod it to 777. This is where new PDFs will be delivered. Share this directory with your network by adding this section to *smb.conf* and restarting Samba:

```
[pdf_output]
comment = Shared PDF Printer Output
path = /home/pdf_printer/output
; this next line is necessary only when security = share
guest ok = yes
browseable = yes
writeable = yes
```

In Windows, this *share* should be visible from the Network Neighborhood
or My Network Places, as shown in Figure 4-16. If not, try digging into
Entire Network → Microsoft Windows Network. Also try the Search for
Computers or Find Computer features. Sometimes, new resources aren't visible immediately. Sometimes, client configurations must be reviewed and
changed, too.

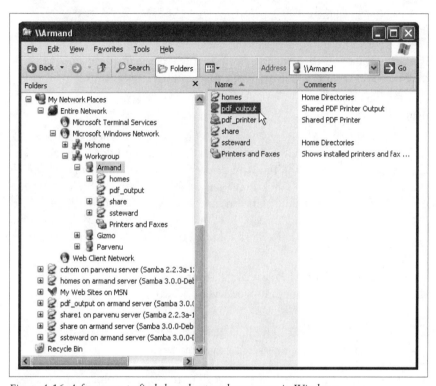

Figure 4-16. A few ways to find shared network resources in Windows

Now, let's add a PDF Printer to Samba. Once you get it working, adapt the
settings to your requirements. Maybe these settings are all you will need.

Download *samba-print-pdf* from *http://ranger.dnsalias.com/mandrake/
samba/*, copy it into your server's */usr/local/bin* directory, and chmod it to 755.
Open this script in an editor to see what it does, and possibly change things,
such as its Ghostscript *OPTIONS*.

Add the following section to *smb.conf*. It should work with Samba's share
security model (security = share) or user security model (security = user).
The user security model requires that a user provide a name and password
before accessing the printer.

```
[pdf_printer]
comment = Shared PDF Printer
path = /tmp
; this next line is necessary only when security = share
guest ok = yes
printable = yes
use client driver = yes
print command = /usr/local/bin/samba-print-pdf %s \
/home/pdf_printer/output //%L/pdf_output %m %I "%J" &
lpq command =
lprm command =
```

Restart Samba and then try accessing the file share *pdf_output* from a client machine. If that works, you are ready to install the client printer.

The Windows Client

Install the Virtual Printer Kit (VPK) [Hack #39]. Right-click our network printer, pdf_printer, under My Network Places in the File Explorer. Select Connect..., and click OK. The Add Printer Wizard will open and ask which printer driver to install. Click Have Disk, browse over to the VPK printer driver that suits your client platform, and click OK. Select the Virtual Post-Script Printer driver and click OK. Your new PDF network printer will appear in the computer's *Printers* folder. Print a test page to make sure it works properly.

Later, copy these Virtual PostScript Printer files to the *pdf_output* share so that you can access them easily across your network.

Print to Image and Other Rasterizing Options
Thumbnail the cover or rasterize the entire document.

You might sometimes need to convert PDF to other graphics formats. You can easily add a "Print to Image" printer by following "Print to PDF with Ghostscript and RedMon on Windows" [Hack #39] and changing a few ingredients. Alternatively, rasterize your PDF documents using Adobe Acrobat or Photoshop. Because Photoshop gives you the most power, you might prefer to "Print to PDF" and then open these pages in Photoshop.

Install a PNG (or JPEG or TIFF) Printer

The procedure for creating a bitmap (e.g., TIFF, JPEG, PNG) printer is the same as the procedure for creating the PDF printer in "Print to PDF with Ghostscript and RedMon on Windows" [Hack #39]. The configuration is just a little different. In this example, we'll configure a PNG printer, but you just as easily can create a JPEG or TIFF printer. The *DEVICE* option determines what gets created. We discuss alternative devices a little later.

Follow the PDF Printer instructions, except:

1. Name the new printer GS png16m Printer instead of GS Pdf Printer.

2. Name the new Redirected Port RPTPNG16M: instead of RPTPDF:.

3. When configuring this new Redirected Port, name the options file *C:\gs\png16m_printer.cfg* instead of *C:\gs\pdf_printer.cfg*.

4. When configuring this new Redirected Port, name the log file *C:\gs\png16m_printer.log* instead of *C:\gs\pdf_printer.log*.

5. Create the file *png16m_printer.cfg*, referenced earlier. It is a text file of additional arguments passed to Ghostscript. An example is included with our Virtual Printer Kit. Change the paths to suit your Ghostscript and system setup.

```
-dSAFER
-dBATCH
-dNOPAUSE
-Ic:\gs\gs8.14\Resource
-Ic:\gs\fonts
-Ic:\gs\gs8.14\lib
-sFONTPATH=c:\WINDOWS\FONTS
-sDEVICE=png16m
-r72
-dTextAlphaBits=4
-dGraphicsAlphaBits=4
-dAlignToPixels=0
```

Using this procedure, you can create one printer for each image file format you commonly use.

"Print to Image" devices and options. The documentation that comes with Ghostscript (*C:\gs\gs8.14\doc\index.htm*) explains the available output devices (*Devices.htm*) and general options (*Use.htm*) that you can use in the configuration file. Tables 4-8 and 4-9 provide a quick, abbreviated reference to give you a glimpse of what's possible.

Table 4-8. Some Ghostscript bitmap devices

Ghostscript device	Description
pnggray	Grayscale PNG
png16	16-Color (4-bit) PNG
png256	256-Color (8-bit) PNG
png16m	16-Million Color (24-bit) PNG
jpeggray	Grayscale JPEG
jpeg	Color JPEG
tiff24nc	16-Million Color (24-bit) TIFF
faxg3	G3 Fax with EOLs

Table 4-9. Some Ghostscript bitmap options

Ghostscript option	Description
-r<dpi resolution>	Sets the resolution of the output file in dots per inch. Screen resolution is commonly 72 dpi. To create thumbnails, set this to a low value, such as 20 dpi.
-dTextAlphaBits=<1|2|4>	Sets the text antialiasing. 4 yields the greatest smoothing.
-dGraphicsAlphaBits=<1|2|4>	Sets the graphics antialiasing. 4 yields the greatest smoothing.
-dJPEGQ=<0-100>	Sets the JPEG quality. Lower values yield greater compression at the expense of image quality.

Image output filenames. When printing a multipage document to one of these bitmap printers, the output filename must include the %d page number variable so that each page gets a unique filename. To pad this variable with three leading zeros, use %03d. On the Windows command line, the % must be represented by %%. Here are some example filenames that you might enter into the Save As… dialog box:

report_page-%d.png
> Yields: report_page-1.png, report_page-2.png, …

book_pg-%03.png
> Yields: book_pg-001.png, book_pg-002.png, …

tome_p-%04.png
> Yields: tome_p-0001.png, tome_p-0002.png, …

Acrobat: Save As Image

Beginning with Acrobat 5, you can open a PDF and then Save As… to JPEG, PNG, or TIFF image files. From the Save As… dialog, click the Settings… button to configure image options. You can set the image resolution, color space, and compression, among other things.

Photoshop: Open PDF

Photoshop is an ideal place to manipulate bitmaps, so it makes sense to open your PDF right in Photoshop. If your original document isn't a PDF, print one using Acrobat Distiller or our GS Pdf Printer [Hack #39]. Open it in Photoshop, then Save As… to whatever format you want.

Mac OS X: Preview

As mentioned in "Read PDFs with Mac OS X's Preview" [Hack #2], the Preview application that comes with Mac OS X lets you open PDF files and save them in a variety of graphics formats.

Print to SVG

#46

Create SVG as easily as PDF using pstoedit, and then embed it into your web page.

Scalable Vector Graphics (SVG) is an emerging web standard for describing vector drawings with XML (*http://www.w3.org/Graphics/SVG/*). It behaves more like PostScript than PDF. In fact, you can transform PostScript into SVG using *pstoedit's* SVG filter. Close the loop by wiring these tools into one of our virtual printers and you'll have "Print to SVG"!

> You can also create SVG using vector-editing programs such as Adobe Illustrator, Corel Draw, or Karbon.

Tool Up

SVG viewers are freely available. Visit *http://www.adobe.com/svg/* or *http://www.corel.com/svgviewer/* to download an SVG plug-in for your web browser. Visit *http://xml.apache.org/batik/svgviewer.html* to learn about Squiggle, the SVG browser.

Follow "Print to PDF with Ghostscript and RedMon on Windows" [Hack #39] to install Ghostscript and our other virtual printer components. Pstoedit requires Ghostscript.

Download the pstoedit installer from *http://www.pstoedit.net/pstoedit/*. This installer includes the shareware SVG filter. During installation, make sure to select this optional component. pstoedit is free software, but this SVG filter is not. The filter distorts its output by altering colors and scrambling text until you purchase and install a registration key. The pstoedit web site has a link to where you can purchase this key.

> pstoedit also includes an alternative, free SVG filter. To use this free filter, replace -f svg with -f plot-svg in the configurations, discussed shortly.

Using pstoedit

Test your installation by running pstoedit from the command line:

```
pstoedit -f svg c:\gs\gs8.14\examples\tiger.eps c:\tiger.svg
```

Open *tiger.svg* in your viewer and you should find this classic character snarling at you. Without its registration key, the SVG filter will deliberately upset tiger's colors, so she might appear blue instead of orange. Try using the plot-svg filter instead to see her true colors:

```
pstoedit -f plot-svg c:\gs\gs8.14\examples\tiger.eps c:\tiger.svg
```

After using this command, I edited the SVG file. I changed the g tag's transform attribute to get all of the tiger back into view for the screenshot in Figure 4-17.

Figure 4-17. Tiger in SVG

Create an SVG Printer

The procedure for creating an SVG printer is the same as the procedure for creating the PDF printer in "Print to PDF with Ghostscript and RedMon on Windows" [Hack #39]. The configuration is just a little different.

Follow the PDF Printer instructions, except:

1. Name the new printer SVG Printer instead of GS Pdf Printer.
2. Name the new Redirected Port RPTSVG: instead of RPTPDF:.
3. When configuring this new Redirected Port, name the log file *C:\gs\svg_ printer.log* and configure the port with the settings shown in Table 4-10.

Table 4-10. RedMon port properties

Field	Value
Redirect this port to the program:	*C:\pstoedit\pstoedit.exe*
Arguments for this program are:	*-f svg - "%1"*
Output:	*Prompt for Filename*
Run:	*Minimized*

Print a test page to see how it works. If the page isn't created, review the log file and double-check your settings. When you look at the SVG test page you will find that TrueType text has lost its encoding and doesn't display properly. This is an unfortunate limitation in the pstoedit SVG filter.

SVG on the Web

Use a belt-and-suspenders approach to adding SVG to your web pages. If the client ignores the OBJECT tag, it can fall back to the enclosed EMBED tag. For example:

```
<object type="image/svg+xml" data="tiger.svg"
title="Roar!" width="400" height="400">
  <embed type="image/svg+xml" src="tiger.svg"
  width="400" height="400"
  pluginspage="http://www.adobe.com/svg/viewer/install/">
</object>
```

Adobe specifically recommends against using the OBJECT tag when embedding SVG in an HTML page. For details, visit *http://www.adobe.com/svg/viewer/install/*.

Print Over the Internet
HACK
#47

Print via HTTP by submitting your print streams as HTML form data.

Printing over the Internet brings the way people like to read and write to the way we plumb information in the 21st century. The idea is to enable authors to create documents using their favorite editor and then print it to a web site. Once on the web server, the PostScript print stream can be converted to PDF and posted online for reading or downloading. In this scenario, the author controls the source document and is responsible for maintenance.

> This hack uses HTTP file submission to transfer PostScript to a web server. A more formal solution would use CUPS (*http://www.cups.org*). For a CUPS-based PDF creation server, try Alambic (*http://alambic.iroise.net*). Alambic supports HTTP and SMTP interfaces.

This hack demonstrates how to "print" a PostScript print stream to a web server. In our examples, we won't be printing to an elaborate document hosting service. Instead, we will print to the simple *http://www.ps2pdf.com* web site.

> Currently, *http://www.ps2pdf.com* uses an old version of Ghostscript, so printing to your own, local version of Ghostscript will yield a better PDF.

Download and Install

Visit *http://www.pdfhacks.com/submit_file/* and download *submit_file-1.0.zip*. Unzip this archive, and then copy *SubmitFile.exe* to a convenient location. This is a simple program that uses the Windows WinInet API to submit a local file to a web server. It then opens the default web browser to view the server's response. The source code is available and you should consult it for HTTP submission details.

Install a ps2pdf.com Printer

The procedure for creating an Internet printer is the same as the procedure for creating the PDF printer in "Print to PDF with Ghostscript and RedMon on Windows" [Hack #39], except you don't need to install Ghostscript. The configuration is also a little different.

Follow the Print to PDF instructions, except:

1. You don't need to install Ghostscript.
2. Name the new printer ps2pdf.com Printer instead of GS Pdf Printer.
3. Name the new Redirected Port RPTWEB: instead of RPTPDF:.
4. When configuring this new Redirected Port, use the settings in Table 4-11.

Table 4-11. RedMon port properties

Field	Value
Redirect this port to the program:	`C:\redmon17\RedRun.exe`

Arguments for this program are:	`C:\pdfhacks\SubmitFile.exe`
	`/convert/convert.cgi`
	`www.ps2pdf.com`
	`inputfile`
	`%1`

Output:	*Program Handles Output*
Run:	*Minimized*

5. Name the Redirected Port log file *C:\pdfhacks\web_printer.log* instead of *C:\gs\pdf_printer.log*.

6. Click OK to accept the new port settings.

7. Click OK to accept the new printer settings and close the dialog.

The RedRun program takes the PostScript print stream and creates a temp file for it. RedRun then runs the program SubmitFile, replacing the %1 with the temp filename. Note that you should not put quotes around this %1, because RedRun seems to pad the temp filename with whitespace that disrupts the SubmitFile arguments.

You can run SubmitFile from the command line, which is useful for debugging. It takes arguments in order:

```
SubmitFile <cgi path> <cgi server name> \
<html form field name> <local filename of upload>
```

Test Your ps2pdf.com Printer

Open the ps2pdf.com Printer properties dialog, click the General tab, and click Print Test Page. When your PDF is ready for download from *http://www.ps2pdf.com*, a browser will open with a hyperlink to follow.

If an error occurs, check the log file for feedback from RedRun or SubmitFile.

Note that the previous configuration is tailored to the current state of *http://www.ps2pdf.com*. The site administrators might choose to alter it at any time, requiring you to change this printer's configuration.

Create a PDF Album of Your Digital Pictures
HACK
#48
Quickly prepare your photos to share with family and friends.

With a digital camera you can easily create hundreds of photographic images. Preparing these pictures to share with your family and friends is a more difficult task. Consider creating a photo album with PDF. It makes a clean package that you can easily distribute, and its thumbnails feature is ideal for rapid navigation.

Most importantly, you can quickly and easily create one, shown in Figure 4-18, with free software. ImageMagick can create a single PDF from a folder of photographs in a snap. Create a lightweight edition suitable for email by simply adding downsample and compression settings.

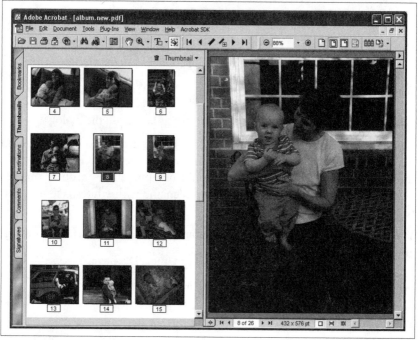

Figure 4-18. Collecting photos into a distributable package that is easy to navigate

Install ImageMagick

Visit *http://www.imagemagick.org* to learn about this powerful toolset and to download a Windows installer. The installer also unpacks documentation. We will use the convert tool, which is described in *convert.html*.

Convert Images to PDF

These examples use JPEG input images, but you can adapt them for use with other image types. Find a folder of images, open a command prompt [Hack #79] in this folder, and whisper this cantrip:

```
convert -density 100 -quality 85 \
-page "800x800>" -resize "800x800>" *.jpg album.pdf
```

When it is done, open *album.pdf* in Acrobat/Reader. Each image gets one PDF page, and they are ordered alphabetically by filename. To view all images with a uniform zoom, select View → Actual Size. View the thumbnails by selecting View → Navigation Tabs → Pages (Acrobat 6) or Window → Thumbnails (Acrobat 5). Select any image and copy it to the clipboard for use elsewhere; this works in Reader as well as Acrobat.

Let's take a look at our command parameters:

density

   This is the resolution of output images measured in dots per inch (dpi). The default is 72 dpi. Changing it doesn't affect the resulting image quality. Rather, it affects the logical, outer dimensions of the image. For example, a 1600×1200–pixel image at 200 dpi is 8×6 inches. At 100 dpi it is 16×12 inches. I chose 100 dpi because it strikes a good balance between on-screen, Actual Size viewing and paper printing (150 dpi is good for printing photos on most 600 dpi printers).

quality

   This is the JPEG compression applied to the images as they are packed into the PDF. 0 yields the poorest image quality but the greatest compression. 100 yields the greatest image quality but the poorest compression. The default is 75.

page

   This describes the outer dimensions of the PDF page, in pixels. If an image is smaller than these dimensions, the page is reduced to fit the image. Omitting this option causes large images to be constrained by (and squeezed into) the default, letter-page size. Set it to match the resize option.

resize

   This describes the maximum dimensions (in pixels) for all output images. The > symbol means that images smaller than this are not changed, and images larger than this are downsampled to fit. Decrease these dimensions to yield a smaller PDF file size. Increase these dimensions to improve image fidelity. Set page to match.

To demonstrate how these work together, here is another example. If your camera creates images at 1600×1200 pixels and you want to create a high-quality archive of these images, consider using:

```
convert -density 200 -quality 95 \
-page "1600x1600>" -resize "1600x1600>" *.jpg archive.pdf
```

Finishing Touches

In Acrobat you can correct image rotation, reorder images, and add book-marks. I like to configure the PDF to open thumbnails automatically. See "Polish Your PDF Edition" [Hack #62] for more information.

> You can create similar PDF albums with Adobe Photoshop Album as well, though it costs around $50.

 Print to Fax on Windows

#49 Treat fax machines like remote printers instead of remote copiers.

Faxing a document traditionally involves two fax machines: one that scans your document and one that prints your document. If the document in question is already stored on a computer, it makes more sense to *print* the document from the computer to the target fax machine. This yields a much higher-quality fax, and it is much more convenient. On a Windows machine with a fax modem, you can install a Fax printer that behaves like any other system printer.

> Faxes tend to look bad because the process of scanning a document adds noise, skews text, and generally degrades the appearance. Artwork and photographs suffer the most corruption. Printing a document to the target fax machine, on the other hand, dispenses with scanning. Text looks sharp, and images are preserved with dithering.

Windows XP and Windows 2000 will create a Fax printer when you install a fax-capable modem (Start → Setting → Control Panel → Phone and Modem Options → Modems → Add...). Using Acrobat or your authoring program, print your document to this Fax printer and a wizard will open. This fax wizard asks for the recipient's phone number and enables you to fill in a cover page. Upon completion, your modem will dial out to the destination fax machine and send your document.

> A useful series of Windows fax articles is available from *http://labmice.techtarget.com/windows2000/printing/fax.htm*.

If you fax PDFs frequently, consider adding a Print to Fax item to the PDF right-click context menu.

Windows XP and 2000:

1. In the Windows File Explorer menu, select Tools → Folder Options… and click the File Types tab. Select the PDF file type and click the Advanced button.

2. Click the New… button and a New Action dialog appears. Give the new action the name Print to Fax.

3. Give the action an application to open by clicking the Browse… button and selecting *Acrobat.exe*, which lives somewhere such as *C:\Program Files\Adobe\Acrobat 6.0\Acrobat*. Or, use Reader *(AcroRd32.exe)* instead of Acrobat.

4. Add arguments after Acrobat.exe or AcroRd32.exe like so:

   `"C:\Program Files\Adobe\Acrobat 6.0\Acrobat\Acrobat.exe" /t "%1" Fax`

5. Click OK, OK, OK and you should be done with the configuration.

To integrate fax features into your network, use HylaFAX. Visit *http://www.hylafax.org* and *http://www.ifax.com*, and consult the *fa.hylafax* newsgroup.

Convert Incoming Faxes to PDF on Linux
#50 Wrap an incoming fax in PDF and deliver it by email.

Before PDF and before email, we had fax. Today, we still have fax. Integrate fax with your 21st-century lifestyle using HylaFAX. HylaFAX turns your Linux box into a fax server. For details, visit *http://www.hylafax.org* and *http://www.ifax.com*. Here, we discuss configuring HylaFAX so that it will deliver incoming faxes to a given email address as a PDF attachment.

Install the HylaFAX server package from your favorite Linux distribution. During installation, a *FaxMaster* email alias should be created that points to the user responsible for maintaining the server. In this hack, all incoming faxes will be emailed to the FaxMaster as PDF. After installation, run faxsetup -server.

After a fax is received, HylaFAX's *faxgetty* invokes the *faxrcvd* script, which in turn executes *FaxDispatch* (typically located in */var/spool/hylafax/etc*) to set configuration parameters. *FaxDispatch* is where you can control how incoming faxes are routed. Your installation might include a sample *FaxDispatch* file, or you might need to create one. Read man faxrcvd for details about *FaxDispatch*.

This sample *FaxDispatch* file configures HylaFAX to email all incoming faxes to the FaxMaster as PDF attachments. Additional, commented-out lines give an idea of what else is possible:

```
## Default FaxDispatch file - routes all inbound faxes to FaxMaster as PDF
## Consult the faxrcvd(8C) man page for more information
##

SENDTO=FaxMaster;            # by default email to FaxMaster
FILETYPE=pdf;                # in PDF format

## This excerpt from the man page gives you an idea of what's possible here
##
## You can route by sender's TSI
#case "$SENDER" in
# *1*510*526*1212*) SENDTO=sam;;        # Sam's test rig in Berkeley
# *1*415*390*1212*) SENDTO=raster@asd;; # 7L Xerox room, used for scanning
# *5107811212)      SENDTO=peebles@mti;; # stuff from home
#esac

## and/or by device
#case "$DEVICE" in
#  ttyS1)            SENDTO=john;;       # all faxes received on ttyS1
#  ttyLT0)           SENDTO=mary@home;;  # all faxes received on ttyLT0
#esac

## and/or by caller id
#case "$CIDNUMBER" in
# 435*)       SENDTO=lee; FILETYPE=pdf;; # all faxes from area code 435
# 5059627777) SENDTO=amy; FILETYPE=tif;; # Amy wants faxes in TIFF
#esac
```

—*Darren Nickerson*

Manipulating PDF Files
Hacks 51–73

A lot of people think of PDFs as frozen files, printed once and then impossible to modify. That isn't the case, however! Whether you have Adobe Acrobat or not, there are lots of ways to manipulate PDF files: breaking them up, making their file sizes smaller, encrypting and decrypting them, and presenting them to users in different ways.

Split and Merge PDF Documents (Even Without Acrobat)

You can create new documents from existing PDF files by breaking the PDFs into smaller pieces or combining them with information from other PDFs.

As a document proceeds through its lifecycle, it can undergo many changes. It might be assembled from individual sections and then compiled into a larger report. Individual pages might be copied into a personal reference document. Sections might be replaced as new information becomes available. Some documents are agglomerations of smaller pieces, like an expense report with all of its lovely and easily lost receipts.

While it's easy to manipulate paper pages by hand, you must use a program to manipulate PDF pages. Adobe Acrobat can do this for you, but it is expensive. Other commercial products, such as pdfmeld from FyTek (*http://www.fytek.com*), also provide this basic functionality. The pdftk PDF toolkit [Hack #79] is a free software alternative.

Quickly Combine Pages in Acrobat

In Acrobat 6, select File → Create PDF → From Multiple Files…. Click the Browse… button (Choose… on a Macintosh) to open a file selector. You can select multiple files at once. On Windows, you can select a variety of file types, including Microsoft Office documents. Arrange the files into the desired order and click OK.

To quickly combine two PDF documents using Acrobat 5, begin by opening the first PDF in Acrobat. In the Windows File Explorer, select the PDF you want to append, drag it over the PDF open in Acrobat, and then drop it. A dialog will open, asking where you want to insert the PDF. Select After Last Page and it will be appended to the first PDF.

If you have a folder of PDF files to combine and their order in the Windows File Explorer is the order you want in the final document, begin by opening the first PDF in Acrobat 5. Next, in the File Explorer, select the remaining PDFs to merge. Finally, click the first PDF in this selection, as shown in Figure 5-1, drag the selection over the PDF currently open in Acrobat, and then drop it. A dialog will open, asking where you want to insert these PDFs. Select After Last Page and they will be appended to the first PDF. Review the document to ensure the PDFs were appended in the correct order.

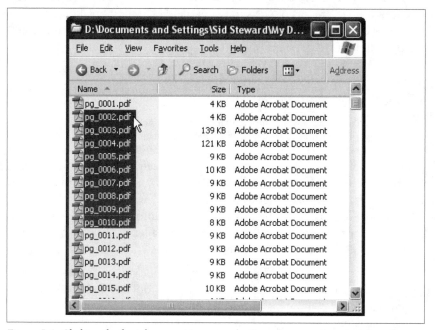

Figure 5-1. Clicking the first document in your selection when you drag-and-drop into Acrobat 5

Acrobat also allows you to arrange, move, and copy PDF pages using its Thumbnails view [Hack #14].

Manipulate Pages with pdftk, the PDF Toolkit

pdftk is a command-line tool for doing everyday things with PDF documents. It can combine PDF documents into a single document or split individual pages out into a new PDF document. Read "Tool Up with pdftk" [Hack #79] to install pdftk and our handy command-line shortcut. pdftk is free software.

Open a command prompt and then change the working directory to the folder that holds the input PDF files. Or, you can open a handy command line by right-clicking the folder that holds your input PDF files and selecting Command from the context menu.

> Instead of typing the input PDF filename, drag-and-drop the PDF file from the Windows File Explorer into the command prompt. Its full filename will appear at the cursor.

To combine pages into one document, invoke pdftk like so:

```
pdftk <input PDF files> cat [<input PDF pages>] output <output PDF filename>
```

A couple of quick examples give you the flavor of it. Here is an example of combining the first page of *in2.pdf*, the even pages in *in1.pdf*, and then the odd pages of *in1.pdf* to create a new PDF named *out.pdf*:

```
pdftk A=in1.pdf B=in2.pdf cat B1 A1-endeven A1-endodd output out.pdf
```

Here is an example of combining a folder of documents to create a new PDF named *combined.pdf*. The documents will be ordered alphabetically:

```
pdftk *.pdf cat output combined.pdf
```

Now, let's dig into the parameters:

<input PDF files>
>   Input PDF filenames are associated with handles like so:
>
>   *<input PDF handle>=<input PDF filename>*
>
>   where a handle is a single, uppercase letter. For example, A=in1.pdf associates the handle A with the file *in1.pdf*.
>
>   Specify multiple input PDF files like so:
>
>   A=in1.pdf B=in2.pdf C=in3.pdf
>
>   A file handle is necessary only when combining specific pages or when the input file requires a password.

[<input PDF pages>]
>   Describe input PDF page ranges like so:
>
>   *<input PDF handle>[<begin page number>[-<end page number>[<qualifier>]]]*
>
>   where the handle identifies one of the input PDF files, and the beginning and ending page numbers are one-based references to pages in that

PDF file. The qualifier can be *even* or *odd*. A few examples make this clearer. If A=in1.pdf:

A1-12

> Means the first 12 pages of *in1.pdf*

A1-12even

> Means pages 2, 4, 6, 8, 10, and 12

A12-1even

> Means pages 12, 10, 8, 6, 4, and 2

A1-end

> Means all the pages from *in1.pdf*

A

> Means the same thing as A1-end

A10

> Means page 10 from *in1.pdf*

You can see from these examples that page ranges also specify the output page order. Notice the keyword end, which refers to the final page in a PDF.

Specify a sequence of page ranges like so:

    A1 B1-end C5

When combining all the input PDF documents in their given order, you can omit the <input PDF pages> section.

> The output PDF filename must be different from any of the input filenames.

If any of the input files are encrypted, you will need to supply their owner passwords [Hack #52].

HACK #52 Encrypt and Decrypt PDF (Even Without Acrobat)

Restrict who can view your PDF and how they can use it.

You can use PDF encryption to lock a file's content behind a password, but more often it is used to enforce lighter restrictions imposed by the author. For example, the author might permit printing pages but prohibit making changes to the document. Here, we continue from "Split and Merge PDF Documents (Even Without Acrobat)" [Hack #51] and explain how pdftk [Hack #79] can encrypt and decrypt PDF documents. We'll begin by describing the Acrobat Standard Security model (called Password Security in Acrobat 6) and the permissions you can grant or revoke.

PDF file attachments get encrypted, too. After opening an encrypted PDF, document file attachments can be opened, changed, or deleted only if the owner granted Modify-Annotations permission.

Page file attachments behave differently than document file attachments. Once you open an encrypted document, you can open files attached to PDF pages regardless of the permissions. Changing or deleting one of these attachments requires the ModifyAnnotations permission. Of course, if you have the owner password, you can do anything you want.

PDF Passwords

Acrobat Standard Security enables you to set two passwords on a PDF: the *user* password and the *owner* password. In Acrobat 6, these are also called the *Open* password and the *Permissions* password, respectively.

The user password, if set, is necessary for viewing the document pages. The PDF encryption key is derived from the user password, so it really is required. When a PDF viewer tries to open a PDF that was secured with a user password, it will prompt the reader to supply the correct password.

The owner password, if set, is necessary for changing the document security settings. A PDF with both its user and owner passwords set can be opened with either password, so you should choose both with equal care.

An owner password by itself does not provide any real PDF security. The content is encrypted, but the key, which is derived from the (empty) user password, is known. By itself, an owner password is a polite but firm request to respect the author's wishes. A rogue program could strip this security in a second. See "Copy-Protect Your PDF" **[Hack #66]** for additional rights management options.

Standard Security Encryption Strength

If your PDF must be compatible with Acrobat 3 or 4, you must use the weaker, 40-bit encryption strength. Otherwise, use the stronger, 128-bit strength. In both cases, the encryption key is created from the user password, so a good, long, random password helps improve your security against brute force attacks. The longest possible PDF password is 32 characters.

Standard Security Permissions

Set the user password if you don't want people to see your PDF. If they don't have the user password, it simply won't open.

You also have some control over what people can do with your document once they have it open. The permissions associated with 128-bit security (Acrobat 5 and 6) are more precise than those associated with 40-bit security (Acrobat 3 and 4). Tables 5-1 and 5-2 list all available permissions for each security model, and Figure 5-2 shows the permissions as seen through Acrobat. The tables also show the corresponding pdftk flags to use.

Table 5-1. Permissions available under 40-bit security

To allow readers to ...	Apply this pdftk permission
Print—pages are top quality	Printing
Modify page or document contents,insert or remove pages, rotate pages or add bookmarks	ModifyContents
Copy text and graphics from pages, extract text and graphics data for use by accessibility devices	CopyContents
Change or add annotations or fill form fields with data	ModifyAnnotations
Reconfigure or add form fields	ModifyContents and ModifyAnnotations
All of the above	AllFeatures

Table 5-2. Permissions available under 128-bit security

To allow readers to ...	Apply this pdftk permission
Print—pages are top quality	Printing
Print—pages are of lower quality	DegradedPrinting
Modify page or document contents, insert or remove pages, rotate pages or add bookmarks	ModifyContents
Insert or remove pages, rotate pages or add bookmarks	Assembly
Copy text and graphics from pages	CopyContents
Extract text and graphics data for use by accessibility devices	ScreenReaders
Change or add annotations or fill form fields with data	ModifyAnnotations
Fill form fields with data	FillIn
Reconfigure or add form fields	ModifyContents and ModifyAnnotations
All of the above, and top-quality printing	AllFeatures

Comparing these two tables, you can see that Assembly is a weaker version of ModifyContents and FillIn is a weaker version of ModifyAnnotations.

DegradedPrinting sends pages to the printer as rasterized images, whereas Printing sends pages as PostScript. A PostScript stream can be intercepted and turned back into (unsecured) PDF, so the Printing permission is a

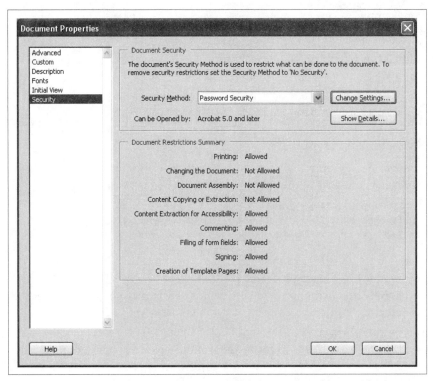

Figure 5-2. PDF Standard Security features, which help you control how readers use your document

security risk. However, DegradedPrinting reduces the clarity of printed pages, so you should test your document to make sure DegradedPrinting yields acceptable, printed pages.

After setting these permissions and/or a user password, changing them requires the owner password, if it is set.

pdftk and Encrypted Input

When using pdftk on encrypted PDF documents, the owner password must be supplied. If an encrypted PDF has no owner password, the user password must be given instead. If an encrypted PDF has neither password set, no password should be associated with this document when calling pdftk.

Input PDF passwords are listed right after the input filenames, like so:

```
pdftk <input PDF files> input_pw <input file passwords> ...
```

The file handles assigned in *<input PDF files>* are used to associate files with passwords in *<input file passwords>* like so:

```
<input PDF handle>=<input PDF password>
```

For example:

```
A=foopass
```

Adding this parameter to our example in "Split and Merge PDF Documents (Even Without Acrobat)" [Hack #51] produces:

```
pdftk A=in1.pdf B=in2.pdf C=in3.pdf \
input_pw A=foopass cat A1 B1-end C5 output out.pdf
```

Use pdftk to Encrypt Output

You can encrypt any PDF created with pdftk by simply adding encryption parameters after the output filename, like so:

```
... output <output filename> \
[encrypt_40bit | encrypt_128bit] [allow <permissions>] \
[owner_pw <owner password>] [user_pw <user password>]
```

Here are the details:

[encrypt_40bit | encrypt_128bit]
Specify an encryption strength. If this strength is not given along with other encryption parameters, it defaults to encrypt_128bit.

[allow <permissions>]
List the permissions to grant users. If this section is omitted, no permissions are granted. See Tables 5-1 and 5-2 for a complete list of available permissions.

[owner_pw <owner password>]
Use this combination to set the owner password. It can be omitted; in which case no owner password is set.

[user_pw <user password>]
Use this parameter to set the user password. It can be omitted; in which case no user password is set.

Adding these parameters to our example in "Split and Merge PDF Documents (Even Without Acrobat)" [Hack #51] yields this:

```
pdftk A=in1.pdf B=in2.pdf C=in3.pdf \
cat A1 B1-end C5 output out.pdf \
encrypt_128bit allow CopyContents Printing \
owner_pw ownpass
```

Simply Encrypting or Decrypting a File

The previous examples were in the context of "Split and Merge PDF Documents (Even Without Acrobat)" [Hack #51]. Here are examples of simply adding or removing encryption from a single file:

Encrypting a single file
```
pdftk A=input.pdf output encrypted.pdf \
encrypt_128bit allow CopyContents \
owner_pw foopass
```

Decrypting a single file
```
pdftk A=encrypted.pdf input_pw A=foopass output decrypted.pdf
```

 ## Add PDF Encryption Actions to Windows Context Menus

Apply or remove encryption from a given PDF with a quick right-click.

"Encrypt and Decrypt PDF (Even Without Acrobat)" [Hack #52] discussed how to apply or remove PDF encryption with pdftk [Hack #79]. Let's streamline these security operations by adding handy Encrypt and Decrypt items to the PDF context menu. The encryption example simply applies a user password to the selected PDF, so nobody can open it without the password. The decryption example removes all (Standard) security, upon success.

Add the Encrypt PDF Context Menu Item

Windows XP and Windows 2000:

1. In the Windows File Explorer menu, select Tools → Folder Options... and click the File Types tab. Select the PDF file type and click the Advanced button.

2. Click the New... button and a New Action dialog appears. Give the new action the name Encrypt.

3. Give the action an application to open by clicking the Browse... button and selecting *cmd.exe*, which lives somewhere such as *C:\windows\ system32* (Windows XP) or *C:\winnt\system32* (Windows 2000).

4. Add these arguments after cmd.exe, changing the path to suit, like so:
   ```
   C:\windows\system32\cmd.exe
   /C C:\windows\system32\pdftk.exe "%1" output "%1.encrypted.pdf"
   encrypt_128bits user_pw PROMPT
   ```

5. Click OK, OK, OK and you should be done with the configuration.

Add the Decrypt PDF Context Menu Item

Follow the preceding procedure, except name the action Decrypt and replace the cmd.exe arguments in step 4 with:
```
C:\windows\system32\cmd.exe
/C C:\windows\system32\pdftk.exe "%1" input_pw PROMPT
output "%1.decrypted.pdf"
```

Using Encrypt or Decrypt

Right-click your PDF of interest and select Encrypt or Decrypt from the context menu. A command prompt will open and ask for the password. Upon success, the command prompt will close. pdftk will create a new PDF file with a name based on the original PDF's filename. If pdftk has trouble executing your request, the command prompt will remain open with a message. Press Enter to close this message.

If you invoke one of these commands on a selection of multiple PDFs, you will get one command prompt for each PDF.

HACK #54 Add Attachments to Your PDF (Even Without Acrobat)

Include live data that your readers can unpack and use.

PDF provides a convenient package for your document. A typical PDF contains fonts, images, page streams, annotations, and metadata. It turns out that you can pack anything into a PDF file, even the source document used to create the PDF! These *attachments* enjoy the benefits of PDF features such as compression, encryption, and digital signatures. Attachments also enable you to provide your readers with document data, such as tables, in a native file format that they can easily use. People often ask, "How do I extract data from my PDF?" [Hack #7]. Attach your document data as HTML or Excel files and give your readers exactly what they need.

This hack explains how to attach files to your PDF. "Easily Attach Your Document's Tables" [Hack #55] goes on to describe how to quickly extract your document's tables for PDF attachment.

Page Attachments Versus Document Attachments

You can attach a file to a particular PDF *page*, where it is visible as an icon. Or, you can attach a file to the PDF *document* so that it keeps a lower profile. After encrypting your PDF, document attachments can't be unpacked without the ModifyAnnotations permission [Hack #52]. Page attachments, on the other hand, can be unpacked at any time, regardless of the security permissions you imposed. Of course, the PDF must be opened first, which could require a user password.

Attach Files to a PDF with Acrobat

Attach your file to a PDF page using the Attach File commenting tool. In Acrobat 6, access this tool using the Advanced Commenting toolbar or from the Tools → Advanced Commenting → Attach menu. In Acrobat 5, access this tool using the Commenting toolbar. The Attach File tool button hides under the Note tool button; click the little down arrow to discover it, as shown in Figure 5-3.

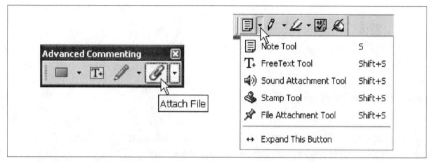

Figure 5-3. Acrobat 6's Attach File paperclip-icon toolbar button and Acrobat 5's hidden Attach File toolbar button, under the Note tool button

Activate the Attach File tool and the cursor becomes a push pin. Click the page where you want the attachment's icon to appear and a file selector dialog opens. Select the file to attach. A properties dialog will open, where you can customize the appearance of your attachment's icon.

As we noted, *document attachments* are different from *page attachments*. In Acrobat 6, access document attachments by selecting Document → File Attachments.... Select Document File Attachments and click Import... to add an attachment. In Acrobat 5, select File → Document Properties → Embedded Data Objects.... Click Import... to add an attachment.

Attach Files to PDFs with pdftk

Our free pdftk [Hack #79] can attach files to PDF documents and pages.

When attaching files to an existing PDF, call pdftk like so:

```
pdftk <PDF filename> attach_file <attachment filename> \
[to_page <page number>] output <output filename>
```

The output filename must be different from the input filename. For example, attach the file *data.xls* to the first page of the PDF *report.pdf* like so:

```
pdftk report.pdf attach_file data.xls to_page 1 output report.page_
attachment.pdf
```

Attach *data.xls* to *report.pdf* as a document attachment instead of a page attachment by simply omitting the to_page parameter:

```
pdftk report.pdf attach_file data.xls output report.doc_attachment.pdf
```

You can include additional output parameters, too, such as PDF encryption options.

Attachments and Encryption

When you encrypt a PDF, you also encrypt its attachments. The permissions you apply can affect whether users can unpack these attachments. See "Encrypt and Decrypt PDF (Even Without Acrobat)" [Hack #52] for details on how to apply encryption using pdftk.

Once the PDF is open in Acrobat/Reader (which might require a password), any files attached to PDF pages can be unpacked, regardless of the PDF's permissions. This enables you to disable copy/paste features, yet still make select data available to your readers.

Document attachments are more restricted than page attachments. You must grant the ModifyAnnotations permission if you want your readers to be able to unpack and view document attachments.

H A C K   Easily Attach Your Document's Tables
#55   Pack your document's essential information into its PDF edition.

Readers copy data from PDF documents to use in their own documents or spreadsheets. Tables usually contain the most valuable data, yet they are the most difficult to extract from a PDF [Hack #7]. Give readers what they need, as shown in Figure 5-4, by automatically extracting tables from your source document, converting them into an Excel spreadsheet, and then attaching them to your PDF.

Copy Tables into a New Document

In Microsoft Word, use the following macro to copy a document's tables into a new document. In Word, create the macro like so.

Open the Macros dialog box (Tools → Macro → Macros…). Type CopyTablesIntoNewDocument into the "Macro name:" field, set "Macros in:" to *Normal.dot*, and click Create.

A window will open where you can enter the macro's code. It already will have two lines of code: Sub CopyTablesIntoNewDocument() and End Sub. You don't need to duplicate these lines.

You can download the following code from *http://www.pdfhacks.com/copytables/*:

```
Sub CopyTablesIntoNewDocument( )
' version 1.0
' http://www.pdfhacks.com/copytables/

Dim SrcDoc, NewDoc As Document
Dim SrcDocTableRange As Range
```

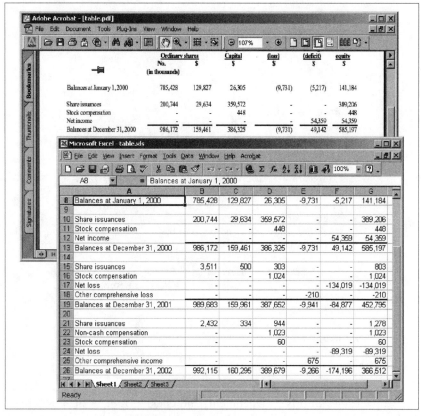

Figure 5-4. Giving your readers live data to work with

```
Set SrcDoc = ActiveDocument
If SrcDoc.Tables.Count <> 0 Then

    Set NewDoc = Documents.Add(DocumentType:=wdNewBlankDocument)
    Set NewDocRange = NewDoc.Range
    Dim PrevPara As Range
    Dim NextPara As Range
    Dim NextEnd As Long
    NextEnd = 0

    For Each SrcDocTable In SrcDoc.Tables
        Set SrcDocTableRange = SrcDocTable.Range

        'output the preceding paragraph?
        Set PrevPara = SrcDocTableRange.Previous(wdParagraph, 1)
        If PrevPara Is Nothing Or PrevPara.Start < NextEnd Then
        Else
            Set PPWords = PrevPara.Words
            If PPWords.Count > 1 Then 'yes
                NewDocRange.Start = NewDocRange.End
```

```
                NewDocRange.InsertParagraphBefore

                NewDocRange.Start = NewDocRange.End
                NewDocRange.InsertParagraphBefore
                NewDocRange.FormattedText = PrevPara.FormattedText
            End If
        End If

        'output the table
        NewDocRange.Start = NewDocRange.End
        NewDocRange.FormattedText = SrcDocTableRange.FormattedText

        'output the following paragraph?
        Set NextPara = SrcDocTableRange.Next(wdParagraph, 1)
        If NextPara Is Nothing Then
        Else
            Set PPWords = NextPara.Words
            NextEnd = NextPara.End
            If PPWords.Count > 1 Then 'yes
                NewDocRange.Start = NewDocRange.End
                NewDocRange.InsertParagraphBefore
                NewDocRange.FormattedText = NextPara.FormattedText
            End If
        End If

    Next SrcDocTable
    End If
    End Sub
```

Run this macro from Word by selecting Tools → Macro → Macro..., selecting Copy Tables Into New Document, and clicking Run. A new document
will open that contains all the tables from your current document. It will
also include the paragraphs immediately before and after each table. This
feature was added to help readers find the table they want. Modify the
macro code to suit your requirements.

Create an HTML or Excel Document from Your Tables Document

Use "Create an HTML Edition from Your Word Processor" **[Hack #35]** to convert this new document into HTML. Make this HTML file act like an Excel
spreadsheet by changing its filename extension from *html* to *xls*. Excel is
perfectly comfortable opening data this way.

> Not only can Excel open HTML files disguised as XLS files,
> but it can also convert Internet web sites into spreadsheets.
> From Excel, select File → Open, enter a web address in the
> "File name:" field, and click Open.

Attach the Tables to Your PDF

See "Add Attachments to Your PDF (Even Without Acrobat)" **[Hack #54]** for the detailed procedure. Speed up attachments with quick attachment actions **[Hack #56]**.

 ## Add PDF Attachment Actions to Windows **#56** Context Menus

Pack or unpack PDF attachments from the Windows File Explorer with a quick right-click.

It's best to perform simple tasks in a simple manner, especially when you must perform them often. Wire pdftk **[Hack #79]** into Windows Explorer so that you can pack or unpack attachments using PDF's right-click context menu.

Create the Attach File Context Menu Item

In Windows XP and Windows 2000:

1. In the Windows File Explorer menu, open Tools → Folder Options… and click the File Types tab. Select the PDF file type and click the Advanced button.

2. Click the New… button and a New Action dialog appears. Give the new action the name Attach File.

3. Give the action an application to open by clicking the Browse… button and selecting *cmd.exe*, which lives somewhere such as *C:\windows\ system32* (Windows XP) or *C:\winnt\system32* (Windows 2000).

4. Add these arguments after cmd.exe, changing the path to suit, like so:

```
C:\windows\system32\cmd.exe
/C C:\windows\system32\pdftk.exe "%1" attach_file PROMPT output PROMPT
```

5. Click OK, OK, OK and you should be done with the configuration.

Create the Unpack Attachments Context Menu Item

Follow the previous procedure, except name the action Unpack Attachments and replace the cmd.exe arguments in step 4 with:

```
/C C:\windows\system32\pdftk.exe "%1" unpack_files
```

Using Attach File or Unpack Attachments

Right-click your PDF of interest and select Attach File or Unpack Attachments from the context menu. A command prompt will open and ask for additional information. Upon success, the command prompt will close. If pdftk has trouble executing your request, the command prompt will remain open with a message. Press Enter to close this message.

Use drag-and-drop to quickly enter the filenames for the files you want to attach. Select a file in Explorer, drag it over to the command-line window, and drop it. Its full filename will appear at the cursor. This works for only one file at a time.

If you invoke one of these commands on a selection of multiple PDFs, you will get one command prompt for each PDF.

HACK #57 Create a Traditional Index Section from Keywords

Add a search feature to your print edition.

Creating a good document Index section is a difficult job performed by professionals. However, an automatically generated index still can be very helpful. Use automatic keywords [Hack #19] or select your own keywords. This hack will locate their pages, build a reference, and then create PDF pages that you can append to your document, as shown in Figure 5-5. It even uses your PDF's page labels (also known as *logical page numbering*) to ensure trouble-free lookup.

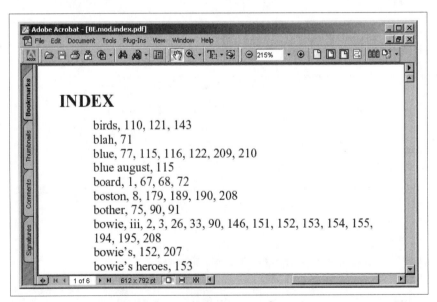

Figure 5-5. Turning document keywords into a PDF Index section

Tool Up

Download and install pdftotext [Hack #19], our kw_index [Hack #19], and pdftk [Hack #79]. You must also have enscript (Windows users visit *http://gnuwin32. sf.net/packages/enscript.htm*) and ps2pdf. ps2pdf comes with Ghostscript [Hack #39]. Our kw_index package includes the kw_catcher and page_refs programs (and source code) that we use in the following sections.

The Procedure

First, set your PDF's logical page numbering [Hack #62] to match your document's page numbering. Then, use pdftk to dump this information into a text file, like so:

```
pdftk mydoc.pdf dump_data output mydoc.data.txt
```

Next, convert your PDF to plain text with pdftotext:

```
pdftotext mydoc.pdf mydoc.txt
```

Create a keyword list [Hack #19] from *mydoc.txt* using kw_catcher, like so:

```
kw_catcher 12 keywords_only mydoc.txt > mydoc.kw.txt
```

Edit *mydoc.kw.txt* to remove duds and add missing keywords. At present, only one keyword is allowed per line. If two or more keywords are adjacent in *mydoc.txt*, our page_refs program will assemble them into phrases.

Now pull all these together to create a text index using page_refs:

```
page_refs mydoc.txt mydoc.kw.txt mydoc.data.txt > mydoc.index.txt
```

Finally, create a PDF from *mydoc.index.txt* using enscript and ps2pdf:

```
enscript --columns 2 --font 'Times-Roman@10' \
--header '|INDEX' --header-font 'Times-Bold@14' \
--margins 54:54:36:54 --word-wrap --output - mydoc.index.txt \
| ps2pdf - mydoc.index.pdf
```

The Code

Of course, the thing to do is to wrap this procedure into a tidy script. Copy the following Bourne shell script into a file named *make_index.sh*, and make it executable by applying chmod 700. Windows users can get a Bourne shell by installing MSYS [Hack #97].

```
#!/bin/sh
# make_index.sh, version 1.0
# usage: make_index.sh <PDF filename> <page window>
# requires: pdftk, kw_catcher, page_refs,
#           pdftotext, enscript, ps2pdf
#
# by Ross Presser, Imtek.com
# adapted by Sid Steward
```

```
# http://www.pdfhacks.com/kw_index/

fname=`basename $1 .pdf`
pdftk ${fname}.pdf dump_data output ${fname}.data.txt && \
pdftotext ${fname}.pdf ${fname}.txt && \
kw_catcher $2 keywords_only ${fname}.txt \
| page_refs ${fname}.txt - ${fname}.data.txt \
| enscript --columns 2 --font 'Times-Roman@10' \
    --header '|INDEX' --header-font 'Times-Bold@14' \
    --margins 54:54:36:54 --word-wrap --output - \
| ps2pdf - ${fname}.index.pdf
```

Running the Hack

Pass the name of your PDF document and the kw_catcher window size to *make_index.sh* like so:

> **make_index.sh** *mydoc.pdf* **12**

The script will create a document index named *mydoc.index.pdf*. Review this index and append it to your PDF document **[Hack #51]** if you desire. The script also creates two intermediate files: *mydoc.data.txt* and *mydoc.txt*. If the PDF index is faulty, review these intermediate files for problems. Delete them when you are satisfied with the PDF index.

The second argument to *make_index.sh* controls the keyword detection sensitivity. Smaller numbers yield fewer keywords at the risk of omitting some keywords; larger numbers admit more keywords and also more noise. "Generate Document Keywords" **[Hack #19]** discusses this parameter and the kw_catcher program that uses it.

HACK #58 Rasterize Intricate Artwork with Illustrator or Photoshop

When distributing a PDF online, some vector drawings outweigh their usefulness.

Vector drawings yield the highest possible quality across all media. For simple illustrations such as charts and graphs, they are also more efficient than bitmaps. However, when preparing a PDF for online distribution, you will sometimes find an intricate vector drawing that has tripled your PDF's file size. With Acrobat and Illustrator (or Photoshop), you can rasterize this detailed drawing in-place and reduce your PDF's file size.

Big Drawings in Little Spaces

How does this happen? Vector artwork scales easily without altering its quality. This means a big, detailed, 2 MB vector drawing can be scaled down perfectly to the size of a postage stamp. Even though most of its detail might no longer be visible on a paper printout or on-screen, the drawing is still 2MB in size. Again, this becomes an issue only when you go to distribute this file online and you want to reduce the document's file size.

Integrate Illustrator or Photoshop into Acrobat

If you have Adobe Acrobat 6 Pro or Acrobat 5 and Adobe Illustrator or Adobe Photoshop, you can rasterize a PDF's drawings. First you must configure Acrobat's *TouchUp Object* tool to open your PDF selections in Illustrator or Photoshop.

In Acrobat, select Edit → Preferences → General… → TouchUp. Click Choose Page/Object Editor and then browse over to *Illustrator.exe*, which might be located somewhere such as *C:\Program Files\Adobe\Illustrator 9.0.1*. Or, use Photoshop instead of Illustrator by browsing over to *Photoshp.exe*, which might be located somewhere such as *C:\Program Files\Adobe\Photoshop 6.0*. Click Open and then click OK to confirm your new Preferences setting.

Rasterize Drawings In-Place with Acrobat

First, make a backup copy of your PDF so that you can go back to where you started at any time.

Open your PDF in Acrobat and locate the drawing you want to rasterize. Activate the TouchUp Object tool (Tools → Advanced Editing → TouchUp Object, in Acrobat 6) and try to select the drawing. This usually requires patience and experimentation because one illustration might use dozens of separate drawing objects. And, it usually is tangled with other items on the page that you don't want to rasterize.

First, try dragging out a selection rectangle that encloses the artwork. If other, unwanted items get caught in your dragnet, try dropping them from your selection by holding down the Shift key and clicking them. If you missed items that you wanted to select, you can add them the same way: Shift-click. The Shift key is a useful way to incrementally add or remove items from your current selection. You can even hold down the Shift key while dragging out a selection rectangle. Items in the rectangle will be toggled in or out of the current selection, depending on their previous state.

If you accidentally move an item, immediately press Ctrl-Z (Edit → Undo) to restore it. If things ever get messed up, close the PDF without saving it and reopen it to start again.

Using Illustrator. After your selection is made in Acrobat, right-click inside the selection and click Edit Objects…. Adobe Illustrator will open and your selected material will appear. Now, you must select the items you want to rasterize. If your selection in Acrobat worked just right, you can simply select the entire page (Edit → Select All). If your original selection included unwanted items, carefully omit these items from this new selection. The Shift key works the same way in Illustrator as it did in Acrobat, as you assemble your selection.

After making your selection in Illustrator, select Object → Rasterize... and a dialog opens. Select a suitable color model (e.g., RGB) and resolution (e.g., 300 pixels per inch) and click OK. Inspect the results to make sure the artwork retained adequate detail. If you like the results, save and close the Illustrator file. Acrobat will automatically update the PDF to reflect your changes. If you still like them, save the PDF in Acrobat. Otherwise, discard them by pressing Ctrl-Z (Edit → Undo) or by closing the PDF and starting over.

Using Photoshop. If you are using Photoshop instead of Illustrator, you won't have a chance to select the objects you want rasterized; Photoshop immediately rasterizes everything you selected in Acrobat. One advantage of using Photoshop is that it won't try to substitute fonts, as Illustrator sometimes does.

After your selection is made in Acrobat, right-click inside the selection and click Edit Objects.... Photoshop will open and ask you for a resolution. Enter a resolution (e.g., 300 pixels per inch), click OK, and the rasterized results will appear. Inspect the results to make sure the artwork retained adequate detail. If you like the results, save the Photoshop file. By default, it should save as PDF, but sometimes you must change the Format to PDF in the Save dialog. Before saving the file, Photoshop will ask which encoding to use (ZIP or JPEG). If you choose JPEG, you can also set its quality level. After saving the rasterized artwork in Photoshop, Acrobat will automatically update the PDF to reflect your changes. If you still like them, save the PDF in Acrobat. Otherwise, discard them by pressing Ctrl-Z (Edit → Undo) or by closing the PDF in Acrobat and starting over.

Reordering Page Layers in Acrobat

Sometimes, when the rasterized artwork is brought back into the PDF, it will cover up and obscure other items on the page. The trick is to place the new bitmap behind the obscured items.

In Acrobat 5, select the bitmap with the TouchUp Object tool, right-click, and select Cut. Right-click the page anywhere and select Paste In Back. The bitmap should appear in the same location, but behind the other items on the page. If it didn't reappear, it is probably being obscured by a larger, background item. Select this obscuring object and cut-and-paste it the same way. Save the PDF when you are done.

In Acrobat 6, open the Content tab (View → Navigation Tabs → Content) and click on the plus symbol to open a hierarchy of document page references. Locate your page and then click on its plus symbol to open a hierarchy of page objects. Lower objects on this stack overlap the higher objects. Identify your image (it will be wrapped inside an XObject node), then click and drag it to a higher level in the page hierarchy. This will take some experimentation. See "Add and Maintain PDF Bookmarks" [Hack #63] for tips on dragging and dropping these nodes. Save the PDF when you are done.

 ## Crop Pages for Clarity

Aggressive page cropping ensures maximum on-screen clarity.

When viewing a PDF in Reader or Acrobat, the page is often scaled to fit its width or its height into the viewer window. This means you can make page content appear larger on-screen by cropping away excess page margins, as shown in Figure 5-6. Cropping has no effect on the printed page's scale, but it might alter the content's position on the printed page.

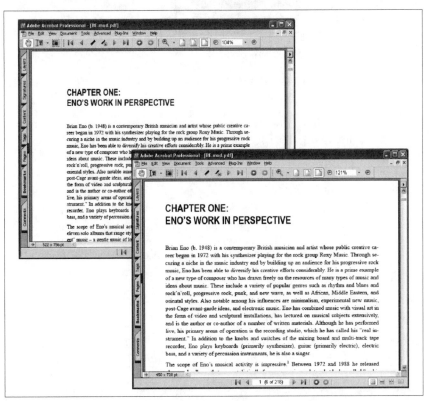

Figure 5-6. Cropping pages to improve on-screen clarity

Acrobat's cropping tool can remove excess page margins. Use it in combination with our freely available BBOX Acrobat plug-in. These two tools make it easy to find the best cropping for a page and then apply this cropping to the entire document.

Acrobat's Crop Tool

With Acrobat's Crop tool, shown in Figure 5-7, you can draw a free-form crop region by clicking the page and dragging out a rectangle. Double-click this new region or simply double-click the page and the Crop Pages dialog opens. The Crop Pages dialog enables you to directly enter the widths you want to trim from each margin. You can also specify a range of document pages to crop according to these settings. The Remove White Margins setting sounds like just what we need, but it is inconsistent and it yields pages with irregular dimensions.

Figure 5-7. The Crop tool on the Advanced Editing toolbar in Acrobat 6 (left) and on the Editing toolbar in Acrobat 5 (right)

Using the Crop tool to draw a free-form region gives you an irregular page size that probably doesn't precisely center your content. The solution is to activate the Snap to Grid feature (View → Snap to Grid). By default, this grid is set to three subdivisions per inch. A more useful setting might be four or eight subdivisions per inch.

 In Acrobat 5, high-precision cropping requires using points instead of inches, because 1/8-inch increments get rounded to two decimals. In the File → Preferences... → Display dialog, change Page Units to Points. There are 72 points to an inch, or 9 points to 1/8 of an inch.

BBOX Acrobat Cropping Plug-In for Windows

BBOX is a simple tool I use in my PDF production. Download it from *http://www.pdfhacks.com/bbox/*, unzip, and copy *pdfhacks_bbox.api* into your Acrobat *plug_ins* folder [Hack #4]. When you restart Acrobat, it will add a menu named Plug-Ins → PDF Hacks → BBOX (the contents of which are shown in Figure 5-8).

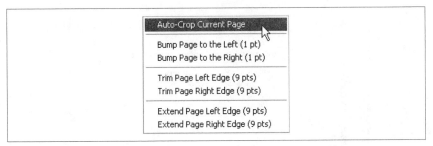

Figure 5-8. Using BBOX to quickly eliminate excess page margins and gutters

The BBOX Auto-Crop feature crops as much as it can from the currently visible page. It trims away multiples of 1/8 inch (9 points), so the resulting page size isn't irregular. It tries to be smart, but it sometimes leaves margins that need additional cropping.

The Trim Page features enable you to trim 1/8 inch from the left or right page edges. If you go too far, use the Extend Page features to add 1/8 inch instead.

Sometimes 1/8-inch units are not fine enough to center a page. For these cases, we have the Bump Page features. These do not alter the page width, but appear to move the page one point at a time. They simply reduce the crop on one side and increase the crop on the other, giving you fine control over page centering.

Document Cropping Procedure

Does your document jog back and forth from one page to the next? Then you have page gutters. You will need to crop your even pages separately from your odd pages.

Find a representative page and crop it to your satisfaction using any combination of the Crop and BBOX tools. If your document has gutters, turn to the next page and give it the same treatment. Flip back and forth between these two pages as you work to remove the gutter, trying to get the pages to stop jogging back and forth.

When your representative page is cropped to your satisfaction, open the Crop Pages dialog by selecting the Crop tool and double-clicking the page. Set the page range to All Pages. If you are cropping even and odd pages separately, set the nearby drop-down box to Even Pages Only or Odd Pages Only depending on which page you currently have displayed. Click OK. *Even* and *odd* in this context refer to the physical page numbers (or *page indexes*) in your document, shown in Figure 5-9, not the logical page numbers (or *page labels*).

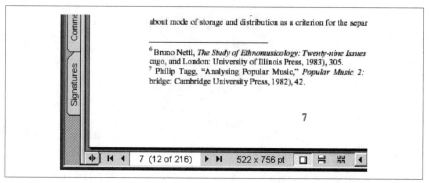

Figure 5-9. Using the physical page number, shown in parentheses, when cropping pages (this one is even)

Refry Before Posting Documents Online

Run your assembled PDF through Acrobat Distiller to reduce its file size. In Acrobat 6, try PDF Optimizer.

You started with two or three PDFs, combined them, and then cropped them. Before going any further, consider running your assembled PDF through Distiller. This *refrying* can reduce duplicate resources and ensures that your PDF is optimized for online reading. It also gives you a chance to improve your PDF's compatibility with older versions of Acrobat and Reader. In Acrobat 6, you can conveniently refry a PDF without Distiller by using the PDF Optimizer feature. Even so, distilling a PDF can yield better results than the PDF Optimizer can.

Traditional Refrying with Distiller

Refrying traditionally has been done with a simple hack, reprinting the PDF out to Distiller, which creates a new PDF file:

1. Save your PDF in Acrobat using the File → Save As... function. Acrobat will consolidate its resources as much as it can. Acrobat 6 does this more aggressively than Acrobat 5 does.

2. Open the Acrobat Print dialog (File → Print...) and select the Adobe PDF printer (Acrobat 6) or the Distiller printer (Acrobat 5).

3. Set the Distiller profile by selecting Properties → Adobe PDF Settings and adjusting the Default Settings (Acrobat 6) or Conversion Settings (Acrobat 5) drop-down box. For online distribution, consider these profiles: eBook, Standard, Screen, or Smallest File Size.

4. If you cropped your PDF, you should set the Print page size to match your PDF page size. In the Acrobat 6 Print dialog, adjust Properties →

Adobe PDF Settings → Adobe PDF Page Size to fit your page. Use the Add Custom Page... button if you can't find your page size among the current options. In the Acrobat 5 Print dialog, adjust Properties → Layout tab → Advanced... → Paper Size to fit your page. Select PostScript Custom Page Size if you can't find your page size among the current options.

5. Print to Distiller. Do not overwrite your original PDF.

6. Review the resulting PDF. Is its file size smaller? Is its fidelity acceptable?

7. Reapply page cropping as needed. You might need to rotate some pages.

8. To restore bookmarks and other features, see "Copy Features from One PDF to Another" [Hack #61].

Refrying with PDF Optimizer in Acrobat 6 Professional

PDF Optimizer (Advanced → PDF Optimizer...) performs this service much more conveniently. Its settings resemble Distiller's, and they enable you to downsample images, remove embedded fonts, or remove unwanted PDF features. You can also change the PDF compatibility to Acrobat 5. Click OK and it will create a new PDF for you. Compare this new PDF with the original and decide whether to keep it or try again. The best time to use the PDF Optimizer is just before you put the PDF online.

> To simply make your Acrobat 6 PDF compatible with Acrobat 5, select File → Reduce File Size... instead of the PDF Optimizer.

The Best Time to Refry Using Distiller

The best time to refry a PDF using Distiller (as opposed to the PDF Optimizer) is after you have assembled it, but before you have added any PDF features. Here is the sequence I typically use when preparing a PDF for online distribution:

1. Assemble the original PDF pages and Save As... to a new PDF.

2. If page sizes are wildly irregular, crop them [Hack #59].

3. Refry the original PDF document and compare the resulting refried PDF to the original. Adjust Distiller settings [Hack #42] as necessary and choose the best results.

4. Crop and rotate the refried PDF pages as needed.

5. If the original document had bookmarks or other PDF features, copy them back to the refried PDF [Hack #61].

6. Add PDF features [Hack #63] or finishing touches [Hack #62].

7. Save again using Save As... to compact the PDF. In Acrobat 6, save the final PDF by selecting File → Reduce File Size... and set the compatibility to Acrobat 5.

HACK #61 Copy Features from One PDF to Another

Restore bookmarks, annotations, and forms after refrying your PDF.

You just refried your high-fidelity PDF [Hack #60] to create a lightweight, online edition and Distiller burned off the nifty PDF navigation features and forms. Let's combine the old PDF's navigation features and forms with the new PDF's pages to get a lightweight, interactive PDF. Here's how:

1. Open the old PDF file (the one with the bookmarks, links, or form fields) in Acrobat.

2. In Acrobat 6, select Document → Pages → Replace. In Acrobat 5, select Document → Replace Pages from the menu.

3. A file selector dialog opens. Select the new PDF file (the one with no PDF features).

4. The Replace Pages dialog opens, requesting which pages to replace. Enter the first and last page numbers of your document.

5. When it is done, select Save As... to save the resulting PDF into a new file.

6. Test the resulting PDF to make sure all your interactive features came through successfully.

Using the Replace Pages feature like this to separate the visible page from its interactive features can be pretty handy. If you ever need to transfer a page and its interactive features, use the Extract Pages, Insert Pages, and Delete Pages functions.

HACK #62 Polish Your PDF Edition

Little things can make a big difference to your readers.

Most creators don't use these basic PDF features, yet they improve the reading experience and they are easy to add. Read "Support Online PDF Reading" [Hack #67] to learn about the additional features required for serving individual PDF pages on demand.

Document Initial View

If your PDF has bookmarks, set your PDF to display them when the document is opened. Otherwise, your readers might never discover them. You can change this, and other settings, from the PDF's document properties. In Acrobat 6, select File → Document Properties... → Initial View to access these setting. In Acrobat 5, select File → Document Properties → Open Options.

Logical Page Numbering

Open your PDF in Acrobat and go to page 1. If your PDF doesn't have logical page numbering, Acrobat thinks its first page is "page 1." Yet your document's "page 1" might actually fall on Acrobat's page 6, as shown in Figure 5-10. Imagine your readers trying to make sense of this, especially when your document refers them to page 52 or when they decide to print pages 42–47.

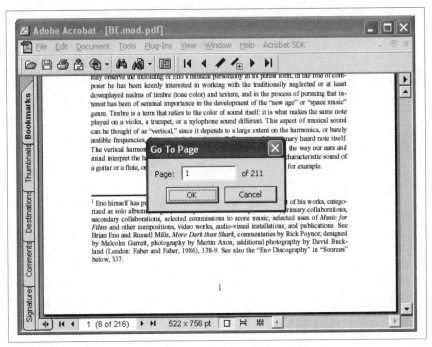

Figure 5-10. Keeping Acrobat synchronized with your document

Synchronize your document's page numbering with Acrobat/Reader by adding logical page numbers to your PDF. In Acrobat 6, select the Pages navigation tab (View → Navigation Tabs → Pages), click Options, and select Number Pages... from the drop-down menu. In Acrobat 5, access the Page Numbering dialog box by selecting Document → Number Pages....

Start from the beginning of your document and work to the end, to minimize confusion. If numbering gets tangled up, reset the page numbers by selecting All Pages, Begin New Section, Style: 1, 2, 3, ..., Prefix: (blank), Start: 1, and clicking OK.

If your document has a front cover, you can give it the logical page number *Cover* by setting its Style to None and giving it a Prefix of Cover.

Does your document have front matter with Roman-numeral page numbers? Advance through your document until you reach page 1. Go back to the page before page 1. Open the Page Numbering dialog. Set the page range From: field to 1. Set the Style to "i, ii, iii, …," and make sure Prefix is empty. Click OK. Now, the pages preceding page 1 should be numbered "i, ii, …," and page 1 should be numbered 1.

Go to the final page in your PDF and make sure the numbering still matches. Sometimes people remove blank pages from a PDF, which causes the document page numbers to skip. If you plan to remove blank pages from your PDF, apply logical page numbering beforehand.

Document Title, Author, Subject, and Keywords

Document metadata doesn't jump out at readers the way bookmarks and logical page numbers do, but your readers can use it to help organize their collections [Hack #22]. Plus, it looks pretty sharp to have them properly filled in. The title and author fields are often filled automatically with nonsense, such as the document's original filename (e.g., *Mockup.doc*) or the typesetter's username.

> You can disable the automatic metadata added by Distiller. Open Distiller and edit your profile's settings. Uncheck Advanced → Preserve Document Information from DSC, and click OK.

In Acrobat 6, view and update this information by selecting File → Document Properties… → Description or Advanced → Document Metadata…. In Acrobat 5, select File → Document Properties → Summary. See "Get and Set PDF Metadata" [Hack #64] for a broader discussion of PDF metadata.

Page Orientation and Cropping

Quickly page through your document from beginning to end, making sure that your page cropping [Hack #59] didn't chop off any data. Also check for rotated pages. Adjust rotated pages to a natural reading orientation by selecting Document → Pages → Rotate (Acrobat 6) or Document → Rotate Pages (Acrobat 5).

Rotating and cropping PDF pages can affect how they print. The user should select "Auto-rotate and center pages" from the Print dialog box when printing PDF to minimize surprises.

Add and Maintain PDF Bookmarks

Bookmarks greatly improve document navigation. Adding them is pretty easy.

Ideally, your document's headings would have been turned into PDF bookmarks when it was created [Hack #32]. If you ended up with no bookmarks or the wrong bookmarks, you can add or change them using Acrobat. Here are a few tricks to speed things up.

Add Bookmarks

Create a bookmark to the current view using the Ctrl-B shortcut (Command-B on the Macintosh). Then, type a label into the new bookmark and press Enter. Note that *current view* means the current page, current viewing mode (e.g., Actual Size, Fit Width, or Fit Page), or current zoom. For example, if you want a bookmark to fill the page with a specific table, zoom in to that table before creating the bookmark. When quickly creating bookmarks to a document's headings, I simply use the Fit Page viewing mode.

Every bookmark needs a text label, and this label usually corresponds to a document heading. Instead of typing in the label, use the Text Select tool to select the heading text on the PDF page. When you create the bookmark (Ctrl-B or Command-B), the selected text appears in the label. Review this text for errors.

Move Bookmarks

New bookmarks don't always appear where you want them. Select a bookmark (use a right-click to keep from activating it), click, and drag it to where it belongs. A little cursor will appear, indicating where the bookmark would go if you dropped it. You can indent a bookmark by dragging it to the left (Acrobat 6, shown in Figure 5-11) or the right (Acrobat 5, shown in Figure 5-12) of the intended parent. The little cursor will jump, showing you where the bookmark would go.

Move an entire block of bookmarks by first creating a multiple selection. In Acrobat 6, the order in which you select bookmarks is the order they will have after you move them, which can be a surprise. To preserve their order, add bookmarks to your multiple selection from top to bottom.

Select the first bookmark, hold down the Shift key, and then select the final bookmark in the block. Hold down the Ctrl key and click a bookmark to add or remove it from your selection. Click the selection and drag it to its new location.

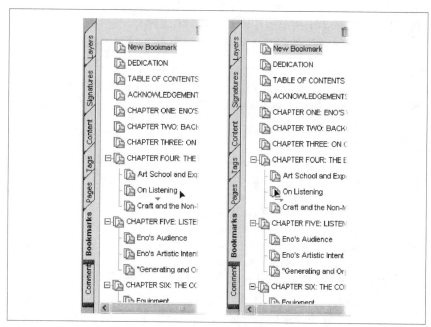

Figure 5-11. In Acrobat 6, dragging a bookmark to the right makes it a sibling (shown on the left), while dragging a bookmark to the left makes it a child (shown on the right)

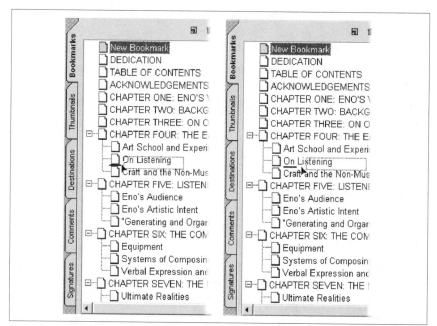

Figure 5-12. In Acrobat 5, dragging a bookmark to the left makes it a sibling (shown on the left), while dragging a bookmark to the right makes it a child (shown on the right)

Get and Set PDF Metadata

Add document information to your PDF, even without using Acrobat.

Traditional *metadata* includes things such as your document's title, authors, and ISBN. But you can add anything you want, such as the document's revision number, category, internal ID, or expiration date. PDF can store this information in two different ways: using the PDF's Info dictionary [Hack #80] or using an embedded Extensible Metadata Platform (XMP) stream. When you change the PDF's title, authors, subject, or keywords using Acrobat, as shown in Figure 5-13, it updates both of these resources. Acrobat 6 also enables you to export or import PDF XMP datafiles. Visit *http://www.adobe. com/products/xmp/* to learn about Adobe's XMP.

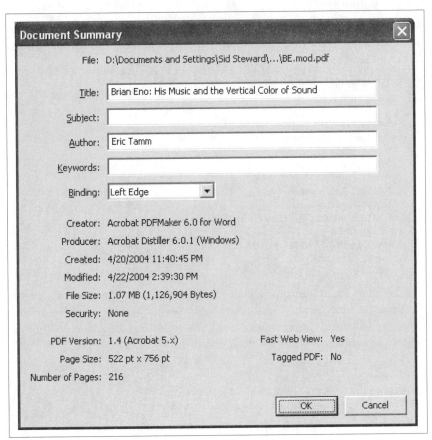

Figure 5-13. Viewing or changing a PDF's basic metadata in Acrobat

In Acrobat 6, view and update metadata by selecting File → Document Properties... → Description or Advanced → Document Metadata.... In

Acrobat 5, select File → Document Properties → Summary. Save your PDF after making changes to the metadata.

Our pdftk [Hack #79] currently reads and writes only the metadata in a PDF's Info dictionary. However, it does not restrict you to just the title, authors, subject, and keywords. This solves the basic problem of embedding information into a PDF document; pdftk allows you to add custom metadata fields to PDF as needed. pdftk is free software.

Xpdf's (*http://www.foolabs.com/xpdf/*) pdfinfo reports a PDF's Info dictionary contents, its XMP stream, and other document data. pdfinfo is free software.

Get Document Metadata

To create a plain-text report of PDF metadata, use pdftk's dump_data operation. It will also report PDF bookmarks and page labels, among other things. The command looks like this:

```
pdftk mydoc.pdf dump_data output mydoc.data.txt
```

Metadata will be represented as key/value pairs, like so:

```
InfoKey: Creator
InfoValue: Acrobat PDFMaker 6.0 for Word
InfoKey: Title
InfoValue: Brian Eno: His Music and the Vertical Color of Sound
InfoKey: Author
InfoValue: Eric Tamm
InfoKey: Producer
InfoValue: Acrobat Distiller 6.0.1 (Windows)
InfoKey: ModDate
InfoValue: D:20040420234132-07'00'
InfoKey: CreationDate
InfoValue: D:20040420234045-07'00'
```

Another tool for reporting PDF metadata is pdfinfo, which is part of the Xpdf project (*http://www.foolabs.com/xpdf/*). In addition to metadata, it also reports page sizes, page count, and PDF permissions [Hack #52]. Running pdfinfo mydoc.pdf yields a report such as this:

```
Title:        Brian Eno: His Music and the Vertical Color of Sound
Author:       Eric Tamm
Creator:      Acrobat PDFMaker 6.0 for Word
Producer:     Acrobat Distiller 6.0.1 (Windows)
CreationDate: 04/20/04 23:40:45
ModDate:      04/22/04 14:39:30
Tagged:       no
Pages:        216
Encrypted:    no
Page size:    522 x 756 pts
File size:    1126904 bytes
```

```
Optimized:     yes
PDF version:   1.4
```

Use pdfinfo's options to fine-tune its behavior. Use its -meta option to view a PDF's XMP stream.

Set Document Metadata

pdftk can take a plain-text file of these same key/value pairs and update a PDF's Info dictionary to match. Currently, it does not update the PDF's XMP stream. The command would look like this:

pdftk *mydoc.pdf* update_info *new_info.txt* output *mydoc.updated.pdf*

This will add or modify the Info keys given by *mydoc.new_data.txt*. Note that the output PDF filename must be different from the input. To remove a key/value pair, simply pass in the key/value with an empty value, like so:

```
InfoKey: MyDataKey
InfoValue:
```

> Use pdftk to strip all *Info* and XMP metadata from a document by copying its pages into a new PDF, like so:
>
> pdftk mydoc.pdf cat A output mydoc.no_metadata.pdf

The PDF specification defines several Info fields. Be careful to use these only as described in the specification. They are Title, Author, Subject, Keywords, Creator, Producer, CreationDate, ModDate, and Trapped.

H A C K #65   Add a Web-Style Navigation Bar to PDF Pages
Ensure that readers see your essential links.

Styles used on the Web suggest that readers love navigation bars, such as the one shown in Figure 5-14. Wherever you are, you can click and jump to where you want to be. PDF documents provide this kind of immediate navigation with bookmarks [Hack #63]. Bookmarks are ideal for representing a detailed document outline, but they lack style.

Creating a PDF navigation bar in Acrobat and then duplicating it across several (or all) document pages is easy. Links can open external web pages or internal PDF pages. Add graphics and other styling elements to make it stand out. Disable printing to prevent it from cluttering printed pages. All of this is possible with PDF form buttons.

Create Buttons and Set Actions

Create and manage buttons using the appropriate Acrobat tool. In Acrobat 6, activate the Button Tool (Tools → Advanced Editing → Forms → Button

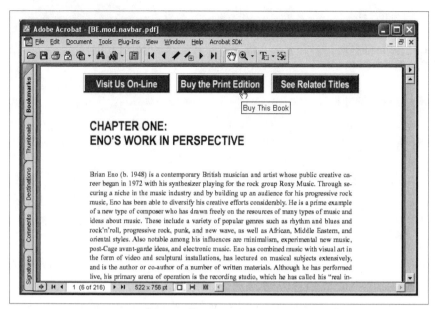

Figure 5-14. Integrating your PDF with the Web using a navigation bar

Tool), then click and drag out a rectangle. Release the mouse and the Button Properties dialog opens. Select the Actions tab and click the Select Action drop-down box. Choose Go to a Page in this Document or Open a Web Link and click Add.... Another dialog opens where you can enter destination details. Click OK and the action should be added to the button's Mouse Up event. Click Close and your button should be functional. Test it by selecting the Hand Tool and clicking the button.

> Improve your button's precision by activating Snap to Grid from View → Snap to Grid. Alter its subdivisions from the Units and Guides (Acrobat 6) or Layout Grid (Acrobat 5) preferences.

In Acrobat 5, select the Form Tool, then click and drag out a rectangle. Release the mouse and a Field Properties dialog opens. Enter the button's name (it can be anything, but it must be unique) and change the Type: to Button. Click the Actions tab, select Mouse Up, and click Add.... Curiously, you do not have the choice to go to a page within the document. Instead, select JavaScript and enter this simple code; JavaScript page numbers are zero-based, so this example goes to page 6, not page 5:

```
this.pageNum = 5;
```

Or, select World Wide Web Link if you want the button to open a web page. Click Set Action and then OK, and your button should be functional. Test it by selecting the Hand Tool and clicking the button.

 Acrobat World Wide Web links should be preceded by http://. Otherwise, they won't work in older versions of Acrobat/Reader.

Styling Buttons and Adding Graphics

By default, buttons are plain, gray rectangles. Change a button's background and border using the Appearance tab in its properties dialog; you can even make a button transparent. Change a button's text label using the Options tab.

The Options tab also enables you to select a graphical icon. Change the Layout: to include an Icon and then click Choose Icon. You can use a bitmap, a PostScript drawing (Acrobat 6), or even a PDF page as a button icon.

Consider creating a *no-op* graphical button as a background to your other (transparent) buttons. This can be easier than trying to split a single navigation bar graphic into several pieces. Just make sure the active buttons end up on top of the graphic layer; otherwise, they won't work. Do this by creating the graphic layer before creating any of the active buttons, or by giving the graphic layer a lower position in the tabbing order.

 Alter form field tab order in Acrobat 6.0.1 by activating the Select Object Tool (Tools → Advanced Editing → Select Object Tool), selecting Advanced → Forms → Fields → Set Tab Order, and then clicking each field in order. Alter form field tab order in Acrobat 5 by activating the Form Tool, selecting Tools → Forms → Fields → Set Tab Order, and then clicking each field in order.

To prevent a button from printing, open its properties and select the General tab (Acrobat 6) or the Appearance tab (Acrobat 5). Change Form Field: to Visible but Doesn't Print.

Copying Buttons Across All Pages

Activate the Button Tool (Acrobat 6) or the Form Tool (Acrobat 5), hold down the Shift key, and select each button until all of them are selected. Right-click the selection and choose Duplicate…. Enter the desired page range and click OK. Your navigation bar now should exist on those pages, too. Page through your document to ensure they are positioned properly.

HACK #66   Copy-Protect Your PDF

Control how far your document can wander by making it difficult to copy.

A large document represents a great deal of work, and PDF is a good way to distribute large documents. Sometimes, it is too good. Perhaps your readers are paying customers, and you don't want them to make copies for their friends. Perhaps you want people to read your work only from your web site, not from a downloaded copy. These kinds of controls go beyond standard PDF security [Hack #52]. This hack discusses some solutions.

Low Tech: Print Editions

Copying and sharing print editions of your document would be too much trouble for most readers. Your price for this security is the cost and trouble of production and shipping. However, readers might prefer a print edition, such as the one shown in Figure 5-15, in which case you are also adding value to your work. "Publish POD and E-books" [Hack #29] discusses how to create print-on-demand (POD) books. Print editions are vulnerable to being converted to unsecured PDF by scanning and OCR.

Online Reading Only

Another idea is to prevent the reader from ever downloading your PDF. A single PDF can always be downloaded. So, burst your document into individual PDF pages and then wrap them in our HTML skins [Hack #71]. When you burst the PDF, supply additional security settings [Hack #52] for the output pages so that the reader won't be able to easily reassemble them. For example:

```
pdftk doc.pdf burst encrypt_128bits owner_pw 23@#5dfa allow DegradedPrinting
```

After integrating your document into your web site, you can employ user accounts, passwords, and other common security devices for enforcing access permissions.

Skinned PDFs are vulnerable to being copied from your site using a recursive HTTP robot. The result would be an exact copy of your site's pages (PDF and HTML) on the user's local machine.

Chain the PDF to the User's Machine

Digital Rights Management (DRM) tools give you fine-grained control over how and when the reader can use your document. Typically, a reader downloads the full PDF, but he can't read it until he purchases a key. After he makes the purchase, a key is created that can open that PDF only on that computer. Some readers find this model too restricting.

Figure 5-15. Old-fangled copy protection

DRM software vendors include Adobe (PDF Merchant), FileOpen Systems, Authentica, and SoftSeal. Their tools tend to be too expensive for the casual user. Consider partnering with a distributor or a self-publishing service [Hack #29].

Support Online PDF Reading

Serve PDF pages on demand and spare readers a long download.

Sometimes readers want to download the entire document; sometimes they want to read just a few pages. If a reader desires to read a single page from your PDF, she shouldn't be stuck downloading the entire document. A large document download will turn her away. The easiest solution is to configure your PDF and your web server for serving individual pages on request. An alternative is to use our PDF skins [Hack #71].

Prepare the PDF

To permit page-at-a-time delivery over the Web, a PDF must be *linearized*. Linearization organizes a PDF's internal structure so that a client can request the PDF resources it needs on a byte-by-byte basis. If the reader wants to see page 12, then the client requests only the data it needs to display page 12.

Test whether a PDF is linearized by opening it in Acrobat/Reader and viewing its document properties. Open File → Document Properties... → Description (Acrobat 6) or File → Document Properties → Summary (Acrobat 5). A linearized PDF shows Fast Web View: Yes.

The Xpdf project (*http://www.foolabs.com/xpdf/*) includes a command-line tool called pdfinfo that can tell you if a PDF is linearized. Pass your PDF to pdfinfo like so:

```
pdfinfo mydoc.pdf
```

pdfinfo will create a text report on-screen that says Optimized: Yes if your PDF is linearized. pdfinfo is free software.

To create a linearized PDF using Acrobat, first inspect your preferences. Select Edit → Preferences → General... and choose the General category (Acrobat 6) or the Options category (Acrobat 5). Place a checkmark next to Save As Optimizes for Fast Web View and click OK.

Open the PDF you want to linearize and then Save As... to the same file-name. In Acrobat 6, you can change the PDF's compatibility level at the same time by selecting File → Reduce File Size instead of *Save As....* Open the document properties to check that it worked.

If you ever make changes to the PDF in Acrobat and then simply File → Save your PDF, it will no longer be linearized. You must use Save As... to ensure that your PDF remains linearized.

Ghostscript [Hack #39] includes a command-line tool called pdfopt that can linearize PDF. To create a linearized PDF using pdfopt, invoke it from the command-line like so:

```
pdfopt input.pdf output.linearized.pdf
```

Prepare the Server

Both Apache, Versions 1.3.17 and greater, and Microsoft IIS, Versions 3 and greater, should serve PDF pages on demand without additional configuration. The key to serving PDF pages on demand is *byte range* support by the web server. HTTP 1.1 describes byte range support (*http://www.freesoft.org/ CIE/RFC/2068/160.htm*). Byte range support means that the client can request a specific range of bytes from the web server. Instead of serving the entire file, the server will send just those bytes.

The web server must indicate its support for byte ranges by sending the "Accept-Ranges: bytes" header in response to a PDF file request. Otherwise, Acrobat might not attempt page-at-a-time downloading. If you want to tell clients to not attempt page-at-a-time serving from your server, send the "Accept-Ranges: none" header instead.

#68 Force PDF Download Rather than Online Reading

Prevent your online PDF from appearing inside the browser.

Some PDF documents on the Web are intended for online reading, but most are intended for download and then offline reading or printing. You can prevent confusion by ensuring your readers get the Save As… dialog when they click your Download Now PDF link. Here are a few ways to do this.

> Keep in mind that any online PDF can be downloaded. If your online PDF is hyperlinked to integrate with your web site, you should take precautions against these links being broken upon download.
>
> One option is to use only absolute URLs throughout your PDF.
>
> Another option is to set the Base URL of your PDF. In Acrobat 6, consult File → Document Properties → Advanced → Base URL. In Acrobat 5, consult File → Document Properties → Base URL.
>
> To prevent people from easily downloading your document, see "PDF Web Skins" [Hack #71].

Zip It Up

The quickest solution for a single PDF is to compress it into a zip file, which gives you a file that simply cannot be read online. This has the added benefit of reducing the download file size a little. The downside is that your readers must have a program to unzip the file. You should include a hyperlink to where they can download such a program (e.g., *http://www.info-zip.org/pub/infozip/*). Stay away from self-extracting executables, because they work on only a single platform.

You can also apply zip compression on the fly with your web server. Here is an example in PHP. Adjust the passthru argument so that it points to your local copy of *zip*:

```php
<?php
// pdfzip.php, zip PDF at serve-time
// version 1.0
// http://www.pdfhacks.com/serving_pdf/
```

Force PDF Download Rather than Online Reading

```
//
// WARNING:
// This script might compromise your server's security.

$fn= $_GET['fn'];
// as a security measure, only serve files located in our directory
if( $fn && $fn=== basename($fn) ) {

    // make sure we're zipping up a PDF (and not some system file)
    if( strtolower( strrchr( $fn, '.' ) )== '.pdf' ) {

      if( file_exists( $fn ) ) {
        header('Content-Type: application/zip');
        header('Content-Disposition: attachment; filename='.$fn.'.zip');
        header('Accept-Ranges: none'); // we don't support byte serving
        passthru("/usr/bin/zip - $fn");
      }
    }
  }
?>
```

If you have a PDF located at *http://www.pdfhacks.com/docs/mydoc.pdf* and
you copied the preceding script to *http://www.pdfhacks.com/docs/pdfzip.php*,
you could serve *mydoc.pdf.zip* with the URL *http://www.pdfhacks.com/docs/
pdfzip.php?fn=mydoc.pdf*.

Create Download-Only Folders Using .htaccess Files

Do you have an entire directory of download-only PDFs on your web server?
You can change that directory's *.htaccess* file so that visitors are always
prompted to download their PDFs. The trick is to send suitable Content-
Type and Content-Disposition HTTP headers to the clients.

This works on Apache and Zeus web servers that have their *.htaccess* features enabled. In your PDF directory, add a file named *.htaccess* that has
these lines:

```
<files *.pdf>
  ForceType application/octet-stream
  Header set Content-Disposition attachment
</files>
```

Serve PDF Downloads with a PHP Script

This next script enables you to serve PDF downloads. It is handy for when
you want to make a single PDF available for both online reading and downloading. You can use its technique of using the Content-Type and Content-
Disposition headers in any script that serves download-only PDF.

```
<?php
// pdfdownload.php
```

```
// version 1.0
// http://www.pdfhacks.com/serving_pdf/
//
// WARNING:
// This script might compromise your server's security.

$fn= $_GET['fn'];
// as a security measure, only serve files located in our directory
if( $fn && $fn=== basename($fn) ) {

    // make sure we're serving a PDF (and not some system file)
    if( strtolower( strrchr( $fn, '.' ) )== '.pdf' ) {

        if( ($num_bytes= @filesize( $fn )) ) {
            // use file pointers instead of readfile( )
            // for better performance, esp. with large PDFs
            if( ($fp= @fopen( $fn, 'rb' )) ) { // open binary read success

                // try to conceal our content type
                header('Content-Type: application/octet-stream');

                // cue the client that this shouldn't be displayed inline
                header('Content-Disposition: attachment; filename='.$fn);

                // we don't support byte serving
                header('Accept-Ranges: none');

                header('Content-Length: '.$num_bytes);
                fpassthru( $fp ); // this closes $fp
            }
        }
    }
}
?>
```

If you have a PDF located at *http://www.pdfhacks.com/docs/mydoc.pdf* and you copied the preceding script to *http://www.pdfhacks.com/docs/pdfdownload.php*, the URL *http://www.pdfhacks.com/docs/pdfdownload.php?fn=mydoc.pdf* would prompt users to download *mydoc.pdf* to their computers.

HACK #69   Hyperlink HTML to PDF Pages

Take readers directly to the information they seek.

You can use HTML hyperlinks, those famous filaments of the Web, to integrate PDF documents with HTML documents. A simple link to a PDF document is not enough, though, because a single PDF might hold hundreds of pages. It is like handing a haystack to somebody searching for a needle. The solution is to modify the HTML link so that it takes the reader directly to the PDF page of interest. This kind of seamless integration of HTML and PDF pages requires some groundwork. See "Support Online PDF Reading" [Hack #67] for details.

To tailor a hyperlink's PDF destination, just add one or more of the suffixes listed in Table 5-3 to the *href* path.

Table 5-3. Suffixes and their impact on Acrobat Reader

PDF viewer behavior	Hyperlink href path suffix
Open the PDF to page number *N* (the first page is 1)	page=*N*
Display PDF bookmarks	pagemode=bookmarks
Display PDF thumbnails	pagemode=thumbs
Conceal PDF bookmarks and thumbnails	pagemode=none
Conceal the Acrobat scrollbars	scrollbar=false
Conceal the Acrobat toolbar	toolbar=false

These are glued together and appended to the *href* path using a special notation. The first suffix follows a hash mark. Each additional suffix follows an ampersand. These options are fully documented in *PDF Open Parameters*, located at *http://partners.adobe.com/asn/acrobat/sdk/public/docs/PDFOpenParams.pdf*.

For example, to open *mydoc.pdf* to page 17 and display its document bookmarks, the hyperlink *href* would look like this:

```
http://pdfhacks.com/mydoc.pdf#page=17&pagemode=bookmarks
```

These special PDF hyperlinks do not work when you're using Internet Explorer and the PDF is on your local disk. For a workaround, see "Create Windows Shortcuts to Local PDF Pages" [Hack #17].

Save Display Settings in the PDF

You can also save these display settings in the PDF file. Whenever and however the PDF is opened, it will be displayed according to your settings. See "Polish Your PDF Edition" [Hack #62] for details.

Create an HTML Table of Contents from PDF Bookmarks
HACK #70

Give web surfers an inviting HTML gateway into your PDF.

When browsing the Web, I usually groan at the sight of a PDF link. You have probably experienced it, too. My research has brought me to this point where I must now download a large PDF before I can proceed. The problem isn't so much with the PDF file, but with my inability to gauge just how much this PDF might help me before I commit to downloading it.

The PDF author might have even gone to great lengths to ensure a good, online read, with nice, clear fonts, navigational bookmarks, and page-at-a-time byte serving for quick, random access. But I can't tell that from looking at this PDF link. Chances are that I'll click and wait, and wait. When it finally opens, I'll probably need to flip, page by page, through illegible text looking for a clue that this tome will help me somehow. I might never find out, especially because I have a dozen other possible lines of inquiry I am pursuing at the same time.

Don't let this happen to your online PDF. If your PDF has bookmarks, use this hack to create an HTML table of contents that hyperlinks every heading directly to its PDF page (see Figure 5-16). If your PDF doesn't have bookmarks, this is a good reason to add them [Hack #63]. Use this table of contents in your web page and smile with the knowledge that you have made the Web a better place.

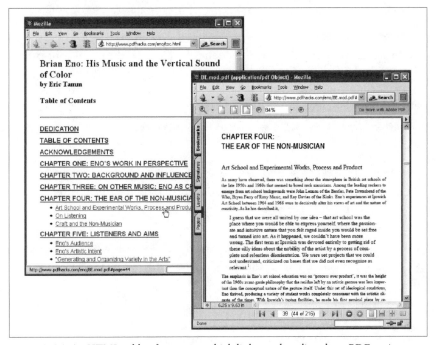

Figure 5-16. An HTML table of contents, which links readers directly to PDF topics

This kind of random access into an online PDF is convenient only if the PDF is linearized and the web server is configured for byte serving [Hack #67]. Without both of these, your readers must download the entire document before viewing a single page.

Create a PDF Table of Contents in HTML with pdftk and pdftoc

pdftk [Hack #79] can report on PDF data, including bookmarks. pdftoc converts this plain-text report into HTML. Visit *http://www.pdfhacks.com/ pdftoc/* and download *pdftoc-1.0.zip*. Unzip, and move *pdftoc.exe* to a convenient location, such as *C:\Windows\system32*. On other platforms, build pdftoc from the source code.

Use pdftk to grab the bookmark data from your PDF, like so:

```
pdftk mydoc.pdf dump_data output mydoc_data.txt
```

Next, use pdftoc to convert this plain-text report into HTML:

```
pdftoc mydoc.pdf < mydoc_data.txt > mydoc_toc.html
```

Alternatively, you can run these two steps together, like so:

```
pdftk mydoc.pdf dump_data | pdftoc mydoc.pdf > mydoc_toc.html
```

The first argument to pdftoc is the document location that you want pdftoc to use in its hyperlinks. The previous example assumes that *mydoc.pdf* and *mydoc_toc.html* will be in the same directory. You can also give a relative path to your PDF, like so:

```
pdftoc ../pdf/mydoc.pdf < mydoc_data.txt > mydoc_toc.html
```

or a full URL:

```
pdftoc http://pdfhacks.com/pdf/mydoc.pdf < mydoc_data.txt > mydoc_toc.html
```

Once readers enter the PDF, they can use its bookmarks for further navigation. To ensure they see your bookmarks, set your PDF to display them upon opening [Hack #62].

You can also add a download link [Hack #68] on the web page that prompts the user to save the PDF on her local disk. As a courtesy to the user, mention the download file size, too.

PDF Web Skins
#71

Split a PDF into pages and frame them in HTML, where the fun begins.

In general, HTML files are called *pages*, while PDF files are called *documents*. By splitting a PDF document into PDF pages we shift it into HTML's paradigm where we now can program the document like a web site. Let's start with a basic document skin, shown in Figure 5-17, which gives us a cool look and handy document navigation.

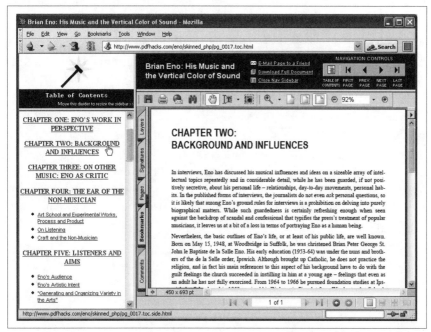

Figure 5-17. The Classic skin, which includes navigation features

Our Classic skin has a number of nice built-in features:

- Table of contents portal page based on PDF bookmarks
- Navigation cluster for flipping through pages
- Table of Contents navigation sidebar based on PDF bookmarks
- A hyperlink to the full, unsplit PDF for download on each page
- Convenient Email This Page link on each page

Test-drive our online version at *http://www.pdfhacks.com/eno/*. The HTML, JavaScript, and user interface icons are freely distributable under the GPL, so feel free to use them in your own templates.

Skinning PDF

First, install pdftk [Hack #79]. Next, visit *http://www.pdfhacks.com/skins/* and download *pdfskins-1.1.zip*. Unzip, and move *pdfskins.exe* to a convenient location, such as *C:\Windows\system32*. On other platforms, compile pdf-skins from the included source code. Just cd pdfskins-1.1 and run make.

Download a skin template from *http://www.pdfhacks.com/skins/*. The template *pdfskins_classic_js* uses client-side JavaScript to create the dynamic pieces. *pdfskins_classic_php* uses server-side PHP instead. Pick one and unzip it into a new directory:

```
unzip pdfskins_classic_js-1.1.zip
```

Copy your PDF document into this new directory and burst it into pages with pdftk. This also creates *doc_data.txt*, which reports on the document's title, metadata, and bookmarks:

```
pdftk full_doc.pdf burst
```

Finally, in this same directory, spin skins using pdfskins. It reads *doc_data.txt*, created earlier, for the document title and other data. Pass the PDF filename as the first argument, if you plan to make the full PDF document available for download. This first argument is used only for constructing the Download Full Document hyperlink. It can be a full or relative URL. Omit this filename, and this hyperlink will not be displayed.

```
pdfskins full_doc.pdf
```

Fire up your web browser and point it at *index.html*, located in the directory where you've been working. The portal should appear, showing the table of contents and graphic placeholders for your logo (*logo.gif*) and document cover thumbnail (*thumb.gif*). If you used the *php* or *comments* templates, the pages must be served to you by a PHP-enabled web server.

 The PDF pages that make up our skinned PDF do not need to be linearized; nor does the web server require byte serving configuration **[Hack #67]**. The only requirement is that the user has Adobe Reader configured to display PDF inside the browser, which is the default Reader configuration.

Changing Colors, Overriding the Title

You can add or change data in the *doc_data.txt* file, or you can pass additional, overriding data to pdfskins on the command line. This is most useful for changing the default colors used in the Classic skin. For example:

```
pdfskins full_doc.pdf -title "Great American Novel" -color1 #336600 \
-color2 white
```

In the Classic skin, color1 is the color of the header and color2 is the color around the upper-left logo. Alternatively, you can add or change these lines in *doc_data.txt*:

```
InfoKey: Color1
InfoValue: #336600
InfoKey: Color2
```

```
InfoValue: white
InfoKey: Title
InfoValue: Great American Novel
```

PDF Skins as Copy Protection

By bursting your PDF into pages and then not making the full document available for download, you compel readers to return to your site when they desire your material. If this is your intent, you should also secure your pages against merging, so nobody can easily reassemble your pages into the original PDF document. Do this when bursting the document. For example:

```
pdftk full_doc.pdf burst encrypt_128bits owner_pw 23@#5dfa \
allow DegradedPrinting
```

See "Encrypt and Decrypt PDF (Even Without Acrobat)" [Hack #52] for more details on how to secure documents with pdftk.

 Test our PHP-based hacks on your Windows machine by installing the Apache web server. See "Collect Data with Online PDF Forms" [Hack #74] for a discussion about installing Apache and PHP on Windows using IndigoPerl.

Hacking the Hack

Now, you control the document. You can take it in any direction you choose. See "Spinning Document Portals" [Hack #21] for some ideas on how to add full-text document search. See "Share PDF Comments Online (Even Without Acrobat)" [Hack #72] to learn how to add online page commenting.

HACK #72 Share PDF Comments Online (Even Without Acrobat)

Use our PDF skins to add commenting features to PDF pages.

Using Acrobat, you can add various comments and annotations to PDF pages. You can also share these comments via email or by configuring Acrobat's Online Comments. These collaboration tools require all contributors to have Acrobat; they do not work with Reader. And, in general, all contributors must have the same version of Acrobat.

Instead, add online commenting features to PDF pages with our PDF skins [Hack #71] and a couple PHP scripts. Users don't need Acrobat, so it works on Mac and Linux as well as Windows. And, you can integrate PDF comments with your site's current commenting system. Our Comments skin, shown in Figure 5-18, will get you up and running. View our online example at *http://www.pdfhacks.com/eno/skinned_comments/*.

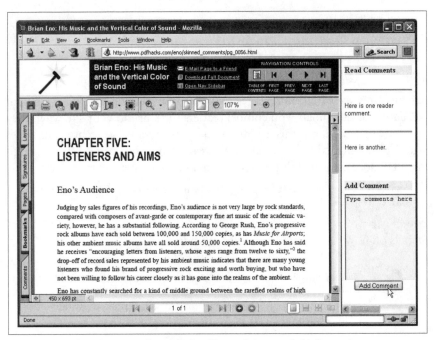

Figure 5-18. The Comments skin, which adds another pane (left) for reader comments

Skinning PDF, Adding Comments

See "PDF Web Skins" **[Hack #71]** to learn how to skin a PDF. Instead of using the template *pdfskins_classic_php-1.0.zip*, download *pdfskins_classic_com-ments-1.0.zip*. This Comments skin is the same as the php skin except it adds *showannot.php* and *saveannot.php*.

Skin a PDF with our *comments* template and move the results into a directory on your web server. Your server must have permission to write in this directory so that it can create and maintain comments. Point your web browser to this URL and the commenting frame should be visible on the right. Enter a comment into the field and click Add Comment. Your comment should appear above.

Hacking the Hack

Our commenting script saves page comments in text files. To reduce the chance of a file access collision, it copies the current comments to a temporary file before appending a new comment. When it is done, it replaces the original comments file with the updated temporary file. Even so, if two users submit comments simultaneously, they still might collide. Consider adapting the script so that it stores comments in a database instead of a text file.

Tally Topic Popularity
#73

Organize PDF page hits by document headings to get a sense of what readers like best.

A single long document can cover dozens of topics. Which topics do readers find most useful? Use our PDF skins [Hack #71] to track hits to individual pages. Then, use our *hit_report* script to map these page hits back into your document's headings, as shown in Figure 5-19. You'll see *topic* hits, not ambiguous page hits. Visit *http://www.pdfhacks.com/eno/* for an example.

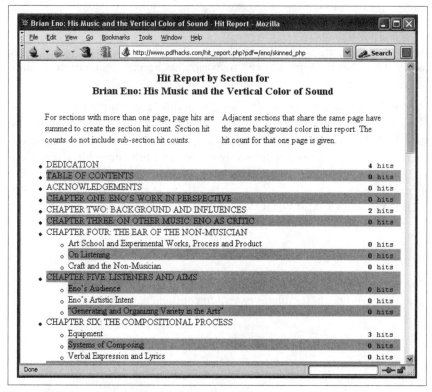

Figure 5-19. hit_report showing hits by topic

Page hit logging is built into the *pdfskins_classic_php* template [Hack #71]. After unpacking this template, activate hit logging by editing *script.include* and setting $log_hits=true. You can do this at any time, before or after skinning your PDF. Page hits get logged into text files located in the same directory as the skinned PDF, so the web server must have write access to that directory.

If a page is named *pg_0025.pdf*, its hit log is named *pg_0025.pdf.hits*. Each hit adds one line to the file. Each line includes the IP number that requested the page, so you can identify unique visitors if you desire.

After skinning your PDF and making sure hit logging works, visit *http://www.pdfhacks.com/skins/* and download *hit_report.php-1.0.zip*. Unpack this single PHP file and copy it onto your web server.

If your skinned PDF is located in the directory:

```
http://pdfhacks.com/eno/skinned_php/
```

pass its location to *hit_report* like so:

```
http://pdfhacks.com/hit_report.php?pdf=/eno/skinned_php
```

The document outline should appear in your browser, just as it does on the skinned PDF's title page. On the right side of the page, a column of numbers shows the number of hits on each outline topic.

For sections that span multiple pages, page hits are summed to create the section-hit count. However, section-hit counts do not include subsection-hit counts. If multiple sections have headings that appear on the same document page, those sections will also share the same hit count. *hit_report* identifies these by giving these sections the same background color. For example, the report in Figure 5-19 shows that the section headings "CHAPTER SIX: THE COMPOSITIONAL PROCESS" and "Equipment" are both on the same page.

Hacking the Hack

Provide this hit information to your readers by merging *hit_report* features with the current skin templates *index.html* and *index.toc.html*.

Dynamic PDF
Hacks 74–92

PDF doesn't have to be stuck in a file, created once and then published. PDF can be dynamic in multiple ways, ranging from interactivity through forms to custom generation of PDFs that meet particular user needs. While PDF seems static to a lot of people, that's more a matter of the way it's typically been used rather than an aspect of the technology itself. If you want to do more with PDF than distribute documents, you can.

HACK #74 Collect Data with Online PDF Forms

Turn your electronic document into a user interface and collect information from readers.

Traditional paper forms use page layout to show how information is structured. Sometimes, as on tax forms, these relationships get pretty complicated. PDF preserves page layout, so it is a natural way to publish forms on the Web. The next decision is, how many PDF form features should you add?

If you add no features, your users must print the form and fill it out as they would any other paper form. Then they must mail it back to you for processing. Sometimes this is all you need, but PDF is capable of more.

If you add fillable form fields to the PDF, your users can fill in the form using Acrobat or Reader. When they are done, they still must print it out and mail it to you. Acrobat users can save filled-in PDFs, but Reader users can't, which can be frustrating.

If you add fillable form fields *and* a Submit button that posts field data to your web server, you have joined the information revolution. Your web server can interactively validate the user's data, provide helpful feedback, record the completed data in your database, and supply the user with a savable PDF copy. *Olé!*

We have gotten ahead of ourselves, though. First, let's create a form that submits data to your web server, such as the one in Figure 6-1. Subsequent hacks will build on this. To see online examples of interactive PDF forms, visit *http://www.pdfhacks.com/form_session/*. You can download our example PDF forms and PHP code from this site, too.

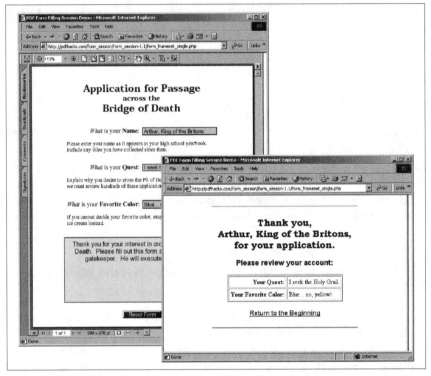

Figure 6-1. A PDF form that delivers data to your web server's doorstep

Create the Form

Open the form's source document and print to PDF **[Hack #39]** or scan a paper copy and create a PDF using OCR. Open the PDF in Acrobat to add form fields.

> PDF forms can be powerful JavaScript programs, but we won't be using any PDF JavaScript. Instead, we will create PDF forms that let the web server do all the work. This gives you the freedom to program the form's logic with any language or database interface you desire.

PDF form fields correspond closely to HTML form fields, as shown in Table 6-1. Add them to your PDF using one or more Acrobat tools.

Table 6-1. PDF fields types compared to HTML field types

HTML form field	PDF form field
input type="text"	Text
input type="password"	Text with Password Option
input type="checkbox"	Checkbox
input type="radio"	Radio Button
input type="submit"	Button with Submit Form Action
input type="reset"	Button with Reset Form Action
input type="hidden"	Text with Hidden Appearance
input type="image"	Button with Icon Option
input type="button"	Button
textarea	Text with Multiline Option
select	Combo Box or List Box

In Acrobat 6, as shown in Figure 6-2, you have one tool for each form field type. Open this toolbar by selecting Tools → Advanced Editing → Forms → Show Forms Toolbar. Select a tool (e.g., Text Field tool), click, and drag out a rectangle where the field goes. Release the rectangle and a Field Properties dialog opens. Select the General tab and enter the field Name. This name will identify the field's data when it is submitted to your web server. Set the field's appearance and behavior using the other tabs. Click Close and the field is done.

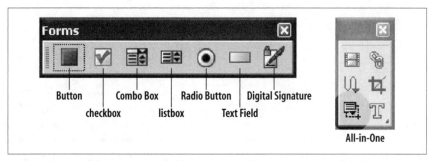

Figure 6-2. A tool for every form field in Acrobat 6 (left); one tool for all fields in Acrobat 5 (right)

In Acrobat 5, use the Form tool shown in Figure 6-2 to create any form field. Click, and drag out a rectangle where the field goes. Release the rectangle and a Field Properties dialog opens. Select the desired field Type (e.g., Text) and enter the field Name. This name will identify the field's data when it is submitted to your web server. Set the field's appearance and behavior using the other tabs. Click OK and the field is done. Using the Form tool, double-click a field at any time to change its properties.

Take care to maximize your PDF form's compatibility with older versions of Acrobat and Reader [Hack #41].

To upload form data to your web server, the PDF must have a Submit Form button. Create a PDF button, open the Actions tab, and then add the Submit a Form (Acrobat 6) or Submit Form (Acrobat 5) action to the *Mouse Up* event, as shown in Figure 6-3.

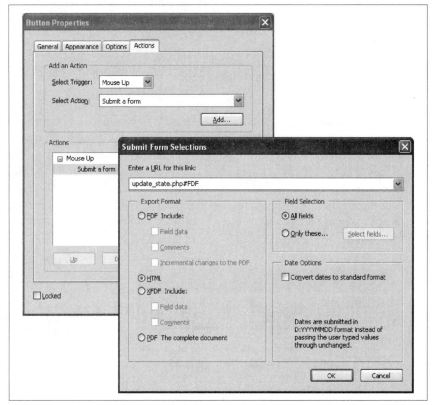

Figure 6-3. *Adding the Submit action to a button's Mouse Up event to create a Submit button (note the #FDF appended to the script's URL)*

Edit the action's properties to include your script's URL; this would be an HTML form's action attribute. Append #FDF to the end of this URL, like this:

```
http://localhost/pdf_hacks/echo.php#FDF
```

Set the Field Selection to include the fields you want this button to submit; All Fields is safest, to start. Set the Export Format to HTML and the PDF form will submit the form data using HTTP's post method.

When you are done, save your PDF form and test it.

Buttons look funny on paper. If users will be printing your form, consider making buttons unprintable. Open the button properties and select the General tab (Acrobat 6) or the Appearance tab (Acrobat 5). Under Common Properties set Form Field: to Visible but Doesn't Print. Click OK.

Install the Apache Web Server on Windows

To test your interactive PDF form, you must have access to a web server. Many of these hacks use server-side PHP scripts, so your web server should also run PHP (*http://www.php.net*). Windows users can download an Apache (*http://www.apache.org*) web server installer called IndigoPerl from IndigoSTAR (*http://www.indigostar.com*). This installer includes PHP (and Perl) modules, so you can run our hacks right out of the box. Apache and PHP are free software.

Visit *http://www.indigostar.com/indigoperl.htm* and download *indigoperl-2004.02.zip*. Unzip this file into a temporary directory and then double-click *setup.bat* to run the installer. When the installer asks for an installation directory, press Enter to choose the default: *C:\indigoperl*. In our discussions, we'll assume IndigoPerl is installed in this location.

After installing IndigoPerl, open a web browser and point it at *http://localhost/*. This is the URL of your local web server, and your browser should display a Web Server Test Page with links to documentation. When you request *http://localhost/*, Apache serves you *index.html* from *C:\indigoperl\apache\htdocs*. Create a *pdf_hacks* directory in the *htdocs* directory, and use this location for our PHP scripts. Access this location from your browser with the URL: *http://localhost/pdf_hacks/*.

Test Your PDF Form

Create a text file named *echo.php* and program it with the following script. IndigoPerl users can save it to *C:\indigoperl\apache\htdocs\pdf_hacks\echo.php*. This PHP script simply reports submitted form data back to your browser. Create a PDF Submit button that posts data to this script's URL (e.g., *http://localhost/pdf_hacks/echo.php#FDF*) as we described earlier.

```
<?php // echo.php, report the data we received
echo '<h2>GET Data</h2>';
foreach( $_GET as $key => $value ) {
  echo '<p>Key: '.$key.', Value: '.$value.'</p>';
}
echo '<h2>POST Data</h2>';
```

```
foreach( $_POST as $key => $value ) {
  echo '<p>Key: '.$key.', Value: '.$value.'</p>';
}
```

A PDF form interacts properly with a web server only when viewed inside a web browser. So, drag and drop your form into a browser, fill some fields, and then click the Submit button. The PDF should be replaced with an echoed data report, like the one shown in Figure 6-4.

> If dragging and dropping PDF into Mozilla causes the PDF to open outside of the browser window, make sure Mozilla's Java is enabled (Edit → Preferences... → Advanced). After enabling Java, restart Mozilla and try again.

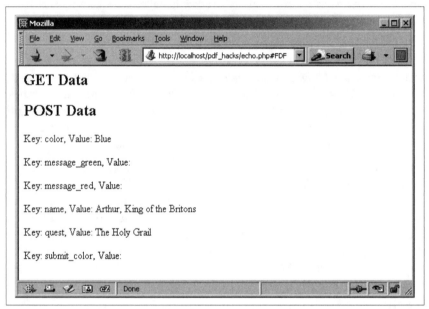

Figure 6-4. Echo PDF form submissions using a local web server and PHP script

Serve Filled-Out PDF Forms

HACK #75

Populate online PDF forms with known data.

To maintain form data, you must display the current state of the data to the user. This enables the user to review the data, update a single field, and submit this change back to the server. With HTML forms, you can set field values as the form is served to the user. With PDF forms, you can use the Forms Data Format (FDF) to populate a form's fields with data, as shown in Figure 6-5.

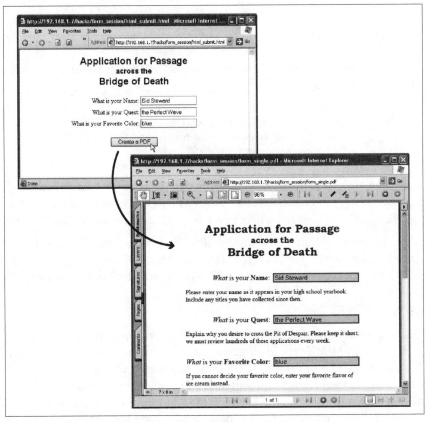

Figure 6-5. Driving PDF forms with active data

FDF, the Forms Data Format

The PDF Reference [Hack #98] describes the FDF file format. Its syntax uses PDF objects [Hack #80] to organize data. To see an example, open your PDF form in Acrobat and fill in some fields. Export this data as FDF by selecting Advanced → Forms → Export Forms Data... (Acrobat 6) or File → Export → Form Data... (Acrobat 5). Our basic PDF form [Hack #74] yields an FDF file that lists fields in name/value pairs and then references the PDF form by filename:

```
%FDF-1.2
1 0 obj
<< /FDF
   << /Fields
      [ << /T (text_field_1) /V (Here is some text) >>
        << /T (text_field_2) /V (More nice text) >> ]
      /F (http://localhost/fine_form.pdf)
   >>
>>
```

```
endobj
trailer
<< /Root 1 0 R >>
%%EOF
```

"PDF Form-Filling Sessions" [Hack #77] offers a PHP script for easily creating FDF from your data.

For XML fans, XFDF is an XML-based subset of FDF features. Acrobat Versions 5 and 6 support XFDF. Its MIME type is *application/vnd.adobe.xfdf*.

Users can store and manage PDF form data using FDF files. Visit *http://segraves.tripod.com/index3.htm* for some examples. For our purpose of serving filled-out PDF forms, the user never sees or handles the FDF file directly.

You have two options for automatically filling an online PDF form with data. You can serve FDF data that references the PDF form, or you can create a URL that references both the PDF form and the FDF data together.

Serve FDF to Fill Forms

One way to automatically fill an online PDF form is to serve a data-packed FDF file (with MIME type *application/vnd.fdf*). The user's browser will open Acrobat/Reader and pass it the FDF data. Acrobat/Reader will read the FDF data to locate the PDF form. It will load and display this PDF and then populate its fields from the FDF. The PDF form in question should be available from your web server and the FDF data should reference it by URL using the /F key, as we do in our preceding example.

Check your web server to make sure it sends the appropriate *Content-type: application/vnd.fdf* header when serving FDF files. Or, send the header directly from your script.

This technique is simple, but it has limitations. First, not all browsers know how to handle FDF data. Second, this technique does not always work inside of HTML frames. The next technique overcomes both of these problems.

Combine PDF and FDF URLs to Fill Forms

Another way to automatically fill an online PDF form is to append an FDF file reference to the PDF form's URL. In this case the FDF file *must omit* the PDF form reference (the /F key). When the user follows the link, Acrobat/Reader opens the PDF and fills the form fields using the FDF data. The FDF file reference must be a full URL:

```
http://localhost/fine_form.pdf#FDF=http://localhost/fine_data.fdf
```

Or, it must reference an FDF-generating script instead of a file. For example:

```
http://localhost/fine_form.pdf#FDF=http://localhost/fdf_data.php?t=42
```

You should use this technique of referencing both the form PDF and the FDF data in a single URL when displaying filled-in forms inside of HTML frames.

> You really must use a web server to test these techniques. Windows users can download IndigoPerl [Hack #74] from *http://www.indigostar.com*. IndigoPerl is an Apache installer for Windows that includes PHP and Perl support.

Hacking the Hack

FDF can also contain PDF annotation (e.g., sticky note) information. Use the preceding techniques to dynamically add annotations to online PDF. Create example FDF or XFDF files by opening a PDF in Acrobat and adding some annotations. Then, select Document → Export Comments... (Acrobat 6) or File → Export → Comments... (Acrobat 5).

H A C K   Drive PDF Forms with Your Data
#76

Convert your data into FDF so that Acrobat or Reader can merge it with a PDF form.

As discussed in "Serve Filled-Out PDF Forms" [Hack #75], you can deliver filled-out PDF forms on the Web by serving FDF data. FDF data contains the URL for your PDF form and the data with which to fill the form. Upon receiving FDF data, Acrobat (or Reader) will open the referenced PDF form and then populate it with the given information. The next problem is how to easily create FDF data on your web server.

The PDF Reference [Hack #98] describes FDF in dizzying detail, and Adobe offers a free-of-charge FDF Toolkit with a dizzying license (*http://partners. adobe.com/asn/acrobat/forms.jsp*). But what you need is usually easy to create from the comfort of your favorite web programming language. We provide such a script written in PHP. It converts form data into an FDF file suitable for filling our basic PDF form [Hack #74].

> In Java, try the FdfWriter and FdfReader classes in iText (*http://www.lowagie.com/iText/*) for creating or parsing FDF data.

Elaborate forms might require the high-caliber Adobe FDF Toolkit to create suitable FDF. Most forms merely require their field data cast into the FDF syntax. We offer the forge_fdf script for this purpose. The FDF example from "Serve Filled-Out PDF Forms" [Hack #75] shows the pattern evident in simple FDF files.

Instead of using a general-purpose FDF function or library, you can also consider exporting an FDF file from your form and then converting it into a template. Replace the form values with variables or other placeholders. Serve this template back to your form after filling the variables with user data. forge_fdf includes functions for encoding PDF strings and names [Hack #80], which you might find useful when filling in your template.

Create FDF with forge_fdf

Pass form data and a PDF's URL into forge_fdf, and it returns the corresponding FDF as a string. Create an FDF file with this string or serve it directly to the client browser with *Content-type: application/vnd.fdf*. We offer an example a little later.

You must remember some FDF peculiarities when passing arguments to forge_fdf.

$pdf_form_url
> Provide the PDF form's URL (or filename) *unless* you plan to pass this FDF data as part of a larger URL that already references the PDF form. For example, if the FDF data will be served to the user like so:
>
> ```
> http://localhost/fine_form.pdf#FDF=http://localhost/fine_data.fdf
> ```
>
> pass an empty string as $pdf_form_url.
>
> To exit a PDF form and replace it with an HTML page in the user's browser, serve the PDF an FDF with $pdf_form_url set to your HTML page's URL.

$fdf_data_strings
> Load text, combo box, and listbox data into this array. It should be an array of string field names mapped to string field values. If you want a form field to be hidden or read-only, you must also add its name to $fields_hidden or $fields_readonly.

$fdf_data_names
> Load checkbox and radio button data into this array. It should be an array of string field names mapped to string field values. Often, true and false correspond to the case-sensitive strings Yes and Off. If you want a form field to be hidden or read-only, you must also add its name to $fields_hidden or $fields_readonly.

$fields_hidden
> If you want a field to disappear from view, add its name to this array. Any field listed here also must be in $fdf_data_strings or $fdf_data_names.

$fields_readonly

If you don't want the user tinkering with a field's data, add its name to this array. Any field listed here also must be in $fdf_data_strings or $fdf_data_names.

For example, the following script uses forge_fdf to serve FDF data that should cause the user's browser to open *http://localhost/form.pdf* and set its fields to match our values:

```php
<?php
require_once('forge_fdf.php');

$pdf_form_url= "http://localhost/form.pdf";

$fdf_data_strings= array( 'text1' => $_GET['t'], 'text2' => 'Egads!' );
$fdf_data_names= array( 'check1' => 'Off', 'check2' => 'Yes' );

$fields_hidden= array( 'text2', 'check1' );
$fields_readonly= array( 'text1' );

header( 'content-type: application/vnd.fdf' );

echo forge_fdf( $pdf_form_url,
                $fdf_data_strings,
                $fdf_data_names,
                $fields_hidden,
                $fields_readonly );
?>
```

To see a more elaborate example of forge_fdf in action, visit *http://www.pdfhacks.com/form_session/*. Tinker with the online example or download PHP source code from this web page.

> If forge_fdf isn't filling your form properly, export the FDF from your form to see exactly how the form expects its data. Try testing your larger program with these pristine example FDF files.

The Code

Copy this code into a file named *forge_fdf.php* and include it in your PHP scripts. Or, adapt this algorithm to your favorite language. Visit *http://www. pdfhacks.com/forge_fdf/* to download the latest version.

```php
<?php
/* forge_fdf, by Sid Steward
   version 1.0
   visit: http://www.pdfhacks.com/forge_fdf/

   For text fields, combo boxes, and list boxes, add
   field values as a name => value pair to $fdf_data_strings.
```

For checkboxes and radio buttons, add field values
as a name => value pair to $fdf_data_names. Typically,
true and false correspond to the (case-sensitive)
names "Yes" and "Off".

Any field added to the $fields_hidden or $fields_readonly
array also must be a key in $fdf_data_strings or
$fdf_data_names; this might be changed in the future

Any field listed in $fdf_data_strings or $fdf_data_names
that you want hidden or read-only must have its field
name added to $fields_hidden or $fields_readonly; do this
even if your form has these bits set already

PDF can be particular about CR and LF characters, so I
spelled them out in hex: CR == \x0d : LF == \x0a
*/

```
function escape_pdf_string( $ss )
{
  $ss_esc= '';
  $ss_len= strlen( $ss );
  for( $ii= 0; $ii< $ss_len; ++$ii ) {
    if( ord($ss{$ii})== 0x28 ||   // open paren
        ord($ss{$ii})== 0x29 ||   // close paren
        ord($ss{$ii})== 0x5c )    // backslash
      {
        $ss_esc.= chr(0x5c).$ss{$ii}; // escape the character w/ backslash
      }
    else if( ord($ss{$ii}) < 32 || 126 < ord($ss{$ii}) ) {
      $ss_esc.= sprintf( "\\%03o", ord($ss{$ii}) ); // use an octal code
    }
    else {
      $ss_esc.= $ss{$ii};
    }
  }
  return $ss_esc;
}

function escape_pdf_name( $ss )
{
  $ss_esc= '';
  $ss_len= strlen( $ss );
  for( $ii= 0; $ii< $ss_len; ++$ii ) {
    if( ord($ss{$ii}) < 33 || 126 < ord($ss{$ii}) ||
        ord($ss{$ii})== 0x23 ) // hash mark
      {
        $ss_esc.= sprintf( "#%02x", ord($ss{$ii}) ); // use a hex code
      }
    else {
      $ss_esc.= $ss{$ii};
    }
  }
  return $ss_esc;
```

```
}

function forge_fdf( $pdf_form_url,
                    $fdf_data_strings,
                    $fdf_data_names,
                    $fields_hidden,
                    $fields_readonly )
{
  $fdf = "%FDF-1.2\x0d%\xe2\xe3\xcf\xd3\x0d\x0a"; // header
  $fdf.= "1 0 obj\x0d<< "; // open the Root dictionary
  $fdf.= "\x0d/FDF << "; // open the FDF dictionary
  $fdf.= "/Fields [ "; // open the form Fields array

  // string data, used for text fields, combo boxes, and list boxes
  foreach( $fdf_data_strings as $key => $value ) {
    $fdf.= "<< /V (".escape_pdf_string($value).")".
      "/T (".escape_pdf_string($key).") ";
    if( in_array( $key, $fields_hidden ) )
      $fdf.= "/SetF 2 ";
    else
      $fdf.= "/ClrF 2 ";

    if( in_array( $key, $fields_readonly ) )
      $fdf.= "/SetFf 1 ";
    else
      $fdf.= "/ClrFf 1 ";

    $fdf.= ">> \x0d";
  }

  // name data, used for checkboxes and radio buttons
  // (e.g., /Yes and /Off for true and false)
  foreach( $fdf_data_names as $key => $value ) {
    $fdf.= "<< /V /".escape_pdf_name($value).
      " /T (".escape_pdf_string($key).") ";
    if( in_array( $key, $fields_hidden ) )
      $fdf.= "/SetF 2 ";
    else
      $fdf.= "/ClrF 2 ";

    if( in_array( $key, $fields_readonly ) )
      $fdf.= "/SetFf 1 ";
    else
      $fdf.= "/ClrFf 1 ";
    $fdf.= ">> \x0d";
  }

  $fdf.= "] \x0d"; // close the Fields array

  // the PDF form filename or URL, if given
  if( $pdf_form_url ) {
    $fdf.= "/F (".escape_pdf_string($pdf_form_url).") \x0d";
  }
```

```
$fdf.= ">> \x0d"; // close the FDF dictionary
$fdf.= ">> \x0dendobj\x0d"; // close the Root dictionary

// trailer; note the "1 0 R" reference to "1 0 obj" above
$fdf.= "trailer\x0d<<\x0d/Root 1 0 R \x0d\x0d>>\x0d";
$fdf.= "%%EOF\x0d\x0a";

    return $fdf;
}
?>
```

 ## PDF Form-Filling Sessions

#77   Walk your users through the form-filling process.

Collecting information with online forms is an interactive process. We have discussed how to collect form data [Hack #74] and how to drive forms [Hack #75]. Now, let's use what we know to program an interactive, online form-filling session, such as the one in Figure 6-6 (visit *http://www.pdfhacks.com/form_session/* to see this example and download PHP source code).

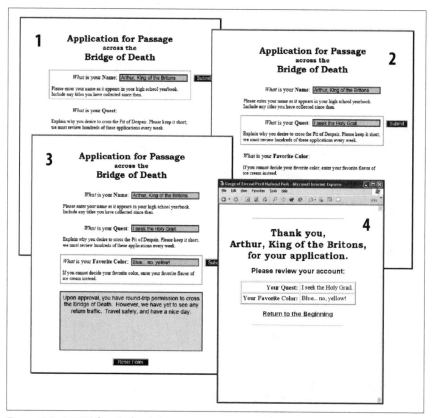

Figure 6-6. A PDF form's dynamic state

Set the Stage

To submit data to your server, the PDF form must be displayed inside a web browser. I recommend displaying it inside an HTML frameset. This enables you to bracket the form with (HTML) instructions and a hyperlinked escape route, so the user won't feel abandoned or trapped. It also adjusts the user to the idea that this isn't any old PDF. Most people experience PDF as something to download and print out. Not only will this look different, but also the frameset conceals the PDF's URL and prevents reflexive downloading.

Here is the HTML frameset code used in our example at *http://www. pdfhacks.com/form_session/*. Note that it uses a PDF+FDF URL to reference the form in order to prevent the PDF from breaking out of the frameset [Hack #75].

```php
<?php
// This is part of form_session
// visit www.pdfhacks.com/form_session/
//

$our_dir= 'http://'.$_SERVER['HTTP_HOST'].dirname($_SERVER['PHP_SELF']);

// The PDF+FDF URL notation respects frames
// and triggers the browser's 'PDF' association
// instead of its 'FDF' association (some browsers
// don't have an FDF association).
//
$form_frame_url= '"'.
$our_dir.'/form_session.pdf#FDF='.
$our_dir.'/update_state.php?reset=1"';

?>
<!DOCTYPE HTML PUBLIC "-//W3C//DTD HTML 4.01 Frameset//EN"
    "http://www.w3.org/TR/html4/frameset.dtd">
<html>
  <head>
    <title>PDF Form Filling Session Demo</title>
  </head>
  <frameset cols="*,200">
    <frame src=<?php echo $form_frame_url ?> name="form" scrolling="no"
marginwidth=0 marginheight=0 frameborder=1>
    <frame src="sidebar_session.html" name="sidebar" scrolling="auto"
marginwidth=5 marginheight=5 frameborder=1>
  </frameset>
</html>
```

Create Your Interactive PDF Form

Here are some ideas for your interactive PDF form design. Keep in mind that a form can have any number of PDF fields, and you can hide fields from the user or set them as read-only at any time. Our forge_fdf script [Hack #77] enables you to set these flags as needed. Just add the field's name to the `$fields_hidden` or `$fields_readonly` arrays.

- Use hidden text fields to store the form's session and state information.

- If your form has multiple sections that require separate, server-side computation, add a Submit Form button for each section. Show only one button at a time by hiding all the others.

  Don't forget to append an #FDF to form submission actions—e.g., `update_state.php#FDF`.

- Highlight specific sections of your form with borders. Create a border using an empty, read-only text field that shows a colored border and a transparent background.

  You must draw these decorative form fields first, so they won't interfere with other, interactive fields. Or, move a decorative field behind the others by giving it a lower tab order.

> Alter form field tab order in Acrobat 6.0.1 by activating the Select Object Tool (Tools → Advanced Editing → Select Object Tool), selecting Advanced → Forms → Fields → Set Tab Order, and then clicking each field in order. Alter form field tab order in Acrobat 5 by activating the Form Tool, selecting Tools → Forms → Fields → Set Tab Order, and then clicking each field in order.

- After the user completes a section, set that section's fields as read-only to lock the data in. Fields that hold the results of server-side calculations also should be read-only.

- If a form's page gets cluttered with PDF fields, consider dividing fields across two or three copies of the same PDF page.

- Consider splitting multiple-page forms into single-page PDFs.

- Create text fields to serve as read-only messages to the user. If the user submits invalid field data, serve the form again and show a suitable message. When creating these message fields in Acrobat, color them so that they stand out from the data. You can change a message's text using FDF.

We employ some of these techniques in our online example at *http://www.pdfhacks.com/form_session/*.

Beginning, Middle, End

A form-filling session has a beginning, a middle, and an end. The middle is the hard part because that is where your form logic is. The tricky parts are the beginning and the end. Here they are, in order:

Dive into the form

Begin the session by using a PDF+FDF URL **[Hack #75]** to open the form. For example:

```
http://localhost/form_session.pdf#FDF=http://localhost/update_state.
php?reset=1
```

The FDF portion is a script that initializes the session state. It must also serve FDF that sets the form's initial appearance.

Store the session's ID and state information in hidden PDF text fields, if necessary.

Respond to data submissions

With each form submission, update the session state and then respond by serving FDF. Use FDF to update the form's appearance. Use it to activate some fields and hide others, as needed. Also use FDF to update read-only field text with calculated data or messages to the user.

Omit the /F key ($pdf_form_url in forge_fdf) from the FDF you serve until you are ready to exit this session.

Bail out of the form

When the form session is done, break out by serving an FDF Forward. This is an FDF with no form data except the /F key ($pdf_form_url in forge_fdf). Set the /F key to the URL of an HTML page or script. This new address will replace the PDF form in the user's browser.

Running the Hack

Visit *http://www.pdfhacks.com/form_session/* to see a live example of this model. Download *form_session-1.1.zip* from this page to examine the PHP scripts and PDF forms. IndigoPerl **[Hack #74]** users can unpack *form_session-1.1.zip* into *C:\indigoperl\apache\htdocs\pdf_hacks\form_session-1.1* and then run the example locally by pointing their browsers at *http://localhost/pdf_hacks/form_session-1.1/start.html*.

Permanently Merge a PDF Form and its Data
H A C K #78
Provide online users with a copy of their completed form to save.

Adobe Reader enables a user to add, change, view, and print form data, but it does not enable a user to save the filled-in PDF form to disk. Saving the file produces a lovely copy of an empty form. How annoying!

Correct this problem server-side by merging the PDF form and its data. Then, offer this filled-in form as a download for the user's records. After merging, the form fields remain interactive, even though they display the user's data. Go a step further and flatten this form so that field data becomes a permanent part of the PDF pages. After flattening, filled-in fields are no longer interactive. You can merge and flatten forms using the iText library or our command-line pdftk. Both are free software.

Merge or Flatten a Form and Its Data in Java

The iText library (*http://www.lowagie.com/iText/* or *http://itextpdf.sf.net*) is a remarkable tool for manipulating PDF documents. The following Java program, merge_pdf_fdf, demonstrates how to merge or flatten a PDF and its form data FDF [Hack #77] using iText. Run this code from your command line, or integrate it into your web application.

```
/*
   merge_pdf_fdf, version 1.0
   merge an input PDF file with an input FDF file
   to create a filled-in PDF; optionally flatten the
   FDF data so that it becomes part of the page
   http://www.pdfhacks.com/merge_pdf_fdf/

   invoke from the command line like this:

     java -classpath ./itext-paulo.jar:. \
     merge_pdf_fdf input.pdf input.fdf output.pdf

   or:

     java -classpath ./itext-paulo.jar:. \
     merge_pdf_fdf input.pdf input.fdf output.pdf flatten

   adjust the classpath to the location of your iText jar
*/

import java.io.*;
import com.lowagie.text.pdf.*;

public class merge_pdf_fdf extends java.lang.Object {

   public static void main(String args[]) {
     if ( args.length == 3 || args.length == 4 ) {
       try {
         // the input PDF
         PdfReader reader =
           new PdfReader( args[0] );
         reader.consolidateNamedDestinations();
         reader.removeUnusedObjects();

         // the input FDF
         FdfReader fdf_reader=
           new FdfReader( args[1] );

         // PdfStamper acts like a PdfWriter
         PdfStamper pdf_stamper=
           new PdfStamper( reader,
```

```
                    new FileOutputStream( args[2] ) );

    if( args.length == 4 ) { // "flatten"
      // filled-in data becomes a permanent part of the page
      pdf_stamper.setFormFlattening( true );
    }
    else {
      // filled-in data will 'stick' to the form fields,
      // but it will remain interactive
      pdf_stamper.setFormFlattening( false );
    }

    // sets the form fields from the input FDF
    AcroFields fields=
      pdf_stamper.getAcroFields( );
    fields.setFields( fdf_reader );

    // closing the stamper closes the underlying
    // PdfWriter; the PDF document is written
    pdf_stamper.close( );
  }
  catch( Exception ee ) {
    ee.printStackTrace( );
  }
}
else { // input error
  System.err.println("arguments: file1.pdf file2.fdf destfile
[flatten]");
  }
 }
}
```

To create a command-line Java program, copy the preceding code into a file named *merge_pdf_fdf.java*. Then, compile *merge_pdf_fdf.java* using javac, setting the classpath to the name and location of your iText jar:

```
javac -classpath ./itext-paulo.jar merge_pdf_fdf.java
```

Finally, invoke merge_pdf_fdf like so:

```
java -classpath ./itext-paulo.jar:. \
merge_pdf_fdf input.pdf input.fdf output.pdf
```

Merge or Flatten a Form and Its Data with pdftk

Use pdftk [Hack #79] to merge a form with an FDF datafile [Hack #77] and create a new PDF. The fields will display the given data, but they also remain interactive. pdftk's fill_form operation takes the filename of an FDF file as its argument. For example:

```
pdftk form.pdf fill_form data.fdf output filled_form.pdf
```

You can't combine the fill_form operation with any other operation (e.g., cat), but you can supply additional output options for encryption [Hack #52].

Flatten form data permanently into the page by adding the flatten_form output option. The resulting PDF data will no longer be interactive.

    pdftk *form.pdf* fill_form *data.fdf* output *filled_form.pdf* flatten_form

Or, if your PDF form already has field data, just flatten it:

    pdftk *filled_form.pdf* output *flattened_form.pdf* flatten_form

Merge or Flatten with pdftk in PHP

After installing pdftk on your web server, you can invoke it from your PHP scripts to merge PDF forms with FDF data. Use our PHP script forge_fdf [Hack #77] to cast your data into FDF. Then, save this FDF data into a temporary file. Finally, call pdftk to create a new PDF from your PDF form and FDF data.

The following PHP code could be used for this purpose:

```php
<?php
// session_fdf is your function for converting
// the user's session state into an FDF string
$fdf_ss= session_fdf( $_GET['id'] );

$temp_fn= tempnam( '/tmp', 'tempfdf' );
$temp_fp= fopen( $temp_fn, 'wb' );
if( $temp_fp ) {
  fwrite( $temp_fp, $fdf_ss );
  fclose( $temp_fp );

  header( 'Content-type: application/pdf' );
  passthru( '/usr/local/bin/pdftk form.pdf fill_form '.$temp_fn.
            ' output - flatten' ); // output to stdout (-)

  unlink( $temp_fn );
}
?>
```

Tool Up with pdftk
HACK #79

Take control of your PDF with pdftk.

If PDF is electronic paper, pdftk is an electronic staple-remover, hole punch, binder, secret-decoder ring, and X-ray glasses. pdftk is a simple, free tool for doing everyday things with PDF documents. It can:

- Split and merge PDF pages [Hack #51]
- Decrypt and encrypt PDF documents [Hack #52]
- Burst a PDF document into single pages [Hack #71]
- Uncompress and recompress page streams [Hack #80]

The pdftk web site (*http://www.AccessPDF.com/pdftk/*) has links to software downloads and instructions for installation and usage. pdftk currently runs on Windows, Linux, Solaris, FreeBSD, and Mac OS X. Some users can download precompiled binaries, while others must download the source code and build pdftk using gcc, gcj, and libgcj (as described on the web site). pdftk is free software.

On Windows, download *pdftk_1.0.exe.zip* to a convenient directory. Unzip with your favorite archiving tool, and move the resulting *pdftk.exe* program to a directory in your *PATH*, such as *C:\windows\system32* or *C:\winnt\ system32*. Test it by opening a command-line DOS prompt and typing pdftk --help. It should respond with pdftk version information and usage instructions.

> Additional free PDF tools include mbtPDFasm (*http:// thierry.schmit.free.fr/dev/mbtPdfAsm/enMbtPdfAsm2.html*) and the Multivalent Tools (*http://multivalent.sourceforge. net/Tools/index.html*). Related commercial tools include pdfmeld (*http://www.fytek.com/*).

Handy Command Line for Windows

Command prompts aren't well suited for quickly navigating large, complex filesystems. Let's configure the Windows File Explorer to open a command prompt in the working directory we select. This will make it easier to use pdftk in a specific directory.

> Be sure to add this new action to the Folder file type, *not* the File Folder file type.

Windows XP and Windows 2000:

1. In the Windows File Explorer menu, select Tools → Folder Options... and click the File Types tab. Select the Folder file type and click the Advanced button.

2. Click the New... button and a New Action dialog appears. Give the new action the name Command.

3. Give the action an application to open by clicking the Browse... button and selecting *cmd.exe*, which lives somewhere such as *C:\windows\ system32*, or *C:\winnt\system32*.

4. Add these arguments after cmd.exe like so:

   ```
   C:\windows\system32\cmd.exe /K cd "%1"
   ```

5. Click OK, OK, OK and you are done.

Windows 98:

1. In the Windows File Explorer menu, select Tools → Folder Options… and click the File Types tab. Select the Folder file type and click the Edit… button.

2. Click the New… button and a New Action dialog appears. Give the new action the name Command.

3. Give the action an application to open by clicking the Browse… button and selecting *command.com*, which lives somewhere such as *C:\windows*.

4. Add these arguments after command.com like so:

   ```
   C:\windows\command.com /K cd "%1"
   ```

5. Click OK, OK, OK and you are done.

Test your configuration by right-clicking a folder in the File Explorer. The context menu should list your new Command action, as shown in Figure 6-7. Choose this action and a command prompt will appear with its working directory set to the folder you selected. *Olé*!

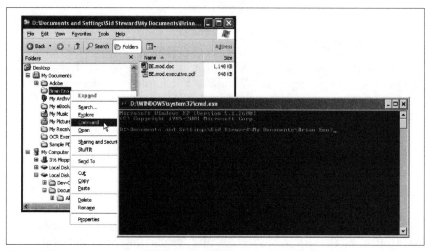

Figure 6-7. Opening a command prompt right where you need it

 Instead of typing long filenames into the command prompt, select a file in the File Explorer and drag it over the command-line window. When you drop it, its full filename will appear at the cursor.

Decipher and Navigate PDF at the Text Level

#80 Turn obfuscated PDF code into transparent data so you can work with it directly.

PDF uses an element framework for organizing data. When editing PDFs at the text level, it helps to know how to navigate these nodes. The data itself usually is compressed and unreadable. pdftk **[Hack #79]** can uncompress these streams, making the PDF more interesting to read and much more hackable.

First, uncompress your PDF document using pdftk:

```
pdftk mydoc.pdf output mydoc.uncompressed.pdf uncompress
```

Next, fire up your text editor. A good text editor enables you to inspect any document at its lowest level by reading its bytes right off of the disk. Not all text editors can handle the mix of human-readable text and machine-readable binary data that PDF contains. Other editors can read and display this data, but they can't write it properly. I recommend using gVim **[Hack #82]**.

> Get the full story on PDF by reading the specification at
> *http://partners.adobe.com/asn/acrobat/sdk/public/docs/*
> *PDFReference15_v5.pdf.*

Open a PDF in your text editor and you will find some plain-text data and some unreadable binary data. All of this data is organized using a few basic objects. The PDF Reference 1.5 section 3.2 describes these in detail. Here is a quick key to get you started.

Names: /...
> A slash indicates the beginning of a name. Examples include /Type and /Page. Most names have very specific meanings prescribed by the PDF Reference. They are never compressed or encrypted.

Strings: (...)
> Strings are enclosed by parentheses. An example is (Now is the time). You use them for holding plain-text data in annotations and bookmarks. You can encrypt them but you can't compress them. Mind escaped characters—e.g., \), \(, or \\.

Dictionaries: << key1 value1 key2 value2 ... >>
> Dictionaries map keys to values. Keys must be names and values can be anything, even dictionaries or arrays.

Arrays: [*object1 object2 ...*]

Arrays represent a list of objects. All PDF objects are part of one big tree, interconnected by arrays and dictionaries.

Streams: << ... >> stream...endstream

Most PDF data is stored in streams. Dictionary data precedes the stream data and holds information about the stream, such as its length and encoding. stream and endstream bracket the actual stream data. Streams are used to hold bitmap images and page-drawing instructions, among other things. Use pdftk to make compressed page streams readable. Some streams use PDF objects (dictionaries, strings, arrays, etc.) to represent information.

Indirect object references: m n R

Indirect object references allow an object to be referenced in one place (or many places) and described in another. The reference is a pair of numbers followed by the letter R, such as: 3528 0 R. You find them in dictionaries and arrays. To locate the object referenced by *m n* R, search for *m n* obj.

Indirect object identifiers: m n obj ... endobj

An *indirect object* is any object that is preceded by the identifying *m n* obj, where *m* and *n* are numbers that uniquely identify the object. Another object can then reference the indirect object by simply invoking *m n* R, described earlier.

Dictionaries tend to be the most interesting objects. They represent things such as pages and annotations. You can tell what a dictionary describes by checking its /Type and /Subtype keys. Conversely, you can find something in a PDF by searching on its type. For example, you can find each page in a PDF by searching for the text /Page. For annotations, search for /Annot, and for images, /Image.

At the end of the PDF file is the XREF lookup table. It gives the byte offset for every indirect object in the PDF file. This allows rapid random access to PDF pages and other data. Text-level PDF editing can corrupt the XREF table, which breaks the PDF. "Edit PDF Code Freely" [Hack #81] solves this problem.

Edit PDF Code Freely
#81   Take control of PDF code by mastering its XREF table.

"Decipher and Navigate PDF at the Text Level" [Hack #80] revealed the hackable plain text behind PDF. Here we edit this PDF text and then use pdftk [Hack #79] to cover our tracks. pdftk can also compress the page streams when we're done.

An unsuitable text editor can quietly damage your PDF. Test your text editor by simply opening a PDF, saving it into a new file, and then trying to open this new file in Acrobat or Reader. If your editor corrupted the PDF's data, Acrobat or Reader should display a brief warning before displaying the PDF. Sometimes, however, this warning flashes by too quickly to notice. After the PDF is repaired, Acrobat and Reader will display the PDF as if nothing happened.

Since Acrobat and Reader aren't the most reliable tools for testing PDFs, you should consider some alternatives. The free command-line pdfinfo program from the Xpdf project (*http://www.foolabs.com/xpdf/*) can tell you whether a PDF is damaged. The Multivalent Tools (*http://multivalent. sourceforge.net/Tools/index.html*) also provide a free PDF validator.

If you need a good text editor, try gVim [Hack #82].

First, uncompress your PDF's page streams [Hack #80]:

```
pdftk mydoc.pdf output mydoc.uncompressed.pdf uncompress
```

Then, open this new PDF in your text editor. Locate your page of interest by searching for the text /pdftk_pageNum *N*, where *N* is the number of your page (the first page is 1, not 0). This text was added to the page dictionaries by pdftk.

Find the /Contents key in your page's dictionary. It is probably mapped to an indirect object reference: *m n* R. Locate this indirect object by searching for the text *m n* obj. This will take you to a stream or to an array of streams. If it is an array, look up any of its referenced streams the same way.

Now you should be looking at a stream of PDF drawing operations that describe your page. These operations and their interactions are best under-stood by studying the PDF Reference [Hack #98]. However, if your page has a lot of text on it, you can probably make it out. An example of a legal change in page text is changing [(gr)17.7(oup)] to [(grip)], or (storey) to (story). Anything inside parentheses this way is fair game. So, change something and save your work.

Editing PDF at the text level typically corrupts the XREF lookup table at the end of the file. Repair your edited PDF using pdftk like so:

```
pdftk mydoc.edited.pdf output mydoc.fixed.pdf
```

Or, if you want to compress the output and remove the /pdftk_pageNum entries, add compress to the end like so:

```
pdftk mydoc.edited.pdf output mydoc.fixed.pdf compress
```

Open your new PDF in Reader and view your page. Do you see the change you made? If it was in the middle of a paragraph, you might be surprised to find that the paragraph hasn't rewrapped to fit your altered word. Most PDFs have no concept of a *paragraph*, so how could it?

This procedure is an unlikely way to fix typos. We put it to better use in "Integrate pdftk with gVim for Seamless PDF Editing" [Hack #82].

HACK #82 Integrate pdftk with gVim for Seamless PDF Editing

Turn gVim into a PDF editor.

gVim is an excellent text editor that can also be handy for viewing and editing PDF code. It handles binary data nicely, it is mature, and it is free. Also, you can extend it with plug-ins, which is what we'll do. First, let's download and install gVim.

Visit *http://www.vim.org*. The download page offers links and instructions for numerous platforms. Windows users can download the installer from *http://www.vim.org/download.php*. As of this writing, it is called *gvim63.exe*. During installation, the default settings should suit most needs. Click through to the end and it will create a Programs menu from which you can launch gVim.

The first-time gVim user should run gVim in *Easy* mode, which will make it behave like most other text editors. On Windows, do this by running gVim Easy from the Programs menu. Or, you can activate Easy mode from inside gVim by typing (the initial colon is essential) :source $VIMRUNTIME/evim.vim into your gVim session.

gVim comes with an interactive tutorial and a good online help system. Learn about it by invoking :help.

> If gVim frequently complains about "Illegal Back Reference" errors, check your HOME environment variable (Start → Settings → Control Panel → System → Advanced → Environment Variables). Some backslash character combinations in HOME, such as \1 or \2, will trigger these errors. Try replacing all the backslashes with forward slashes in HOME.

Plug pdftk into gVim

The pdftk plug-in turns gVim into a PDF editor. When opening a PDF it automatically uncompresses page streams so that you can read and modify them [Hack #80]. When closing a PDF, it automatically compresses page streams. If any changes were made to the PDF, it also fixes internal PDF byte offsets [Hack #81].

Visit *http://www.AccessPDF.com/pdftk/* and download *pdftk.vim.zip*. Unzip and then move the resulting file, *pdftk.vim*, to the gVim plug-ins directory. This usually is located someplace such as *C:\Vim\vim63\plugin*. To help find this directory, try searching for the file *gzip.vim*, which should be there already. The pdftk plug-in will be sourced the next time you run gVim, so restart gVim if necessary.

Use care when testing the plug-in for the first time. Copy a PDF to create a test file named *test1.pdf*. Launch gVim and use it to open *test1.pdf*. There will be a delay while pdftk uncompresses it. Data should then appear in the editor as readable text, as shown in Figure 6-8. Any graphic bitmaps still will appear as unreadable gibberish.

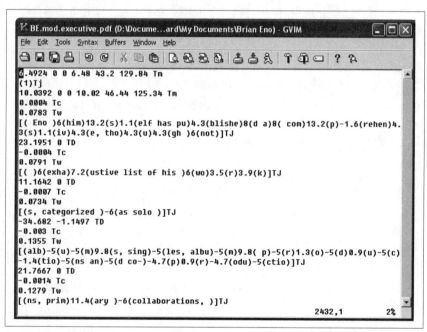

Figure 6-8. Clear text from compressed PDF streams, thanks to our gVim plug-in

Without making any changes to the file, save it as *test2.pdf* and close it. gVim will pause again while it compresses *test2.pdf*. Now, open *test2.pdf* in Acrobat or Reader. If everything is in place, it should open just fine. If Acrobat or Reader complains about the file being damaged, double-check the installation.

Acrobat and Reader display a warning as they repair a corrupted PDF file, but sometimes this warning flashes by too quickly to notice. After the PDF is repaired, they will display the PDF as if nothing happened. So, Acrobat and Reader aren't the most reliable tools for testing PDFs. Consider these alternatives.

The free, command-line pdfinfo program from the Xpdf project (*http://www.foolabs.com/xpdf/*) can tell you whether a PDF is damaged. The Multivalent Tools (*http://multivalent.sourceforge.net/Tools/index.html*) also provide a free PDF validator.

Hacking the Hack

With our PDF extensions, gVim enables you to conveniently edit PDF code. You can bring power and beauty together by configuring Acrobat's TouchUp tool to use gVim for editing PDF objects.

In Acrobat, select Edit → Preferences → General → TouchUp. Click Choose Page/Object Editor… and a file selector will open. Select *gvim.exe*, which usually lives somewhere such as *C:\Vim\vim63*. Click OK and you are done.

Test out your new configuration on a disposable document. Open the PDF in Acrobat and select the TouchUp Object tool (it might be hidden by the TouchUp Text tool), as shown in Figure 6-9.

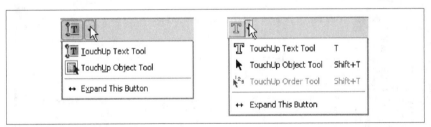

Figure 6-9. The TouchUp Object tool button, which can be found hiding under the TouchUp Text tool button in Acrobat 6 (left) and Acrobat 5 (right)

Click a paragraph and a box appears, outlining the selection. Right-click inside this box and choose Edit Object…. gVim will open, displaying the PDF code used to describe this selection, as shown in Figure 6-10. It will be a full PDF document, with fonts and an XREF table.

Find some paragraph text and make some small changes [Hack #80]. When you save the gVim file, Acrobat should promptly update the visible page to reflect your change. Sometimes this update looks imperfect, temporarily. You can make many successive PDF edits this way.

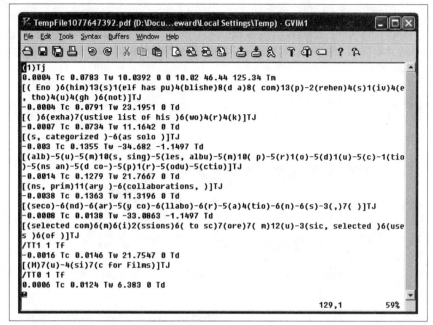

Figure 6-10. The PDF code behind selected sections

You might notice occasional warnings from gVim about the data having been modified on the disk by another program. You can safely ignore these.

Modify PDF Hyperlinks at Serve-Time
#83   Add live session data to your PDF on its way down the chute.

After publishing your PDF online, it can be hard to gauge what impact it had on readers. Get a clearer picture of reader response by modifying the PDF's hyperlinks so that they pass document information to your web server.

For example, if your July newsletter's PDF edition has hyperlinks to:

```
http://www.pdfhacks.com/index.html
```

you can append the newsletter's edition to the PDF hyperlinks using a question mark:

```
http://www.pdfhacks.com/index.html?edition=0407
```

When somebody reading your PDF newsletter follows this link into your site, your web logs record exactly which newsletter they were reading.

Take this reader response idea a step further by adding data to PDF hyperlinks that identifies the user who originally downloaded the PDF. With a little preparation, this is easy to do as the PDF is being served.

Add Hyperlinks to Your PDF Using Links or Buttons

A PDF page can include hyperlinks to web content. You can create them using the Link tool, the Button tool (Acrobat 6), or the Form tool (Acrobat 5). Use the Link tool shown in Figure 6-11 if you want to add a hyperlink to existing text or graphics. Use the Button/Form tool if you want to add a hyperlink *and* add text/graphics to the page, as shown in Figure 6-12. For example, you would use the Button/Form tool to create a web-style navigation bar [Hack #65].

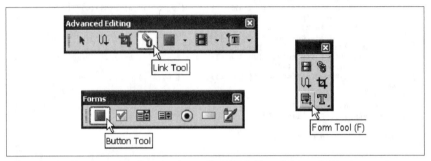

Figure 6-11. The Button tool in Acrobat 6 (bottom left) and the general-purpose Form tool in Acrobat 5 (right)

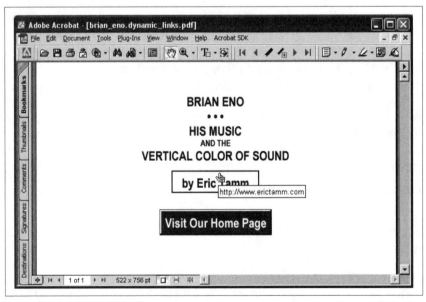

Figure 6-12. Adding a hyperlink (top) to existing page text, and using a button (bottom) to add a hyperlink and text/art to the page

To create a hyperlink button in Acrobat 6, select the Button tool (Tools →
Advanced Editing → Forms → Button Tool). Click the PDF page and drag
out a rectangle. Release the rectangle and a Field Properties dialog opens.
Set the button's appearance using the General, Appearance, and Options
tabs.

Open the Actions tab. Set the Trigger to Mouse Up, set the Action to Open
a Web Link, and then click Add…. A dialog will open where you can enter
the hyperlink URL.

> When creating hyperlink buttons, the button's Name is not
> important. However, it can't be left blank, either. Set it to any
> unique identifier. Acrobat 6 does this for you automatically.

To create a hyperlink button in Acrobat 5, select the Form tool. Click the
PDF page and drag out a rectangle. Release the rectangle and a Field Properties dialog opens. Set the field type to Button and enter a unique Name. Set
the button's appearance using the Appearance and Options tabs.

Open the Actions tab. Select Mouse Up and click Add…. Set the Action
Type to World Wide Web Link. Click Edit URL… and enter the hyperlink
URL.

Use Placeholders for Hyperlink URLs

When entering your link or button URL, use an identifying name, such as
urlbeg_userhome, instead of the actual URL. Pad this placeholder with asterisks (*) so that it is at least as long as your longest possible URL, as shown in
Figure 6-13. Use a constant prefix across all these names (e.g., urlbeg) so
that they are easy to find later using grep.

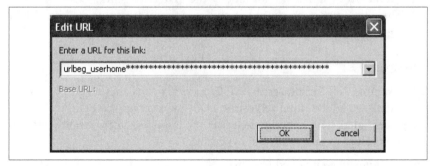

*Figure 6-13. Identifying placeholders for URLs, padded with asterisks so that they are
long enough to fit your longest possible URL*

Format the PDF Code with pdftk

When your PDF is ready to distribute online, run it through pdftk [Hack #79]. This formats the PDF code to ensure that each URL is on its own line. Add the extension *pdfsrc* to the output filename instead of *pdf*:

```
pdftk mydocument.pdf output mydocument.pdfsrc
```

From this point on, you should not treat the file like a PDF, and this *pdfsrc* extension will remind you.

Add Placeholder Offsets to the PDF

Find the byte offsets to your URL placeholders with grep (Windows users visit *http://gnuwin32.sf.net/packages/grep.htm* or install MSYS [Hack #97] to get grep). grep will tell you the byte offset and display the specific placeholder located on that line in the PDF. For example:

```
ssteward@armand:~$ grep -ab urlbeg mydocument.pdfsrc
9202:<</URI (urlbeg_userhome******************)
11793:<</URI (urlbeg_userhome******************)
17046:<</URI (urlbeg_newsletters******************)
```

In your text editor [Hack #82], open your *pdfsrc* file and add one line for each offset to the beginning. Each line should look like this:

```
#-urlname-urloffset
```

For example, this is how the previous grep output would appear at the start of *mydocument.pdfsrc*:

```
#-userhome-9202
#-userhome-11793
#-newsletters-17046
%PDF-1.3...
```

After adding these lines, do not modify the PDF with pdftk, gVim, or Acrobat. The *pdfsrc* extension should remind you to not treat this file like a PDF. Altering the PDF could break these byte offsets.

The Code

This example PHP script, *serve_newsletter.php*, opens a *pdfsrc* file, reads the offset data we added, then serves the PDF. As it serves the PDF, it replaces the placeholders with hyperlinks. It uses the input GET query string's edition and user values to tailor the PDF hyperlinks.

For example, when invoked like this:

```
http://www.pdfhacks.com/serve_newsletter.php?edition=0307&user=84
```

it opens the PDF file *newsletter.0307.pdfsrc* and serves it, replacing all userhome hyperlink placeholders with:

```
http://www.pdfhacks.com/user_home.php?user=84
```

and replacing all newsletters placeholders with:

```
http://www.pdfhacks.com/newsletter_home.php?user=84&edition=0307
```

Tailor *serve_newsletter.php* to your purpose:

```php
<?php
// serve_newsletter.php, version 1.0
// http://www.pdfhacks.com/dynamic_links/

$fp= @fopen( "./newsletter.{$_GET['edition']}.pdfsrc", 'r' );
if( $fp ) {

  if( $_GET['debug'] ) {
    header("Content-Type: text/plain"); // debug
  }
  else {
    header('Content-Type: application/pdf');
  }

  $pdf_offset= 0;
  $url_offsets= array( );

  // iterate over first lines of pdfsrc file to load $url_offsets
  while( $cc= fgets($fp, 1024) ) {
    if( $cc{0}== '#' ) { // one of our comments
      list($comment, $name, $offset)= explode( '-', $cc );

      if( $name== 'userhome' ) {
        $url_offsets[(int)$offset]=
          'http://www.pdfhacks.com/user_home.php?user=' . $_GET['user'];
      }
      else if( $name== 'newsletters' ) {
        $url_offsets[(int)$offset]=
          'http://www.pdfhacks.com/newsletter_home.php?user=' .
          $_GET['user'] . '&edition=' . $_GET['edition'];
      }
      else { // default
        $url_offsets[(int)$offset]= 'http://www.pdfhacks.com';
      }
    }
    else { // finished with our comments
      echo $cc;
      $pdf_offset= strlen($cc)+ 1;

      break;
    }
  }
}
```

```
// sort by increasing offsets
ksort( $url_offsets, SORT_NUMERIC );
reset( $url_offsets );

$output_url_line_b= false;
$output_url_b= false;
$closed_string_b= false;

list( $offset, $url )= each( $url_offsets );
$url_ii= 0;
$url_len= strlen($url);

// iterate over rest of file
while( ($cc= fgetc($fp))!= "" ) {

  if( $output_url_line_b && $cc== '(' ) {
    // we have reached the beginning of our URL
    $output_url_line_b= false;
    $output_url_b= true;

    echo '(';
  }
  else if( $output_url_b ) {
    if( $cc== ')' ) { // finished with this URL
      if( $closed_string_b ) {
        // string has already been capped; pad
        echo ' ';
      }
      else {
        echo ')';
      }

      // get next offset/URL pair
      list( $offset, $url )= each( $url_offsets );
      $url_ii= 0;
      $url_len= strlen($url);

      // reset
      $output_url_b= false;
      $closed_string_b= false;
    }
    else if( $url_ii< $url_len ) {
      // output one character of $url
      echo $url{$url_ii++};
    }
    else if( $url_ii== $url_len ) {
      // done with $url, so cap this string
      echo ')';
      $closed_string_b= true;
      $url_ii++;
    }
    else {
      echo ' '; // replace padding with space
```

```
        }
      }
      else {
        // output this character
        echo $cc;

        if( $offset== $pdf_offset ) {
          // we have reached a line in pdfsrc where
          // our URL should be; begin a lookout for '('
          $output_url_line_b= true;
        }
      }

      ++$pdf_offset;
    }

    fclose( $fp );
  }
  else { // file open failure
    echo 'Error: failed to open: '."./newsletter.{$_GET['edition']}.pdfsrc";
  }
?>
```

Running the Hack

Upload this file to your web server along with your modified PDF file. Invoke the script with an information-packed URL, such as this one:

```
http://www.pdfhacks.com/newsletters.php?ed=0307&u=84572
```

HACK #84 Tailor PDF Text at Serve-Time

Create a PDF template that you can populate as it is served.

Sometimes a PDF needs to include dynamic information. For example, you could fashion the cover of your personalized PDF sales brochure [Hack #89] to include the customer's name: "Created for Mary Jane Doe on March 15, 2004." To do this, let's use what we know about modifying PDF text in a plain-text editor [Hack #80] to create a PDF template. Then we'll fill in this template using a web server script.

The overall process resembles "Modify PDF Hyperlinks at Serve-Time" [Hack #83]. Instead of PDF links, you will add placeholders to the PDF's page streams. As it is served, these placeholders can be replaced with your data.

Create the PDF

Design the document using your favorite authoring application. Add placeholder text where you want the dynamic data to appear. Placeholders should have a common prefix, such as *textbeg_customer*. Style this text to taste, but align it to the left (not the center). Before creating a PDF, be careful with the placeholder fonts to avoid results such as the one in Figure 6-14.

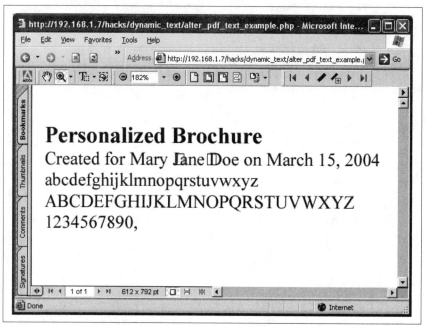

Figure 6-14. Acrobat displaying parentheses around "Jane" as empty rectangles, because we omitted them from our alphabet soup

Whichever font you choose for your placeholder, you must make sure the font gets adequately embedded into the PDF [Hack #43]. An embedded font is often *subset*, which means it includes only the characters that are used in your document. If your placeholder text uses a Type 1 font, you can configure Distiller to not subset this font [Hack #43]. If your placeholder text uses a TrueType or OpenType font, you must be sure that every character you might need occurs in your document. To be safe, create a separate page that includes every letter in the alphabet, every number, and every punctuation mark you'll need. Set this alphabet soup to the font of your placeholder.

Print to PDF and delete this alphabet page.

Convert the PDF into a Template

Prepare the PDF for text editing with pdftk [Hack #79] like this (if you use gVim and our plug-in [Hack #82] to edit PDF, this step isn't necessary):

```
pdftk mydoc.pdf output mydoc.plain.pdf uncompress
```

Open the results in your editor and search for your placeholder text. If you can't find it, search on its page number—e.g., pageNum 5—and then dig down [Hack #81] to find the page stream that has your placeholder. Distiller probably split it into pieces—e.g., textbeg_customer might end up as [(text)5(b)-1.7(eg_cust)5(o)-1.7(mer)].

When creating PDF with Ghostscript, text that uses True-Type fonts ends up getting a strange, custom encoding. This means your PDF code will be incomprehensible. The solution is to use Type 1 fonts in your document instead of TrueType.

Make a few changes to this page stream. First, repair your placeholder text so that grep can find it. So:

```
[(text)5(b)-1.7(eg_cust)5(o)-1.7(mer)]TJ
```

becomes:

```
[(textbeg_customer)]TJ
```

Or, if your string ends in Tj, such as this:

```
(Created for textbeg_customer on textbeg_date)Tj
```

rewrite it like this, adding square brackets and changing the Tj at the end to TJ:

```
[(Created for textbeg_customer on textbeg_date)]TJ
```

Next, isolate each placeholder on its own line, if necessary. So, the previous example becomes:

```
[(Created for )
(textbeg_customer)
( on )
(textbeg_date)]JT
```

Finally, pad the placeholders with asterisks (*). Add enough asterisks so that the placeholder is longer than any possible data you might write there. Padding the previous example would look like this:

```
[(Created for )
(textbeg_customer*******************************)
( on )
(textbeg_date*********************)]JT
```

Save and close your altered PDF.

What happens to excess padding when the file is served? Our script replaces it with whitespace *outside* of the PDF string, so it won't be rendered on the page. The preceding example might look like this, after it is served by our script:

```
[(Created for )
(Mary Jane Doe)
( on )
(March 15, 2004)                    ]JT
```

where (Mary Jane Doe) and (March 15, 2004) are followed by numerous space characters.

Add Placeholder Offsets to the PDF

If you used gVim and our plug-in to edit the PDF, now you must uncompress the PDF. If you did not use gVim, now you must repair the PDF's XREF table and stream lengths. One command accomplishes both tasks:

```
pdftk mydoc.plain.pdf output mydoc.pdfsrc uncompress
```

From this point on, you should not treat the file like a PDF, and this *pdfsrc* extension will remind you.

Find the byte offsets to your placeholders with grep (Windows users visit *http://gnuwin32.sf.net/packages/grep.htm* or install MSYS **[Hack #97]** to get grep):

```
ssteward@armand:~$ grep -ab textbeg mydoc.pdfsrc
9202:(textbeg_customer**************************)
9247:(textbeg_date**************************)]TJ
11793:(textbeg_customer**************************)
```

In your text editor, add one line for each offset to the beginning of your *pdfsrc* file. Each line should look like this:

```
#-dataname-dataoffset
```

The *dataname* is used in the following script code to identify the data to be written into the PDF. In this example, customer will be replaced with the customer's name. For example, here is how the preceding grep output would appear at the beginning of a *pdfsrc* file:

```
#-customer-9202
#-date-9247
#-customer-11793
%PDF-1.3...
```

After adding these lines, do not modify the PDF with pdftk, gVim, or Acrobat. The *pdfsrc* extension should remind you to not treat this file like a PDF. Altering the PDF could invalidate these byte offsets.

The Code

This example PHP script, *alter_pdf_text_example.php*, opens a *pdfsrc* file, reads the offset data we added, and then serves the PDF. As it serves the PDF, it replaces the placeholders with the given text. Note how the replacement text is escaped using escape_pdf_string.

```php
<?php
// alter_pdf_text_example.php, version 1.0
// http://www.pdfhacks.com/dynamic_text/

// the filename of the source PDF file, which
// contains placeholders for our dynamic text
$pdfsrc_fn= './cover.pdfsrc';

// the data we will place into the PDF text;
$customer_text= "Mary Jane Doe";
$date_text= "March 15, 2004";

function escape_pdf_string( $ss )
{
  $ss_esc= '';
  $ss_len= strlen( $ss );
  for( $ii= 0; $ii< $ss_len; ++$ii ) {
    if( ord($ss{$ii})== 0x28 ||  // open paren
        ord($ss{$ii})== 0x29 ||  // close paren
        ord($ss{$ii})== 0x5c )   // backslash
      {
        $ss_esc.= chr(0x5c).$ss{$ii}; // escape the character w/ backslash
      }
    else if( ord($ss{$ii}) < 32 || 126 < ord($ss{$ii}) ) {
      $ss_esc.= sprintf( "\\%03o", ord($ss{$ii}) ); // use an octal code
    }
    else {
      $ss_esc.= $ss{$ii};
    }
  }
  return $ss_esc;
}

// open the source PDF file, which contains placeholders
$fp= @fopen( $pdfsrc_fn, 'r' );
if( $fp ) {

  if( $_GET['debug'] ) {
    header("Content-Type: text/plain"); // debug
  }
  else {
    header('Content-Type: application/pdf');
  }

  $pdf_offset= 0;
```

```
    $text_offsets= array( );

    // iterate over first lines of pdfsrc file to load $text_offsets;
    while( $cc= fgets($fp, 1024) ) {
      if( $cc{0}== '#' ) { // one of our comments
        list($comment, $name, $offset)= explode( '-', $cc );

        if( $name== 'customer' ) {
          $text_offsets[(int)$offset]=
            escape_pdf_string( $customer_text );
        }
        else if( $name== 'date' ) {
          $text_offsets[(int)$offset]=
            escape_pdf_string( $date_text );
        }
        else { // default
          $text_offsets[(int)$offset]=
            escape_pdf_string( '[ERROR]' );
        }
      }
      else { // finished with our comments
        echo $cc;
        $pdf_offset= strlen($cc)+ 1;

        break;
      }
    }

    // sort by increasing offsets
    ksort( $text_offsets, SORT_NUMERIC );
    reset( $text_offsets );

    $output_text_line_b= false;
    $output_text_b= false;
    $closed_string_b= false;

    list( $offset, $text )= each( $text_offsets );
    $text_ii= 0;
    $text_len= strlen($text);

    // iterate over rest of file
    while( ($cc= fgetc($fp))!= "" ) {

      if( $output_text_line_b && $cc== '(' ) {
        // we have reached the beginning of our TEXT
        $output_text_line_b= false;
        $output_text_b= true;

        echo '(';
      }
      else if( $output_text_b ) {
```

```
      if( $cc== ')' ) { // finished with this TEXT
        if( $closed_string_b ) {
          // string has already been capped; pad
          echo ' ';
        }
        else {
          echo ')';
        }

        // get next offset/TEXT pair
        list( $offset, $text )= each( $text_offsets );
        $text_ii= 0;
        $text_len= strlen($text);

        // reset
        $output_text_b= false;
        $closed_string_b= false;
      }
      else if( $text_ii< $text_len ) {
        // output one character of $text
        echo $text{$text_ii++};
      }
      else if( $text_ii== $text_len ) {
        // done with $text, so cap this string
        echo ')';
        $closed_string_b= true;
        $text_ii++;
      }
      else {
        echo ' '; // replace padding with space
      }
    }
    else {
      // output this character
      echo $cc;

      if( $offset== $pdf_offset ) {
        // we have reached a line in pdfsrc where
        // our TEXT should be; begin a lookout for '('
        $output_text_line_b= true;
      }
    }

    ++$pdf_offset;
  }

  fclose( $fp );
}
else { // file open failure
  echo 'Error: failed to open: '.$pdfsrc_fn;
}
?>
```

Running the Hack

IndigoPerl users (see "Install the Apache Web Server on Windows" in "Collect Data with Online PDF Forms" [Hack #74]) can copy *alter_pdf_text_example.php* into *C:\indigoperl\apache\htdocsdf_hacks* along with a PDF template named *cover.pdfsrc*. Point your browser to *http://localhost/pdf_hacks/alter_pdf_text_example.php*, and a PDF should appear. All instances of textbeg_customer should be replaced with "Mary Jane Doe," and all instances of textbeg_date should be replaced with "March 15, 2004." Naturally, you will need to adapt this script to your own purposes.

Use HTML to Create PDF

Format your content in HTML and then transform it into PDF.

HTML pages are easy to create on the fly. PDF pages are hard. One simple way to create dynamic PDF is to first create the document in HTML and then use HTMLDOC to transform it into PDF, as shown in Figure 6-15. This works for single pages and long documents.

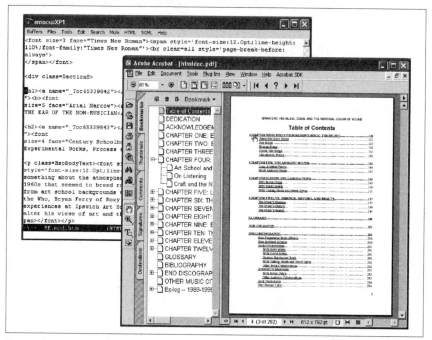

Figure 6-15. Using HTMLDOC to create bookmarks and TOC pages from your HTML headings, and to convert hyperlinks into live PDF links

HTMLDOC creates PDF documents from HTML 3.2 data. It provides document layout options, such as running headers and footers. It can add PDF features, such as bookmarks, links, metadata, and encryption. Invoke HTMLDOC from the command line or use its GUI. Visit *http://www.easysw. com/htmldoc/software.php* to download Windows binaries or source that can be compiled on Linux, Mac OS X, or a variety of other operating systems.

The detailed documentation that comes with HTMLDOC also is available online at *http://www.easysw.com/htmldoc/documentation.php*.

In Perl, you can automate PDF generation with HTMLDOC by using the HTML::HTMLDoc module to interface with HTMLDOC.

Use Perl to Create PDF
Create or modify PDF with a Perl script.

Many web sites use Perl for creating dynamic content. You can also use Perl to script Acrobat on your local machine [Hack #95]. Given the great number of packages that extend Perl, it is no surprise that packages exist for creating and manipulating PDF. Let's take a look.

Install Perl and the PDF::API2 Package on Windows

"Script Acrobat Using Perl on Windows" [Hack #95] explains how to install Perl on Windows. After installing Perl, use the Perl Package Manager to easily install the PDF::API2 package.

Launch the Programmer's Package Manager (PPM, formerly called Perl Package Manager) by selecting Start → Programs → ActiveState ActivePerl 5.8 → Perl Package Manager. A command prompt will open with its ppm> prompt awaiting your command. Type help to see a list of commands. Type search pdf to see a list of available packages. To install PDF::API2, enter install pdf-api2. The Package Manager will fetch the package from the Internet and install it on your machine. The entire session looks something like this:

```
PPM - Programmer's Package Manager version 3.1.
Copyright (c) 2001 ActiveState SRL. All Rights Reserved.

Entering interactive shell. Using Term::ReadLine::Stub as readline library.

Type 'help' to get started.

ppm> install pdf-api2
====================
Install 'pdf-api2' version 0.3r77 in ActivePerl 5.8.3.809.
====================
Transferring data: 74162/1028845 bytes.

...
```

```
Installing C:\Perl\site\lib\PDF\API2\CoreFont\verdanaitalic.pm
Installing C:\Perl\site\lib\PDF\API2\CoreFont\webdings.pm
Installing C:\Perl\site\lib\PDF\API2\CoreFont\wingdings.pm
Installing C:\Perl\site\lib\PDF\API2\CoreFont\zapfdingbats.pm
Installing C:\Perl\site\lib\PDF\API2\Chart\Pie.pm
Successfully installed pdf-api2 version 0.3r77 in ActivePerl 5.8.3.809.
ppm> quit
```

The PDF::API2 package is used widely to create and manipulate PDF. You can download documentation and examples from *http://pdfapi2.sourceforge. net/dl/*.

Hello World in Perl

This Perl script creates a PDF named *HelloWorld.pdf*, adds a page, and then adds text to that page. It gives you an idea of how easily you can create PDF. Figure 6-16 shows the PDF document created by this script.

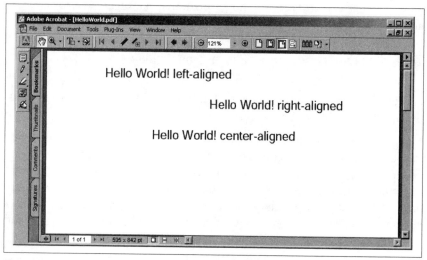

Figure 6-16. Creating PDF content using Perl

```perl
#!/usr/bin/perl
# HelloWorld.pl; adapted from 0x_test-pl

use PDF::API2;

my $pdf  = PDF::API2->new(-file => "HelloWorld.pdf");
$pdf->mediabox(595,842);
my $page = $pdf->page;
my $fnt = $pdf->corefont('Arial',-encoding => 'latin1');
my $txt = $page->hybrid;
$txt->textstart;
$txt->font($fnt, 20);
```

```
$txt->translate(100,800);
$txt->text("Hello World! left-aligned");
$txt->translate(500,750);
$txt->text_right("Hello World! right-aligned");
$txt->translate(300,700);
$txt->text_center("Hello World! center-aligned");
$txt->textend;
$pdf->save;
$pdf->end();
```

Discover Perl Packages with CPAN

CPAN (*http://www.cpan.org*) is the Comprehensive Perl Archive Network, where you will find "All Things Perl." Visit *http://search.cpan.org* to discover several other PDF packages. Drill down to find details, documentation, and downloads. For example, PDF::Extract (*http://search.cpan.org/~nsharrock/*) creates a new PDF from the pages of a larger, input PDF.

HACK #87 Use PHP to Create PDF

Generate PDF from within your PHP script.

A number of libraries enable you to create PDF using PHP. The standard PHP documentation includes a PDF Functions section that describes the popular PDFlib module (*http://www.pdflib.com*). However, this PDF extension is not free software. Typically, you must purchase a license and then recompile PHP to take advantage of these functions.

Consider some of these free alternatives. They are native PHP, so they are easy to install; just include one in your script.

R&OS PDF-PHP

With the R&OS PDF-PHP library (*http://www.ros.co.nz/pdf/*), you can add text, bitmaps, and drawings to new PDF pages. Formatting includes running headers and footers, multicolumn layout, and tables. PDF features include page labels, links, and encryption. Programming features include callbacks and transactions.

```
<?php // hello world with R&OS, from readme.pdf
include ('class.ezpdf.php');

$pdf =& new Cezpdf();
$pdf->selectFont('./fonts/Helvetica.afm');
$pdf->ezText('Hello World!', 50);
$pdf->ezStream();
?>
```

FPDF

FPDF (*http://www.fpdf.org*) enables you to add text, bitmaps, lines, and rect-angles to new PDF pages. Formatting includes running headers and footers, multicolumn layout, and tables. PDF features include metadata and links. The home page provides an active user forum and user-contributed scripts. The following PHP script produces the PDF document shown in Figure 6-17.

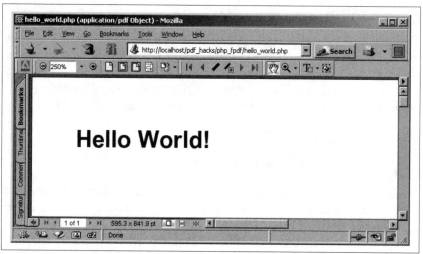

Figure 6-17. Dynamically generated PDF from FPDF

```php
<?php // hello world with FPDF, adapted from the tutorial for IndigoPerl
users
define('FPDF_FONTPATH','C:\\indigoperl\\apache\\htdocs\\pdf_hacks\\fpdf\\
font\\');
require('C:\\indigoperl\\apache\\htdocs\\pdf_hacks\\fpdf\\fpdf.php');

$pdf=new FPDF();
$pdf->AddPage();
$pdf->SetFont('Arial','B',16);
$pdf->Cell(40,10,'Hello World!');
$pdf->Output();
?>
```

pdf4php

pdf4php (*http://www.gnuvox.com/pdf4php/*) provides basic operations for creating PDFs. Add text, JPEG bitmaps, lines, and rectangles to new PDF pages. PDF features include compression. The PHP library file size is smaller, so runtime parsing goes faster.

```php
<?php // hello world with pdf4php, adapted from the home page
include('pdf4php.php');
```

```
$pdf=new PDFClass();
$pdf->startPage(8.5 * 72, 11 * 72);
$pdf->SetFont(48, 'Helvetica');
$pdf->SetStrokeColor(1,0,0);
$pdf->DrawTextAt(4.25*72, 45, "Hello World!", ALIGN_CENTER);
$pdf->endPage();
$pdf->end();
?>
```

phppdflib

phppdflib (*http://www.potentialtech.com/ppl.php*) provides basic operations for creating PDFs. You can add text, bitmaps, lines, rectangles, and circles to new PDF pages. Special features include templates.

```
<?php // hello world with phppdflib, adapted from example.php
require('phppdflib.class.php');

$pdf=new pdffile;
$pdf->set_default('margin', 0);
$firstpage=$pdf->new_page("letter");
$pdf->draw_text(10, 100, "Hello World!", $firstpage);
$temp=$pdf->generate();
header("Content-type: application/pdf");
header("Content-length: '.strlen($temp));
echo $temp;
?>
```

 Use Java to Create PDF
#88   Generate PDF from within your Java program.

When you're programming in Java, the free iText library should serve most of your dynamic PDF needs. Not only can you create PDF, but you can also read existing PDFs and incorporate their pages into your new document. Visit *http://www.lowagie.com/iText/* for documentation and downloads. You can download an alternative, development branch from *http://itextpdf. sourceforge.net.*

 Another free PDF library written in Java is Etymon's PJX (*http://etymon.com/epub.html*). It supports reading, combining, manipulating, and writing PDF documents.

When creating a new PDF, iText can add text, bitmaps, and drawings. Formatting includes running headers and footers, lists, and tables. PDF features include page labels, links, encryption, metadata, bookmarks, and annotations. Programming features include callbacks and templates.

You can also use iText to manipulate existing PDF pages. For example, you can combine pages to create a new document [Hack #89] or use a PDF page as the background for your new PDF [Hack #90].

Here is *Hello World!* using iText:

```
// Hello World in Java using iText, adapted from the iText tutorial
import java.io.FileOutputStream;
import java.io.IOException;

// the iText imports
import com.lowagie.txt.*;
import com.lowagie.text.pdf.PdfWriter;

public class HelloWorld {
  public static void main(String[] args) {
    Document pdf= new Document();
    PdfWriter.getInstance(pdf, new FileOutputStream("HelloWorld.pdf"));
    pdf.open();
    pdf.add(new Paragraph("Hello World!"));
    pdf.close();
  }
}
```

HACK #89 Assemble Pages and Serve PDF

Collate an online document at serve-time.

Imagine that you have a travel web site. A user visits to learn what packages you offer. She enters her preferences and tastes into an online form and your site returns several suggestions. Now, take this scenario to the next level. Create a custom PDF report based on these suggestions by assembling your literature into a single document. She can download and print this report, and the full impact of your literature is preserved. She can share it with her friends, read it in a comfortable chair, and leave it on her desk as a reminder to follow up—a personal touch with professional execution.

Assembling PDFs into a single document should be easy, and it is. In Java use iText. Elsewhere, use our command-line pdftk [Hack #79].

Assemble Pages in Java with iText

If your web site runs Java, consider using the iText library (*http://www. lowagie.com/iText/*) to assemble PDF documents. The following code demonstrates how to use iText to combine PDF pages. Compile and run this Java program from the command-line, or use its code in your Java application:

```
/*
  concat_pdf, version 1.0, adapted from the iText tools
  concatenate input PDF files and write the results into a new PDF
  http://www.pdfhacks.com/concat/
```

```
This code is free software. It may only be copied or modified
if you include the following copyright notice:

This class by Mark Thompson. Copyright (c) 2002 Mark Thompson.

This code is distributed in the hope that it will be useful,
but WITHOUT ANY WARRANTY; without even the implied warranty of
MERCHANTABILITY or FITNESS FOR A PARTICULAR PURPOSE.
*/

import java.io.*;

import com.lowagie.text.*;
import com.lowagie.text.pdf.*;

public class concat_pdf extends java.lang.Object {

  public static void main( String args[] ) {
    if( 2<= args.length ) {
      try {
        int input_pdf_ii= 0;
        String outFile= args[ args.length-1 ];
        Document document= null;
        PdfCopy writer= null;

        while( input_pdf_ii < args.length- 1 ) {
          // we create a reader for a certain document
          PdfReader reader= new PdfReader( args[input_pdf_ii] );
          reader.consolidateNamedDestinations( );

          // we retrieve the total number of pages
          int num_pages= reader.getNumberOfPages( );
          System.out.println( "There are "+ num_pages+
                              " pages in "+ args[input_pdf_ii] );

          if( input_pdf_ii== 0 ) {
            // step 1: creation of a document-object
            document= new Document( reader.getPageSizeWithRotation(1) );

            // step 2: we create a writer that listens to the document
            writer= new PdfCopy( document, new FileOutputStream(outFile) );

            // step 3: we open the document
            document.open( );
          }

          // step 4: we add content
          PdfImportedPage page;
          for( int ii= 0; ii< num_pages; ) {
            ++ii;
            page= writer.getImportedPage( reader, ii );
            writer.addPage( page );
            System.out.println( "Processed page "+ ii );
          }
```

```
            PRAcroForm form= reader.getAcroForm( );
            if( form!= null ) {
              writer.copyAcroForm( reader );
            }

            ++input_pdf_ii;
          }

          // step 5: we close the document
          document.close( );
        }
        catch( Exception ee ) {
          ee.printStackTrace( );
        }
      }
    }
    else { // input error
      System.err.println("arguments: file1 [file2 ...] destfile");
    }
  }
}
```

To create a command-line Java program, copy the preceding code into a file named *concat_pdf.java*. Then, compile *concat_pdf.java* using javac, setting the classpath to the name and location of your iText jar:

```
javac -classpath ./itext-paulo.jar concat_pdf.java
```

Finally, invoke concat_pdf to combine PDF documents, like so:

```
java -classpath ./itext-paulo.jar:. \
concat_pdf in1.pdf in2.pdf in3.pdf out123.pdf
```

Assemble Pages in PHP with pdftk

This example of using pdftk with PHP demonstrates how easily it assembles server-side PDF. Pass pdftk a hyphen instead of an output filename, and it will deliver its work on *stdout*.

```
<?php
// the input PDF filenames
$brochure_dir= '/var/www/brochures/';
$report_pieces=
    array( 'our_cover.pdf', 'boston.pdf', 'yorktown.pdf', 'our_info.pdf' );

// the command and its arguments
$cmd= '/usr/local/bin/pdftk ';
foreach( $report_pieces as $ii => $piece ) {
    $full_fn= $brochure_dir.$piece;
    if( is_readable( $full_fn ) ) {
        $cmd.= ' '.$full_fn;
    }
}
$cmd.= ' cat output -'; // hyphen means output to stdout
```

```
// serve it up
header( 'Content-type: application/pdf' );
passthru( $cmd ); // command output gets passed to client
?>
```

See Also

Consider some of these other free tools for assembling PDF:

- Multivalent Document Tools (*http://multivalent.sourceforge.net/Tools/ index.html*) are Java tools for manipulating PDF documents.
- PDFBox (*http://www.pdfbox.org*) is a Java library that can combine PDF documents.
- PDF::Extract (*http://search.cpan.org/~nsharrock/*) is a Perl module for extracting pages from a PDF document.
- PDF::Reuse (*http://search.cpan.org/~larslund/*) is a Perl module designed for mass-producing PDF documents from templates.

 ## Superimpose PDF Pages
#90
Merge your PDF pages with a background letterhead, form, or watermark.

Sometimes it makes sense to divide document creation into layers. For example, you need to create an invoice's background form, with its logo and rules, only once. You can create the invoice data dynamically as needed and then superimpose it on this form to yield the final invoice.

Perform this final merge in Java with iText, or elsewhere with our command-line pdftk [Hack #79], producing the results in Figure 6-18.

Superimpose Pages in Java with iText

iText (*http://www.lowagie.com/iText/*) is a powerful library for creating and manipulating PDF. The following Java program uses iText to apply one watermark PDF page to every page in a document. This watermark page can be any PDF page, such as a company letterhead design or an invoice form. The watermark will appear as though it is behind each page's content. Compile and run this program, or use its code in your Java application.

```
/*
  watermark_pdf, version 1.0
  http://www.pdfhacks.com/watermark/

  place a single "watermark" PDF page "underneath" all
  pages of the input document

  after compiling, invoke from the command line like this:
```

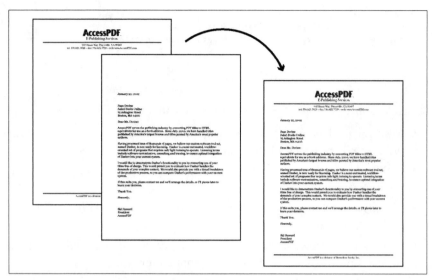

Figure 6-18. Document creation split into layers

```
java -classpath ./itext-paulo.jar:. \
watermark_pdf doc.pdf watermark.pdf output.pdf

  only the first page of watermark.pdf is used
*/

import java.io.*;
import com.lowagie.text.*;
import com.lowagie.text.pdf.*;

public class watermark_pdf {

  public static void main( String[] args ) {
    if( args.length== 3 ) {
      try {
        // the document we're watermarking
        PdfReader document= new PdfReader( args[0] );
        int num_pages= document.getNumberOfPages();

        // the watermark (or letterhead, etc.)
        PdfReader mark= new PdfReader( args[1] );
        Rectangle mark_page_size= mark.getPageSize( 1 );

        // the output document
        PdfStamper writer=
          new PdfStamper( document,
                          new FileOutputStream( args[2] ) );

        // create a PdfTemplate from the first page of mark
        // (PdfImportedPage is derived from PdfTemplate)
```

```
      PdfImportedPage mark_page=
        writer.getImportedPage( mark, 1 );

      for( int ii= 0; ii< num_pages; ) {
        // iterate over document's pages, adding mark_page as
        // a layer 'underneath' the page content; scale mark_page
        // and move it so that it fits within the document's page;
        // if document's page is cropped, this scale might
        // not be small enough

        ++ii;
        Rectangle doc_page_size= document.getPageSize( ii );
        float h_scale= doc_page_size.width()/mark_page_size.width();
        float v_scale= doc_page_size.height()/mark_page_size.height();
        float mark_scale= (h_scale< v_scale) ? h_scale :  v_scale;

        float h_trans= (float)((doc_page_size.width()-
                               mark_page_size.width()* mark_scale)/2.0);
        float v_trans= (float)((doc_page_size.height()-
                               mark_page_size.height()* mark_scale)/2.0);

        PdfContentByte contentByte= writer.getUnderContent( ii );
        contentByte.addTemplate( mark_page,
                              mark_scale, 0,
                              0, mark_scale,
                              h_trans, v_trans );
      }

      writer.close();
    }
    catch( Exception ee ) {
      ee.printStackTrace();
    }
  }
  else { // input error
    System.err.println("arguments: in_document in_watermark out_pdf_fn");
  }
 }
}
```

To create a command-line Java program, copy the preceding code into a file named *watermark_pdf.java*. Then, compile *watermark_pdf.java* using javac, setting the classpath to the name and location of your iText jar:

```
javac -classpath ./itext-paulo.jar watermark_pdf.java
```

Finally, invoke watermark_pdf to apply the first page of *form.pdf* to every page of *invoice.pdf* to create *watermarked.pdf*, like so:

```
java -classpath ./itext-paulo.jar:. \
watermark_pdf invoice.pdf form.pdf watermarked.pdf
```

Superimpose Pages with pdftk

pdftk packs iText's power into a standalone program. Apply a single PDF page to the background of an entire document like so:

```
pdftk mydoc.pdf output mydoc.marked.pdf background watermark.pdf
```

pdftk will use the first page of *watermark.pdf*, if it has more than one page. You can combine this background option with additional input operations (such as assembling PDFs [Hack #51]) and other output options (such as encryption [Hack #52]).

#91 Generate PDF Documents from XML and CSS

Produce PDF documents for XML documents styled with CSS using YesLogic Prince.

YesLogic (*http://www.yeslogic.com*) of Melbourne, Australia, offers an extremely simple little tool for converting XML documents styled with CSS into PDF or PostScript. It's called Prince and it's currently at Version 3.0. It runs on Windows or Red Hat Linux (Versions 7.3 and 8.0). Prince comes with a set of examples, default stylesheets, and DTDs.

You can download a free demo version from *http://yeslogic.com/prince/demo/*. This demo is fully featured but outputs the word *Demo* in an outline font across every page it creates. If you like it, you can purchase a copy from *http://yeslogic.com/prince/purchasing/*.

This simple XML document represents a time:

```
<?xml version="1.0" encoding="UTF-8"?>

<!-- a time instant -->
<time timezone="PST">
 <hour>11</hour>
 <minute>59</minute>
 <second>59</second>
 <meridiem>p.m.</meridiem>
 <atomic signal="true" symbol="&#x25D1;"/>
</time>
```

The CSS stylesheet provides detailed formatting information for it:

```
time {font-size:40pt; text-align: center }
time:before {content: "The time is now: "}
hour {font-family: sans-serif; color: gray}
hour:after {content: ":"; color: black}
minute {font-family: sans-serif; color: gray}
minute:after {content: ":"; color: black}
second {font-family: sans-serif; color: gray}
second:after {content: " "; color: black}
meridiem {font-variant: small-caps}
```

After downloading and installing Prince, open the application and follow these steps:

1. Select Documents → Add and then select the document *time.xml* from the directory of working examples.

2. Select Stylesheets → Add and select *time.css* from the same location.

3. Select the Output menu and select PDF if it isn't already selected.

4. Click Go and Prince produces a PDF based on *time.xml* combined with *time.css*. The application should look like Figure 6-19.

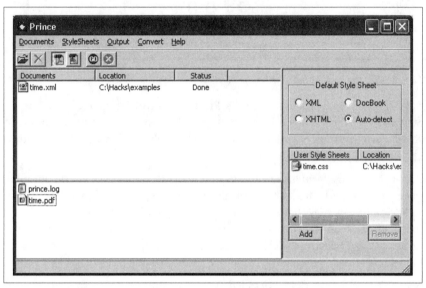

Figure 6-19. YesLogic Prince after converting time.xml styled with time.css into time.pdf

5. Select *time.pdf* in the lower-left pane and right-click it. If Adobe Reader is installed on your computer, you should be able to open *time.pdf* with it. If it is not installed, get a free copy from *http://www.adobe.com/products/acrobat/readstep2.html*.

Figure 6-20 shows you *time.pdf* in Adobe Reader Version 6.0.

—Michael Fitzgerald

Create PDF with XSL-FO and FOP

#92   Use Apache's FOP engine together with XSL-FO to generate PDF output.

Apache's Formatting Objects Processor (FOP, available at *http://xml.apache.org/fop/*) is an open source Java application that reads an XSL-FO (*http://www.w3.org/TR/xsl/*) tree and renders the result primarily as PDF, although

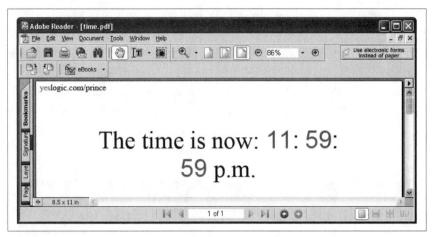

Figure 6-20. time.pdf in Adobe Reader 6.0

other formats are possible, such as Printer Control Language (PCL), Post-Script (PS), Scalable Vector Graphics (SVG), an area tree representation of XML, Java Abstract Windows Toolkit (AWT), FrameMaker's Maker Interchange Format (MIF), and text.

XSL-FO defines *formatting objects* that help describe blocks, paragraphs, pages, tables, and such. These formatting objects are aided by a large set of *formatting properties* that control things such as fonts, text alignment, spacing, and the like, many of which match the properties used in CSS (*http://www.w3.org/Style/CSS/*). XSL-FO's formatting objects and properties provide a framework for creating attractive, printable pages.

XSL-FO is a huge, richly detailed XML vocabulary for formatting documents for presentation. XSL-FO is the common name for the XSL specification produced by the W3C. The spec is nearly 400 pages long. At one time, XSL-FO and XSLT (finished spec is less than 100 pages) were part of the same specification, but they split into two specs in April 1999. XSLT became a recommendation in November 1999, but XSL-FO did not achieve recommendation status until October 2001.

To get you started, we'll go over a few simple examples. The first example, *time.fo*, is a XSL-FO document that formats the contents of the elements in *time.xml*:

```
<fo:root xmlns:fo="http://www.w3.org/1999/XSL/Format">
 <fo:layout-master-set>
  <fo:simple-page-master master-reference="Time" page-height="11in"
      page-width="8.5in" margin-top="1in" margin-bottom="1in"
      margin-left="1in" margin-right="1in">
   <fo:region-body margin-top=".5in"/>
   <fo:region-before extent="1.5in"/>
```

```
      <fo:region-after extent="1.5in"/>
    </fo:simple-page-master>
  </fo:layout-master-set>
  <fo:page-sequence master-name="Time">
    <fo:flow flow-name="xsl-region-body">

      <!-- Heading -->
      <fo:block font-size="24px" font-family="sans-serif" line-height="26px"
        space-after.optimum="20px" text-align="center" font-weight="bold"
        color="#0050B2">Time</fo:block>

      <!-- Blocks for hour/minute/second/atomic status -->
      <fo:block font-size="12px" font-family="sans-serif" line-height="16px"
        space-after.optimum="10px" text-align="start">Hour: 11 </fo:block>
      <fo:block font-size="12px" font-family="sans-serif" line-height="16px"
        space-after.optimum="10px" text-align="start">Minute: 59</fo:block>
      <fo:block font-size="12px" font-family="sans-serif" line-height="16px"
        space-after.optimum="10px" text-align="start">Second: 59</fo:block>
      <fo:block font-size="12px" font-family="sans-serif" line-height="16px"
        space-after.optimum="10px" text-align="start">Meridiem: p. m.</fo:block>
      <fo:block font-size="12px" font-family="sans-serif" line-height="16px"
        space-after.optimum="10px" text-align="start">Atomic? true</fo:block>

    </fo:flow>
  </fo:page-sequence>
</fo:root>
```

XSL-FO Basics

The root element of an XSL-FO document is (surprise) root. The namespace name is http://www.w3.org/1999/XSL/Format, and the conventional prefix is fo. Following root is the layout-master-set element where basic page layout is defined. simple-page-master holds a few formatting properties such as page-width and page-height, and some margin settings (you could use page-sequence-master for more complex page layout, in place of simple-page-master). The region-related elements such as region-body are used to lay out underlying regions of a simple page master. The master-reference attribute links with the master-name attribute on the page-sequence element.

The page-sequence element contains a flow element that essentially contains the flow of text that will appear on the page. Following that are a series of block elements, each of which has properties for the text they contain (blocks are used for formatting things such as headings, paragraphs, and figure captions). Properties specify formatting such as the font size, font family, text alignment, and so forth.

Generating a PDF

FOP is pretty easy to use. To generate a PDF from this XSL-FO file, download and install FOP from *http://xml.apache.org/fop/download.html*. At the time of this writing, FOP is at Version 20.5. In the main directory, you'll find a *fop.bat* file for Windows or a *fop.sh* file for Unix. You can run FOP using these scripts.

To create a PDF from *time.fo*, enter this command:

```
fop time.fo time-fo.pdf
```

time.fo is the input file, and *time-fo.pdf* is the output file. FOP will let you know of its progress with a report such as this:

```
[INFO] Using org.apache.xerces.parsers.SAXParser as SAX2 Parser
[INFO] FOP 0.20.5
[INFO] Using org.apache.xerces.parsers.SAXParser as SAX2 Parser
[INFO] building formatting object tree
[INFO] setting up fonts
[INFO] [1]
[INFO] Parsing of document complete, stopping renderer
```

Figure 6-21 shows the result of formatting *time.fo* with FOP in Adobe Acrobat.

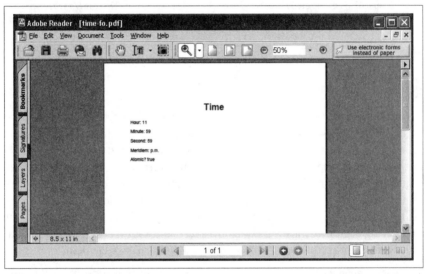

Figure 6-21. time-fo.pdf in Adobe Acrobat 6.0.1

You also can incorporate XSL-FO markup into an XSLT stylesheet, then transform and format a document with just one FOP command. Here is a stylesheet (*time-fo.xsl*) that incorporates XSL-FO:

```
<xsl:stylesheet version="1.0" xmlns:xsl="http://www.w3.org/1999/XSL/
Transform"
xmlns:fo="http://www.w3.org/1999/XSL/Format">
<xsl:output method="xml" encoding="utf-8" indent="yes"/>
```

```
<xsl:template match="/">
<fo:root>
 <fo:layout-master-set>
  <fo:simple-page-master master-reference="Time" page-height="11in"
      page-width="8.5in" margin-top="1in" margin-bottom="1in"
      margin-left="1in" margin-right="1in">
   <fo:region-body margin-top=".5in"/>
   <fo:region-before extent="1.5in"/>
   <fo:region-after extent="1.5in"/>
  </fo:simple-page-master>
 </fo:layout-master-set>
 <fo:page-sequence master-name="Time">
  <fo:flow flow-name="xsl-region-body">
   <xsl:apply-templates select="time"/>
  </fo:flow>
 </fo:page-sequence>
</fo:root>
</xsl:template>

<xsl:template match="time">
 <!-- Heading -->
 <fo:block font-size="24px" font-family="sans-serif" line-height="26px"
     space-after.optimum="20px" text-align="center" font-weight="bold"
     color="#0050B2">
     Time
 </fo:block>

 <!-- Blocks for hour/minute/second/atomic status -->
 <fo:block font-size="12px" font-family="sans-serif" line-height="16px"
     space-after.optimum="10px" text-align="start">
     Hour: <xsl:value-of select="hour"/>
 </fo:block>
 <fo:block font-size="12px" font-family="sans-serif" line-height="16px"
     space-after.optimum="10px" text-align="start">
     Minute: <xsl:value-of select="minute"/>
 </fo:block>
 <fo:block font-size="12px" font-family="sans-serif" line-height="16px"
     space-after.optimum="10px" text-align="start">
     Second: <xsl:value-of select="second"/>
 </fo:block>
 <fo:block font-size="12px" font-family="sans-serif" line-height="16px"
     space-after.optimum="10px" text-align="start">
     Meridiem: <xsl:value-of select="meridiem"/>
 </fo:block>
 <fo:block font-size="12px" font-family="sans-serif" line-height="16px"
     space-after.optimum="10px" text-align="start">
     Atomic? <xsl:value-of select="atomic/@signal"/>
 </fo:block>
</xsl:template>

</xsl:stylesheet>
```

The same XSL-FO markup you saw in *time.fo* is interspersed with templates and instructions that transform *time.xml*. Now with this command, you can generate a PDF like the one you generated with *time.fo*:

```
Fop -xsl time-fo.xsl -xml time.xml -pdf time-fo.pdf
```

For more information on these technologies, see Michael Fitzgerald's *Learning XSLT* (O'Reilly) or Dave Pawson's *XSL-FO* (O'Reilly).

—*Michael Fitzgerald*

Scripting and Programming Acrobat

Hacks 93–100

Although most users think of Acrobat as a GUI interface to PDF documents, you can also automate and extend it. Some automation features are built into Acrobat, especially Acrobat 6 Professional, and you can create your own automated processing sequences using a variety of other tools.

 Modify or Convert Batches of Documents

#93

Automate repetitive tasks using Acrobat, such as converting folders of Word documents to PDF.

If you have a folder of PDFs that you must alter or convert, consider using Acrobat's built-in batch processing feature. After you create a batch sequence, you can use it to process large quantities of PDFs hands-free. You can also apply a batch sequence to a single PDF, which means you can create batch sequences for use as macros.

Acrobat batch processing isn't just for manipulating PDF. You can use it to convert Microsoft Office documents, PostScript files, or graphic bitmaps into PDF documents. Or, use batch processing to convert PDF documents to HTML, PostScript, RTF, text, or graphic bitmaps. Many of these options are not available in Acrobat 5. In Acrobat 6, you can also apply OCR to bitmaps or refry PDFs to prepare them for online distribution [Hack #60].

You can automate many of the basic things you do in Acrobat with batch processing. We'll describe a couple of examples.

Refry a Folder Full of PDFs (Acrobat 6 Pro)

Before publishing a PDF online for wide distribution, you should try reducing its file size by refrying it [Hack #60]. With Acrobat 6, you can refry a PDF using its Optimizer feature (Advanced → PDF Optimizer...). Let's create an Acrobat 6 batch sequence that applies the Optimizer to an entire folder of

PDF documents. While we're at it, we can also add metadata or other finishing touches [Hack #62].

Create a batch sequence in Acrobat 6 Professional by selecting Advanced → Batch Processing... and clicking New Sequence.... Name the new sequence Refry and click OK. The Batch Edit Sequence dialog will open.

If you want to also add metadata (title, subject, author, or keywords) to the PDFs, click Select Commands... and the Edit Sequence dialog will open. Select the Description command from the list on the left and click Add. In the right column, double-click this command and a dialog opens where you can set the metadata values, shown in Figure 7-1. Click OK to close the Edit Sequence dialog and to return to the Batch Edit Sequence dialog.

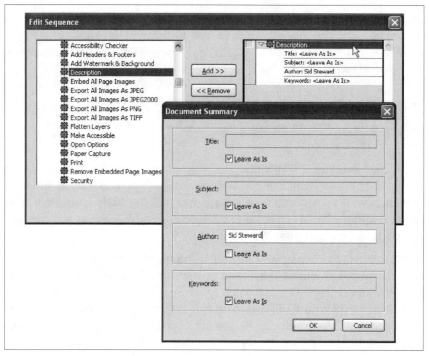

Figure 7-1. Adding PDF metadata using the Description batch sequence command

> Fine-tune a batch sequence using the Execute JavaScript batch command. If JavaScript is not powerful enough, you can develop your own batch processing commands using an Acrobat plug-in. See the BatchCommand and BatchMetadata plug-in samples that come with the Acrobat SDK [Hack #98].

Set Run Commands On to Ask When Sequence is Run. Set Select Output Location to Same Folder as Original(s). Click Output Options....

On the Output Options dialog, shown in Figure 7-2, select Add to Original
Base Name(s) and then set Insert After to .opt. Under Output Format, set
Save File As to Adobe PDF Files. Place checkmarks next to Fast Web View
and PDF Optimizer. Click Settings… to configure the Optimizer, as shown
in Figure 7-3.

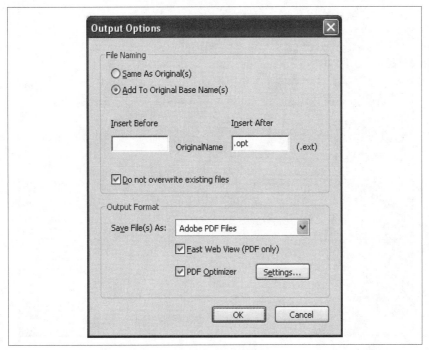

Figure 7-2. The Output Options dialog, where you can access Optimizer settings

Configure the Optimizer to suit your requirements. Set its compatibility to
Acrobat 5.0 and Later or Acrobat 4.0 and Later for maximum PDF portability [Hack #41]. Click OK when you're done.

Click OK to close the Output Options dialog. Click OK to close the Batch
Edit Sequence dialog. Your new Refry batch sequence now should be visible
in the Batch Sequences dialog, as shown in Figure 7-4.

> To make a batch sequence recurse into subfolders, set Run
> Commands On to Selected Folder. Then click Browse… to
> select the folder you want to process. Whenever you run the
> sequence, it will process that same folder (and its subfolders).

Test your batch sequence on a temporary folder of disposable PDFs. In the
Batch Sequences dialog, select Refry and click Run Sequence. Click OK on
the Confirmation dialog. A file selector will open. Select one or more PDFs

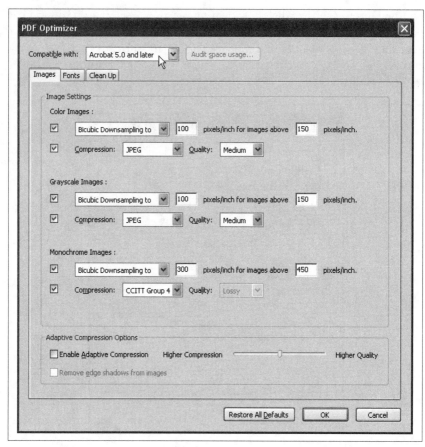

Figure 7-3. Using the PDF Optimizer to prepare your PDFs for online distribution

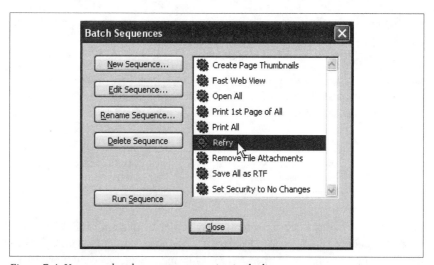

Figure 7-4. Your new batch sequence appearing in the list

and click Select to continue. Acrobat will create new PDFs based on your Optimizer settings. The new PDFs will have the same filenames as the original PDFs, except they will have *.opt.pdf* instead of *.pdf* at the end. When Acrobat is done, check the new PDFs to make sure the results are satisfactory.

> Disable the batch processing confirmation dialog using the Acrobat preferences: Edit → Preferences → General... → Batch Processing.

Convert Microsoft Office Documents to PDF

If you have Acrobat 6 and Microsoft Word, you can use Acrobat's preconfigured Open All batch sequence to convert Word documents into PDFs hands-free. As the name suggests, you actually can use the Open All batch sequence on any kind of file that Acrobat knows how to handle, including bitmap and PostScript files. Acrobat 5 also has an Open All batch sequence, but it does not handle as many file types as Acrobat 6 does.

> To merge a number of Word documents into a single PDF with Acrobat 6, use the File → Create PDF → From Multiple Files... feature instead.

First, you must configure Acrobat 6 to create the kind of PDF you desire. Do this using the Acrobat preferences, located at Edit → Preferences → General... → Convert to PDF. Select Microsoft Office and click Settings..., and a dialog opens, shown in Figure 7-5. Set Adobe PDF Settings to your desired Distiller profile [Hack #38]; the Standard profile works well for most purposes. Set the other options (bookmarks, links, and security) to suit your requirements and click OK. I recommend disabling Enable Accessibility & Reflow, because enabling this feature slows down the process and creates very large PDFs [Hack #34].

In Acrobat 6, start the Open All batch sequence by selecting Advanced → Batch Processing... → Open All and clicking Run Sequence. In Acrobat 5, start the Open All batch sequence by selecting File → Batch Processing → Open All. Click OK to close the confirmation dialog (if necessary), and a file selector will open. Change Files of Type to All Files, select one or more input files, and then click Select. Acrobat will create one PDF for each input document. Acrobat 5 can't process Word documents this way, but it can handle bitmap images.

Exploring Batch Sequences

The previous examples are pretty simple. You can also create fancier sequences to perform specific tasks. The Acrobat 5 CD-ROM includes batch

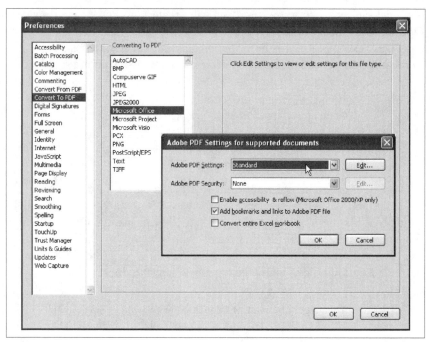

Figure 7-5. Acrobat's preferences, which control PDFs created with Acrobat

sequence examples and documentation in its *Batch* folder. Also, visit *http://www.planetpdf.com/mainpage.asp?webpageid=1511* for more examples and commentary.

 The Acrobat 5 CD-ROM batch sequence examples are set as read-only. After you copy them to a local folder, change this file attribute to view their JavaScripts in Acrobat.

Batch sequences are stored as text files, so they are easy to maintain. System-level sequences are located somewhere such as *C:\Program Files\Adobe\Acrobat 6.0\Acrobat\Sequences\ENU*. With Acrobat 6, user-level sequences are located somewhere such as *C:\Documents and Settings\Sid Steward\Application Data\Adobe\Acrobat\6.0\Sequences*. With Acrobat 5, user-level sequences are located somewhere such as *C:\Documents and Settings\Sid Steward\My Documents\Adobe\Acrobat\Sequences*.

 ### HACK Script Acrobat Using Visual Basic on Windows
#94
Drive Acrobat using VB or Microsoft Word's Visual Basic for Applications (VBA).

Adobe Acrobat's OLE interface enables you to access or manipulate PDFs from a freestanding Visual Basic script or from another application, such as

Word. You can also use Acrobat's OLE interface to render a PDF inside your own program's window. The Acrobat SDK [Hack #98] comes with a number of Visual Basic examples under the *InterAppCommunicationSupport* directory. The SDK also includes OLE interface documentation. Look for *IACOverview.pdf* and *IACReference.pdf*. These OLE features do not work with the free Reader; you must own Acrobat.

> Acrobat Distiller also has an OLE interface. It is documented in *DistillerAPIReference.pdf*, which comes with the full Acrobat SDK.

The following example shows how easily you can work with PDFs using Acrobat OLE. It is a Word macro that scans the currently open PDF document for readers' annotations (e.g., sticky notes). It creates a new Word document and then builds a summary of these annotation comments.

The Code

To add this macro to Word, select Tools → Macro → Macros…, type in the macro name SummarizeComments, and click Create. Word will open a text editor where you can enter the code shown in Example 7-1. Save, and then test. You can download this code from *http://www.pdfhacks.com/summarize*.

Example 7-1. VBA code for summarizing comments

```
Sub SummarizeComments( )
Dim app As Object
Set app = CreateObject("AcroExch.App")
If (0 < app.GetNumAVDocs) Then
  ' a PDF is open in Acrobat
  ' create a new Word doc to hold the summary
  Dim NewDoc As Document
  Dim NewDocRange As Range
  Set NewDoc = Documents.Add(DocumentType:=wdNewBlankDocument)
  Set NewDocRange = NewDoc.Range

  Dim found_notes_b As Boolean
  found_notes_b = False

  ' get the active doc and drill down to its PDDoc
  Dim avdoc, pddoc As Object
  Set avdoc = app.GetActiveDoc
  Set pddoc = avdoc.GetPDDoc

  ' iterate over pages
  Dim num_pages As Long
  num_pages = pddoc.GetNumPages
  For ii = 0 To num_pages - 1
```

Example 7-1. VBA code for summarizing comments (continued)

```
    Dim pdpage As Object
    Set pdpage = pddoc.AcquirePage(ii)
    If (Not pdpage Is Nothing) Then

      ' iterate over annotations (e.g., sticky notes)
      Dim page_head_b As Boolean
      page_head_b = False
      Dim num_annots As Long
      num_annots = pdpage.GetNumAnnots
      For jj = 0 To num_annots - 1

        Dim annot As Object
        Set annot = pdpage.GetAnnot(jj)
        ' Popup annots give us duplicate contents
        If (annot.GetContents <> "" And _
            annot.GetSubtype <> "Popup") Then

          If (page_head_b = False) Then ' output the page number
            NewDocRange.Collapse wdCollapseEnd
            NewDocRange.Text = "Page: " & (ii + 1) & vbCr
            NewDocRange.Bold = True
            NewDocRange.ParagraphFormat.LineUnitBefore = 1
            page_head_b = True
          End If

          ' output the annotation title and format it a little
          NewDocRange.Collapse wdCollapseEnd
          NewDocRange.Text = annot.GetTitle & vbCr
          NewDocRange.Italic = True
          NewDocRange.Font.Size = NewDocRange.Font.Size - 1
          NewDocRange.ParagraphFormat.LineUnitBefore = 0.6

          ' output the note text and format it a little
          NewDocRange.Collapse wdCollapseEnd
          NewDocRange.Text = annot.GetContents & vbCr
          NewDocRange.Font.Size = NewDocRange.Font.Size - 2

          found_notes_b = True
        End If
      Next jj
    End If
  Next ii

  If (Not found_notes_b) Then
    NewDocRange.Collapse wdCollapseEnd
    NewDocRange.Text = "No Notes Found in PDF" & vbCr
    NewDocRange.Bold = True
  End If
End If
End Sub
```

Running the Code

Open a PDF in Acrobat, as shown in Figure 7-6. In Word, run the macro by selecting Tools → Macro → Macros… → SummarizeComments and then clicking Run. After a few seconds, a new Word document will appear, as shown in Figure 7-7. It will list all the comments that readers have added to each page of the currently visible PDF.

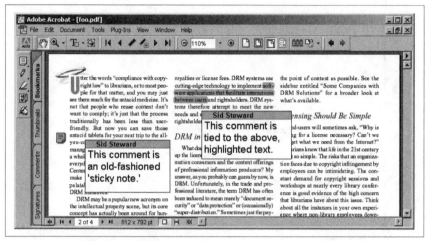

Figure 7-6. PDF Comments displayed in Acrobat

Hacking the Hack

This script demonstrates the typical process of drilling down through layers of PDF objects to find desired information. Here is a simplified sketch of the layers:

app

>   The currently running Acrobat program. Use the app to alter the user interface or Acrobat's preferences.

avdoc

>   The PDF currently displayed in Acrobat. Use the avdoc to change how the PDF appears in the viewer or to print pages.

pddoc

>   Represents the underlying PDF document. Use the pddoc to access or manipulate the PDF's pages or metadata.

pdpage

>   Represents the underlying PDF page. Use the pdpage to access or manipulate a page's annotations, its rotation, or its cropping.

These OLE objects closely resemble the objects exposed by the Acrobat API [Hack #97]. The API gives you much more power, however.

Figure 7-7. The PDF Comments in Word after extraction via SummarizeComments

 ## Script Acrobat Using Perl on Windows
#95   Install Perl and use it instead of Visual Basic to drive Acrobat.

Depending on your tastes or requirements, you might want to use the Perl scripting language instead of Visual Basic [Hack #94] to program Acrobat. Perl can access the same Acrobat OLE interface used by Visual Basic to manipulate PDFs. Perl is well documented, is widely supported, and has been extended with an impressive collection of modules. A Perl installer for Windows is freely available from ActiveState.

We'll describe how to install the ActivePerl package from ActiveState, and then we'll use an example to show how to access Acrobat's OLE interface using Perl.

  Acrobat OLE documentation comes with the Acrobat SDK [Hack #98]. Look for *IACOverview.pdf* and *IACReference.pdf*. Acrobat Distiller also has an OLE interface. It is documented in *DistillerAPIReference.pdf*.

Install Perl on Windows

The ActivePerl installer for Windows is freely available from *http://www. ActiveState.com/Products/ActivePerl/*. Download and install. It comes with excellent documentation, which you can access by selecting Start → Programs → ActiveState ActivePerl 5.8 → Documentation.

ActivePerl also includes the OLE Browser, shown in Figure 7-8, which enables you to browse the OLE servers available on your machine (Start → Programs → ActiveState ActivePerl 5.8 → OLE-Browser). The OLE Browser is an HTML file that must be opened in Internet Explorer to work properly.

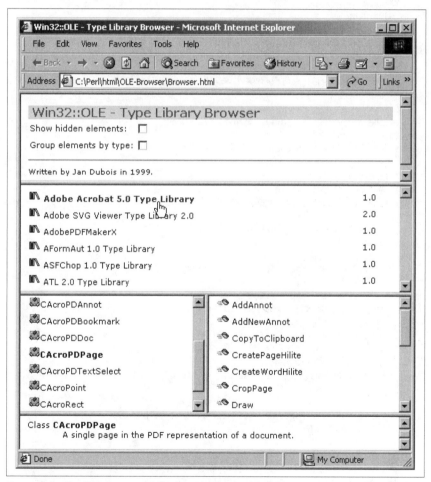

Figure 7-8. The OLE Browser, which you can use to discover OLE servers available on your machine

The Code

In this example, the Perl script will use Acrobat to read annotation (e.g., sticky notes) data from the currently open PDF. The script will format this data using HTML and then output it to *stdout*.

Copy the script in Example 7-2 into a file named *SummarizeComments.pl*. You can download this code from *http://www.pdfhacks.com/summarize/*.

Example 7-2. Perl code for summarizing comments

```perl
# SummarizeComments.pl ver. 1.0
use strict;
use Win32::OLE;

my $app = Win32::OLE->new("AcroExch.App");
if( 0< $app->GetNumAVDocs ) { # a PDF is open in Acrobat
  # open the HTML document
  print "<html>\n<head>\n<title>PDF Comments Summary</title>\n</head>\n<body>\n";
  my $found_notes_b= 0;

  # get the active PDF and drill down to its PDDoc
  my $avdoc= $app->GetActiveDoc;
  my $pddoc= $avdoc->GetPDDoc;

  # iterate over pages
  my $num_pages= $pddoc->GetNumPages;
  for( my $ii= 0; $ii< $num_pages; ++$ii ) {

    my $pdpage= $pddoc->AcquirePage( $ii );
    if( $pdpage ) {

      # interate over annotations (e.g., sticky notes)
      my $page_head_b= 0;
      my $num_annots= $pdpage->GetNumAnnots;
      for( my $jj= 0; $jj< $num_annots; ++$jj ) {

        my $annot= $pdpage->GetAnnot( $jj );
        # Pop-up annots give us duplicate contents
        if( $annot->GetContents ne '' and
          $annot->GetSubtype ne 'Popup' ) {

          if( !$page_head_b ) { # output the page number
            print "<h2>Page: " . ($ii+ 1) . "</h2>\n";
            $page_head_b= 1;
          }

          # output the annotation title and format it a little
          print "<p><i>" . $annot->GetTitle . "</i></p>\n";

          # output the note text; replace carriage returns
          # with paragraph breaks
          my $comment= $annot->GetContents;
```

Example 7-2. Perl code for summarizing comments (continued)

```
        $comment =~ s/\r/<\/p>\n<p>/g;
        print "<p>" . $comment . "</p>\n";

        $found_notes_b= 1;
      }
    }
  }
}
if( !$found_notes_b ) {
  print "<h3>No Notes Found in PDF</h3>\n";
}

# close the HTML document
print "</body>\n</html>\n";
}
```

Running the Hack

Open a PDF in Acrobat, as shown in Figure 7-6, and then run this script from the command line by typing:

```
C:\> perl SummarizeComments.pl > comments.html
```

It will take a few seconds to complete. When it is done, you can open *comments.html* in your browser to see a summary of the PDF's comments, as shown in Figure 7-9.

As noted in "Script Acrobat Using Visual Basic on Windows" [Hack #94], this example demonstrates the relationships between several fundamental PDF objects.

Customize Acrobat Using JavaScript

HACK #96

Create custom Acrobat menu items and batch processing scripts.

Acrobat can do most of the things that you need. Yet, there's always something you wish it did a little differently. Acrobat enables you to add custom features using plain-text JavaScripts. These scripts can add menu items to Acrobat's menus or add tailored sequences to Acrobat's batch processing.

Acrobat JavaScript builds on the language core familiar to web developers, but its document object model is completely different from the DOM used by web browsers. Acrobat's JavaScript objects are documented in Technical Note 5186: Acrobat JavaScript Object Specification. Access it online from *http://partners.adobe.com/asn/developer/pdfs/tn/5186AcroJS.pdf*. Another useful document is the *Acrobat JavaScript Scripting Guide* from *http://partners. adobe.com/asn/acrobat/sdk/public/docs/AcroJSGuide.pdf*.

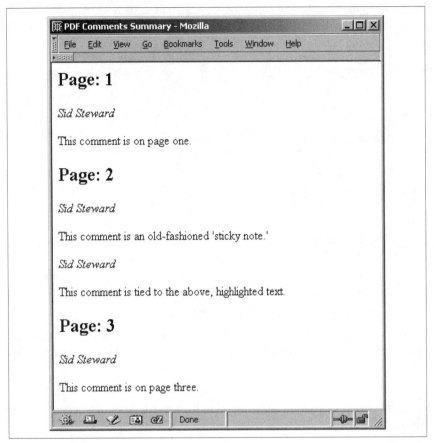

Figure 7-9. The PDF Comments in Mozilla after extraction via SummarizeComments.pl

Test Scripts Using the Debugger

The JavaScript Debugger (Acrobat 6 Pro) or Console (Acrobat 5) is the place to test new ideas. Open it by selecting Advanced → JavaScript → Debugger... (Acrobat 6 Pro) or Tools → JavaScript → Console... (Acrobat 5).

Add New Acrobat Features with Startup JavaScripts

When Acrobat starts up, it runs any JavaScripts it finds in either the system-level *JavaScripts* folder or the user-level *JavaScripts* folder. The locations of these folders are given shortly. You might need to create some of these folders if you can't find them.

Use startup JavaScripts to add menu items to Acrobat or to set global Java-Script variables. "Bookmark PDF Pages in Reader" [Hack #15] demonstrates how to add a menu item and how to set/query a persistent global variable.

Acrobat stores these persistent global variables in a file named *glob.js*. "Pace Your Reading or Present a Slideshow in Acrobat or Reader" [Hack #10] shows one use of making Acrobat execute a JavaScript periodically.

These JavaScripts even enable you to add features to the free Reader, although Reader won't perform the more powerful commands. Our various JavaScript hacks all work with Reader. JavaScripts are also platform-independent, so our JavaScript hacks all run on Windows, Mac, and Linux.

Windows startup JavaScripts. For Versions 5 or 6 of Acrobat or Reader, the system-level *JavaScripts* folder is located somewhere such as *C:\Program Files\Adobe\Acrobat 6.0\Acrobat\Javascripts* or *C:\Program Files\Adobe\ Acrobat 6.0\Reader\Javascripts*.

For Acrobat or Reader 6, the user-level folder is located somewhere such as *C:\Documents and Settings\Sid Steward\Application Data\Adobe\Acrobat\6.0\ JavaScripts*. Both Acrobat and Reader use this one folder.

For Acrobat 5, the user-level folder is located somewhere such as *C:\Documents and Settings\Sid Steward\My Documents\Adobe\Acrobat\JavaScripts*. Both Acrobat and Reader use this one folder.

Sometimes you must create a *JavaScripts* folder, if one does not already exist.

Mac startup JavaScripts. For Acrobat 6, the system-level *JavaScripts* folder is located inside the Acrobat 6 package. Right-click or control-click the Acrobat application icon, and choose Show Package Contents. The system-level *JavaScripts* folder is located at *Contents : MacOS : JavaScripts*.

The Acrobat 6 user-level *JavaScripts* folder is in the user's home folder: ~ : *Library : Acrobat User Data : JavaScripts*.

The Acrobat 5 system-level *JavaScripts* folder is located at : *Adobe Acrobat 5. 0 : JavaScripts*. The user-level folder is located in the user's home folder: ~ : *Documents : Acrobat User Data : JavaScripts*.

Linux startup JavaScripts. For Reader 5, the system-level *JavaScripts* directory is located somewhere such as */usr/local/Acrobat5/Reader/intellinux/ plug_ins/JavaScripts*. The user-level directory is located in the user's home directory: *~/.acrobat/JavaScripts*. Create these directories if they don't already exist.

Create Custom Batch Sequence Commands

Acrobat 6 Professional's batch processing [Hack #93] uses batch sequences to modify or process collections of PDF documents. Acrobat provides basic commands for creating sequences, such as Insert Pages. Among these commands you will also find Execute JavaScript. Use this command to apply a JavaScript to each PDF in the batch, as shown in Figure 7-10. You can use the *global* object to store the accumulated state of your running batch process, if necessary. Visit *http://www.planetpdf.com/mainpage.asp?webpageid=1511* for some interesting examples and commentary.

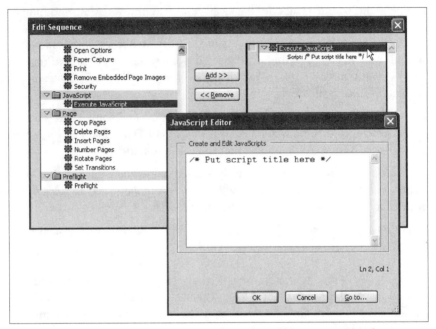

Figure 7-10. Using the Execute JavaScript command to add logic to your batch sequences

 Configure Acrobat to use your favorite text editor for editing JavaScripts. Select Edit → Preferences → General... → JavaScript and tell it how to launch your editor.

Tool Up for Acrobat Plug-In Development
HACK #97
Compile Acrobat plug-ins on Windows using GCC.

The Acrobat API gives you the most powerful tools for accessing and modifying PDF data. The typical way to access the API is with an Acrobat plug-in.

A plug-in is a DLL (on Windows), and it is created from C or C++ source code using a compiler such as Microsoft's Visual C++ or the GNU Compiler Collection (GCC). In this hack, we'll explain how to install the free (and fabulous) GCC compiler on Windows. Then, we'll install the Acrobat SDK. Finally, we'll build a sample plug-in using GCC.

You can also compile Acrobat plug-ins for Macintosh and Unix. Adobe provides separate SDKs for each platform. Typically, you compile Macintosh Acrobat plug-ins using Metrowerks CodeWarrior.

Install GCC on Windows with MinGW and MSYS

You can get GCC on your Windows machine using a couple of different methods. I prefer using the packages provided by the MinGW (*http://www. mingw.org*) folks. They provide a set of installers that you can choose from according to your needs. They also provide software updates that you can unpack and copy on top of the original installation.

Visit *http://www.mingw.org/download.shtml* and download the following packages. Each file is named according to its version. If newer versions are available under the Current section of the web page, use those instead. For example, download *MSYS-1.0.10.exe* instead of *MSYS-1.0.9.exe*.

> *MSYS-1.0.10.exe*
> *MinGW-3.1.0-1.exe*
> *gcc-core-3.3.1-20030804-1.tar.gz*
> *gcc-g++-3.3.1-20030804-1.tar.gz*

First, install MinGW. Throughout this discussion, I'll assume you installed MinGW on the *C:* drive so that you ended up with *C:\MinGW*.

Next, install MSYS. Throughout this discussion, I'll assume you installed MSYS on the *C:* drive so that you ended up with *C:\msys\1.0*. The MSYS post-install script will configure MSYS to your environment. When it asks where MinGW is installed, tell it `C:/MinGW` (note the forward slash).

MSYS gives you many of the GNU (*http://www.gnu.org*) tools that are common on Linux systems, such as grep, less, and diff. MSYS also gives you a Bourne shell (a.k.a. *command prompt*) environment that makes a Linux user feel more at home. In fact, it creates a home directory for you; in my case it is *C:\msys\1.0\home\Sid Steward*. When you run MSYS (Start → Programs → MinGW → MSYS → msys), a colorful command prompt opens, and it opens in your home directory by default. It is like a little slice of Linux, right there on your Windows machine. Run `dir` and it doesn't understand. Use `ls` instead. Run `pwd` and you'll see that even the filesystem looks different. Your current directory is */home/Sid Steward/*, not *C:\msys\1.0\home\Sid Steward*. You can access the traditional DOS drive names like so:

```
cd "/c/Program Files"
```

Test whether MSYS can find MinGW by running:

```
$ gcc --version
```

If it replies command not found, MSYS can't see MinGW. In that case, you will need to edit the text file *C:\msys\1.0\etc\fstab* so that it includes the line:

```
c:/MinGW /mingw
```

Note the forward slashes, and replace *c:/MinGW* with the location of MinGW on your machine.

> To access the MSYS and MinGW tools from the Windows command prompt, you will need to add `C:\msys\1.0\bin` and `C:\MinGW\bin` to your Windows Path environment variable. Access environment variables by selecting Start → Settings → Control Panel → System → Advanced → Environment Variables.

Finally, we'll apply the 3.3.1 updates to the installation. Copy the *.tar.gz* files to your MinGW directory (e.g., *C:\MinGW*). Open the MSYS shell (*Start → Programs → MinGW → MSYS → msys*) and then change into the */mingw* directory (cd /mingw). Unpack the *.tar.gz* archives like so:

```
Sid Steward@GIZMO /mingw
$ tar -xzf gcc-core-3.3.1-20030804-1.tar.gz

Sid Steward@GIZMO /mingw
$ tar -xzf gcc-g++-3.3.1-20030804-1.tar.gz
```

Now, test to make sure the upgrades worked by checking the versions. For example:

```
Sid Steward@GIZMO /mingw
$ gcc --version
gcc.exe (GCC) 3.3.1 (mingw special 20030804-1)
```

Success!

Download and Install the Acrobat SDK

The full Acrobat SDK from Adobe includes documentation, samples, and API header files. Presently, only (fee-paying) ASN Developer members can download the full Acrobat 6 SDK. So, we'll download the freely available Acrobat 5 SDK instead. This free download does require that you sign up for a (free) ASN Web Account.

Visit *http://partners.adobe.com/asn/acrobat/download.jsp*, and download the Acrobat 5.0 Full SDK Installation. For Windows, it is a zipped-up installer named *acro5sdkr4.zip*.

> In addition to the Acrobat SDK documentation, you should also download the latest PDF Reference from *http://partners.adobe.com/asn/tech/pdf/specifications.jsp*.

Unzip, and then run the installer. Throughout this discussion, I'll assume you installed the SDK in a directory named *C:\acro5sdkr4*.

Open *C:\msys\1.0\etc\fstab* in a text editor and add this line (note the forward slashes):

```
C:/acro5sdkr4 /acro5sdkr4
```

Mapping Windows directories to MSYS directories like this makes life easier in MSYS. Regardless of where you installed the SDK, its location in MSYS is always */acro5sdkr4*. We'll take advantage of this fact in our plug-in sample project. It expects to find the Acrobat API headers at */acro5sdkr4/PluginSupport/Headers/Headers/*.

Download and Install Our Sample Plug-In

The Acrobat SDK Windows installer comes with many sample plug-in projects, but they all use Visual C++ project files. Visit *http://www.pdfhacks.com/jumpsection/* and download *jumpsection-1.0.tar.gz,* which is the source code for our jumpsection Acrobat plug-in [Hack #13]. It demonstrates the basic elements of an Acrobat plug-in project built using MinGW.

Move *jumpsection-1.0.tar.gz* to your MSYS home directory and unpack it in MSYS like so:

```
Sid Steward@GIZMO ~
$ tar -xzf jumpsection-1.0.tar.gz
```

This creates a directory named *jumpsection-1.0*. Change into this directory and compile jumpsection using make:

```
Sid Steward@GIZMO ~
$ cd jumpsection-1.0
Sid Steward@GIZMO ~/jumpsection-1.0
$ make
```

make will use the instructions in *Makefile* to create the Acrobat plug-in *jumpsection.api*. When it is done, copy *jumpsection.api* to the Acrobat *plug_ins* directory [Hack #4] and restart Acrobat to test it. It works in both Acrobat 5 and Acrobat 6. It won't load in Reader.

This toolset is the bare minimum you will need to build Acrobat plug-ins. To develop plug-ins, you will also need a good text editor such as vim [Hack #82] or Emacs (*http://www.gnu.org/software/emacs/windows/ntemacs.html*). Or, you might prefer a GUI environment such as Dev-C++ (*http://www.bloodshed.net/devcpp.html*).

HACK #98
Explore the Acrobat SDK Documentation and Examples

Look under Acrobat's hood, and explore the possibilities.

The Acrobat 5 SDK for Windows includes more than 26 documents, 15 interapplication (e.g., OLE, DDE) examples, and 52 Acrobat plug-in examples, as shown in Figure 7-11. Acrobat SDKs are also available for Macintosh and Unix. This material is the foundation for all PDF, Acrobat, and Distiller programming. And, it is freely available from *http://partners.adobe.com/asn/ acrobat/download.jsp*. For a fee, you can also access the Acrobat 6 SDK.

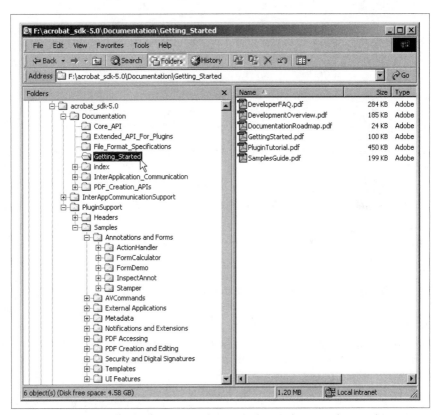

Figure 7-11. The Acrobat 5 SDK for Windows, which includes more than 26 documents and 67 programming examples

Here is a list of the most notable documents included with the Acrobat SDK.

PDF Reference

The most important document is the PDF Reference (*PDFReference.pdf*). The one that comes with the Acrobat 5 SDK is old, so visit *http://partners. adobe.com/asn/tech/pdf/specifications.jsp* and download the latest version.

"Maximize PDF Portability" [Hack #41] discusses how each new version of Acrobat is coupled with a new release of the PDF Reference. Check the "what's new" section of the reference to get a glimpse of what was added to the corresponding version of Acrobat. In the PDF Reference Version 1.5 (that was released with Acrobat 6), new PDF features are described in section 1.2.

The PDF Reference sometimes refers to the PostScript Reference. Download this venerable document from *http://partners.adobe.com/asn/tech/ps/ specifications.jsp*.

Acrobat Core API Reference

The API Reference (*CoreAPIReference.pdf*) lists all the objects, methods, and callbacks available to your Acrobat plug-in [Hack #97]. It is a reference, so it doesn't offer deep explanations. For explanations of the concepts behind the API, consult the Acrobat Core API Overview (*CoreAPIOverview.pdf*).

Acrobat Interapplication Communication (IAC) Reference

The Acrobat Interapplication Communication (IAC) Reference (*IACReference.pdf*) lists all the different interfaces you can use to access Acrobat from external programs or scripting languages. It includes Acrobat's OLE objects and their methods, Acrobat's Apple Event objects and their properties, and the DDE messages that Acrobat supports. For an introduction to IAC programming, read the Acrobat Interapplication Communication Overview (*IACOverview.pdf*).

Guide to SDK Samples

Read the SDK Samples Guide (*SamplesGuide.pdf*) to get a sense of what you can do with the Acrobat SDK. Consult the included sample code to see exactly how Adobe made their samples work. One of the samples might provide a good foundation for creating exactly what you need.

Acrobat Distiller Parameters

Acrobat Distiller uses different settings [Hack #38] to create different kinds of PDFs. A PDF created for online distribution should be lightweight, while a

PDF created for a service bureau should have the highest fidelity. The Distiller Parameters document (*DistillerParameters.pdf* or *distparm.pdf*) explains all the available settings. As discussed in "Configure Distiller and Ghostscript for Your Purpose" [Hack #42], the Distiller GUI interface does not give you access to all these parameters.

pdfmark Reference Manual

The pdfmark Reference Manual (*pdfmarkReference.pdf*) provides information on pdfmark operators. Acrobat Distiller and Ghostscript both convert PostScript pages to PDF pages. By adding pdfmark operators to the input PostScript, you can also make Distiller or Ghostscript add features to the output PDF, such as annotations, links, bookmarks, and metadata. Various word processor macros [Hack #32] use pdfmark operators for this purpose.

HACK #99 Use Acrobat Plug-Ins to Extend PDF
The Acrobat API gives you the power to adapt PDF to your needs.

Some of our Acrobat hacks add features to Adobe Acrobat using plug-ins. But plug-ins also have the power to extend Acrobat with custom tools, or to extend PDF with custom PDF *annotations*. The best illustration of this power is the fact that Adobe uses plug-ins [Hack #4] to implement Acrobat's most interesting features, as shown in Figure 7-12. PDF form fields, for example, are implemented as PDF annotations. A specific plug-in (*AcroForm.api*) handles them in Acrobat. This plug-in adds tools to Acrobat for creating and editing form field annotations, and then this plug-in handles user interaction with the form fields.

Likewise, you can extend PDF by adding custom annotations to PDF pages. Your Acrobat plug-in would need a way to add annotations to the page; you can do this with a custom tool. Then, your plug-in must register an *annotation handler* with Acrobat. An annotation handler is responsible for drawing the annotation's appearance on the PDF page and for responding to user interaction with the annotation.

When would you want to use custom PDF annotations? Annotations are ideal for adding things to PDF pages. You control how these things appear, print, and behave.

Learn about PDF annotations by reading the PDF Reference Version 1.5, section 8.4, and consulting the Acrobat SDK [Hack #98]. The SDK includes the Stamper sample plug-in that demonstrates how to create a custom tool and a custom annotation handler. Take a look at the other plug-in samples included in this Annotations and Forms section to get a sense of what else is possible.

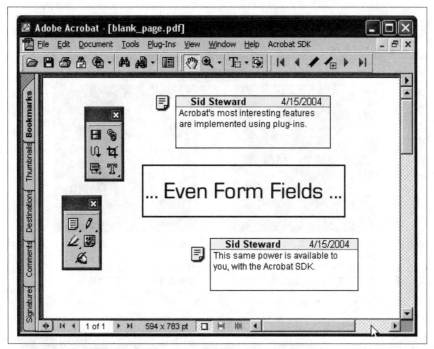

Figure 7-12. Implementing PDF and Acrobat features using plug-ins

Many other Adobe products offer plug-in interfaces for extending the application, including Photoshop, Illustrator, and InDesign.

PostScript and PDF Games

HACK 100

Have some fun, thanks to PostScript and PDF programming.

PostScript is a full-fledged programming language, and you can animate PDF using JavaScript. Folks have hacked PDFs to do all sorts of things.

Naval Battle and Tic-Tac-Toe in PDF

Naval Battle, shown in Figure 7-13, is a PDF game in which you try to sink the computer's ships before it sinks yours. Craig Connor of Adobe Systems, Inc. created it, and you can download it from *http://www.math.uakron.edu/~dpstory/acrotex.html*. This site offers many other interactive PDF games, including Tic-Tac-Toe by D. P. Story.

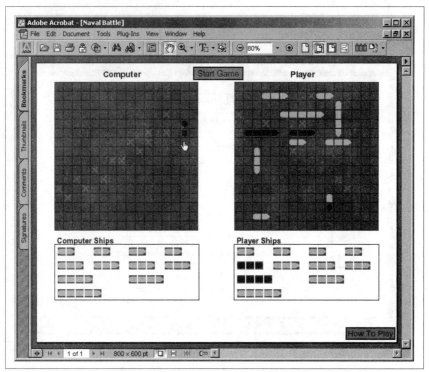

Figure 7-13. The PDF game Naval Battle

Programming PostScript

PostScript is more than marks on a page; it is a full-fledged programming language. This means it can compute the drawing as it creates the drawing. For example, Michel Charpentier has a PostScript program that computes prime numbers (*http://www.cs.unh.edu/~charpov/Programming/PostScript-primes/*). Naturally, it reports its results as a printed page. If you send such a program to your PostScript printer, its interpreter actually performs the computation. If you don't have a PostScript printer or Acrobat Distiller, you can use Ghostscript to run these PostScript programs and see their results on-screen [Hack #3].

PostScript and Fractals

Because PostScript is a programming language, it is possible to describe large, intricate patterns using lightweight PostScript procedures. In particular, PostScript is a clever way to generate fractals (see Figure 7-11). Michel Charpentier provides good examples and a good discussion for generating

(L-system) fractals at *http://www.cs.unh.edu/~charpov/Programming/L-systems/*. Stijn van Dongen provides another source of interesting examples at *http://www.micans.org/stijn/ps/*. Finally, if you are serious about mathematical PostScript, visit *http://www.math.ubc.ca/~cass/graphics/text/www/* to read Bill Casselman's *Mathematical Illustrations*.

Figure 7-14. An elegant way to generate fractals

PostScript Web Server

The PostScript web server, PS-HTTPD, is a lark on par with the RFC 1149 implementation for Linux (*http://www.blug.linux.no/rfc1149/*). Visit *http://www.pugo.org* or *http://public.planetmirror.com/pub/pshttpd/* to learn more about PS-HTTPD and to download source code.

Index

We'd like to hear your suggestions for improving our indexes. Send email to *index@oreilly.com*.

Colophon

Our look is the result of reader comments, our own experimentation, and feedback from distribution channels. Distinctive covers complement our distinctive approach to technical topics, breathing personality and life into potentially dry subjects.

The tool on the cover of *PDF Hacks* is a sledge hammer. The sledge hammer is a heavy hammer with a long handle designed to drive wedges or stakes. While handheld hammers rarely weigh more than four pounds, sledge hammers generally range in weight from six to twelve pounds. The head of the sledge hammer is usually fashioned from forged steel, and the handle is typically wood or fiberglass. In olden times, blacksmiths used the sledge hammer to forge metal.

Brian Sawyer was the production editor and proofreader for *PDF Hacks*. Audrey Doyle was the copyeditor. Emily Quill and Darren Kelly provided quality control. Julie Hawks wrote the index.

Hanna Dyer designed the cover of this book, based on a series design by Edie Freedman. The cover image is a photograph from the Stockbyte Work Tools CD. Emma Colby produced the cover layout with QuarkXPress 4.11 using Adobe's Helvetica Neue and ITC Garamond fonts.

David Futato designed the interior layout. This book was converted by Julie Hawks to FrameMaker 5.5.6 with a format conversion tool created by Erik Ray, Jason McIntosh, Neil Walls, and Mike Sierra that uses Perl and XML technologies.

Brian Sawyer saved this book's FrameMaker source files to PostScript format and then used Acrobat Distiller to create final PDF versions to send to the printer.

The text font is Linotype Birka; the heading font is Adobe Helvetica Neue Condensed; and the code font is LucasFont's TheSans Mono Condensed. The illustrations that appear in the book were produced by Robert Romano and Jessamyn Read using Macromedia FreeHand 9 and Adobe Photoshop 6. This colophon was written by Sanders Kleinfeld.

Need in-depth answers fast?

Related Titles Available from O'Reilly

Hacks

Amazon Hacks

BSD Hacks

Digital Photography Hacks

eBay Hacks

Excel hacks

Google Hacks

Harware Hacking Projects for Geeks

Linux Server Hacks

Mac OS X Hacks

Mac OS X Panther Hacks

Spidering Hacks

TiVo Hacks

Windows Server Hacks

Windows XP Hacks

Wireless Hacks

Keep in touch with O'Reilly

1. Download examples from our books

To find example files for a book, go to:

www.oreilly.com/catalog

select the book, and follow the "Examples" link.

2. Register your O'Reilly books

Register your book at *register.oreilly.com*

Why register your books? Once you've registered your O'Reilly books you can:

- Win O'Reilly books, T-shirts or discount coupons in our monthly drawing.
- Get special offers available only to registered O'Reilly customers.
- Get catalogs announcing new books (US and UK only).
- Get email notification of new editions of the O'Reilly books you own.

3. Join our email lists

Sign up to get topic-specific email announcements of new books and conferences, special offers, and O'Reilly Network technology newsletters at:

elists.oreilly.com

It's easy to customize your free elists subscription so you'll get exactly the O'Reilly news you want.

4. Get the latest news, tips, and tools

http://www.oreilly.com

- "Top 100 Sites on the Web"—PC Magazine
- CIO Magazine's Web Business 50 Awards

Our web site contains a library of comprehensive product information (including book excerpts and tables of contents), downloadable software, background articles, interviews with technology leaders, links to relevant sites, book cover art, and more.

5. Work for O'Reilly

Check out our web site for current employment opportunities:

jobs.oreilly.com

6. Contact us

O'Reilly & Associates
1005 Gravenstein Hwy North
Sebastopol, CA 95472 USA

TEL: 707-827-7000 or 800-998-9938
       (6am to 5pm PST)

FAX: 707-829-0104

order@oreilly.com
For answers to problems regarding your order or our products.
To place a book order online, visit:

www.oreilly.com/order_new

catalog@oreilly.com
To request a copy of our latest catalog.

booktech@oreilly.com
For book content technical questions or corrections.

corporate@oreilly.com
For educational, library, government, and corporate sales.

proposals@oreilly.com
To submit new book proposals to our editors and product managers.

international@oreilly.com
For information about our international distributors or translation queries. For a list of our distributors outside of North America check out:

international.oreilly.com/distributors.html

adoption@oreilly.com
For information about academic use of O'Reilly books, visit:

academic.oreilly.com